HONOR AMONG CHRISTIANS

HONOR AMONG CHRISTIANS

THE CULTURAL KEY TO THE MESSIANIC SECRET

DAVID F. WATSON

Fortress Press
Minneapolis

HONOR AMONG CHRISTIANS
The Cultural Key to the Messianic Secret

Cover image: Museo Pio Cristiano, Vatican Museums, Vatican State. Vanni / Art Resource, NY.
Cover design: Brad Norr
Book design: Jessica Hillstrom

Library of Congress Cataloging-in-Publication Data
Watson, David F., 1970-
  Honor among Christians : the cultural key to the Messianic secret / David
F. Watson.
    p. cm.
  Includes bibliographical references (p.   ) and indexes.
  ISBN 978-0-8006-9709-9 (alk. paper)
  1. Bible. N.T. Mark--Criticism, interpretation, etc. 2.   Honor--Biblical
teaching. I. Title.
  BS2585.6.H634W38 2010
  226.3'06--dc22
                              2010018954

Manufactured in the U.S.A.

14   13   12   11   10   1   2   3   4   5   6   7   8   9   10

To my parents, David and Valrie,
with love and gratitude

CONTENTS

PREFACE

My fascination with the Gospel of Mark goes back to my days as a seminary student. During one semester, I took an upper-level course on Mark. I found myself after each class session variously energized, puzzled, frustrated, and always desirous to learn more. Careful study of Mark's Gospel can in itself inspire this kind of intellectual curiosity, but I was helped by having an exceptional instructor. Many thanks to Clifton Black for his outstanding teaching in this class.

Over the course of the writing of this work, I have benefited from the insights of a number of very fine scholars. Abraham Smith, Joseph Tyson, and Jerome Neyrey all provided very important feedback on the ideas in this book. I am especially grateful to Jouette Bassler, a scholar of the highest caliber under whom it was my privilege to study. Her feedback on this work was crucial for its completion.

I also wish to express my gratitude to my colleagues at United Theological Seminary, who are people of deep faith and intellectual rigor. I could not ask for a finer group of colleagues. Larry Welborn, who is now on the faculty at Fordham University, was extremely helpful in providing guidance with regard to primary texts. My senior Bible colleague Tom Dozeman offered invaluable assistance in the preparation of this manuscript, not only by reading and critiquing chapters, but by talking through arguments, helping me to sharpen and clarify them. I am also grateful to my highly capable research assistant, Justin Williams.

Most of all I am grateful to my wife, Harriet, who not only proofread each chapter, but has supported me with unfailing encouragement and patiently dealt with a husband who has been glued to a laptop for more time than should be allowed.

INTRODUCTION

Mark's Gospel is a puzzling piece of ancient literature, and the more one studies it, the more puzzling it is likely to become. To a greater extent than either Matthew or Luke, Mark leaves things unexplained. Mark's story can be abrupt and cryptic, at least for modern readers. Perhaps the writer of this Gospel knew the audience well enough to know what they would and would not assume, what stories they had already heard time and again, what they thought about Jesus and his culturally unusual way of acting and teaching. Perhaps it was perfectly obvious to them why Jesus was baptized for the forgiveness of sins (1:9), or exactly what Jesus meant by the "mystery of the kingdom of God" (4:11), or why Jesus would call the Syrophoenician woman a dog (7:27). Be that as it may, many of the assumptions of these earliest hearers of Mark's story are not readily available to us today. Some

1

are utterly lost to us. The ideas, values, experiences, and worldview that we bring to the text are different from those of ancient hearers of Mark's Gospel. Even the act of reading Mark, rather than hearing the story read aloud as the ancients would have, changes the ways in which we interpret it. Nevertheless, we are not totally at a loss. Our efforts to make sense of Mark's Gospel often involve efforts to reconstruct the assumptions and experience of these earliest Christians, and then to interpret the text in light of our reconstructions.

One puzzle of particular interest over the last century involves a number of Markan passages collectively known as the "messianic secret." This term has been around since the earliest years of the twentieth century. It is a translation of William Wrede's term *Messiasgeheimnis*, which might also be translated "messianic mystery."[1] Many scholars since Wrede have offered explanations of the significance of Mark's messianic secret. Nevertheless, no scholarly consensus has emerged on this issue. Part of the reason that no consensus has emerged is that scholars do not agree on exactly which passages constitute the messianic secret. The term functions essentially as a cipher: scholars have used it to refer to a wide variety of Markan themes and passages.[2] In general, some combination of the following sets of passages have been thought to constitute the messianic secret. Many scholars focus on only one or a few of these:

1. Jesus' commands that people whom he has healed tell no one about what he has done (1:40-45; 5:21-24, 35-43; 7:31-37; 8:22-26)
2. Jesus' healing of people in private settings (5:21-24, 35-43; 7:31-37; 8:22-26)
3. Jesus' silencing of demons, who are aware of his special status (1:23-28; 1:34; 3:12)
4. Jesus' commands that the disciples tell no one what Peter has revealed in his confession at Caesarea Philippi, and that those disciples who were with him at the transfiguration tell no one what they had witnessed (8:30; 9:9). It is often noted in this connection that Jesus took only three disciples with him during the transfiguration scene
5. Jesus' seeking solitude and his attempts to escape from the crowds (e.g., 1:35; 4:35-36; 6:32)

6. Jesus' teaching an inner circle of followers in private settings (4:10ff.; 4:34; 7:17-23; 9:28; 10:10; 13:3ff.)
7. The "mystery of the kingdom of God" to which Jesus refers in 4:10-12
8. The disciples' failure to understand Jesus and to respond to him in faith (e.g., 4:13; 4:35-41; 8:31-32; 9:33-37; 10:35-45)[3]

In subsequent chapters, when referring to the passages in these eight categories as a group, I will refer to them as the Markan concealment passages. One of the points I wish to make in this book is that, from the perspective of Mark's audience, secrecy is not the most appropriate category for thinking about these passages. In the present chapter's review of Wrede and subsequent scholarship, however, I will maintain the use of terms such as "messianic secret" and "secrecy motif," since such terms are part of the technical vocabulary that scholars use to talk about these passages.

WILLIAM WREDE

Modern critical debate on the "messianic secret" began with William Wrede's work, *Das Messiasgeheimnis in den Evangelien*, widely recognized today as a landmark in New Testament studies. In this work, Wrede takes issue with nineteenth-century scholars who considered the Gospel of Mark to be a historically reliable source for writing accounts of the life of Jesus.[4] Wrede identifies a division between the historical and theological facets of the Gospels, especially with regard to the Gospel of Mark. He holds that "the Gospel of Mark belongs to the history of dogma," and consequently the presentation of Jesus in this Gospel is governed primarily by dogmatic concerns.[5] Mark's Gospel offers only "pale residues" of the historical life of Jesus.[6]

For Wrede, the key to Mark's dogmatic presentation lies in the collection of passages in which Jesus' identity, deeds, and teachings are obscured. Together, these passages form a unified motif, a "messianic secret," in which Jesus' messianic identity and the necessity of his suffering, death, and resurrection are kept hidden from all but a small group of his followers.[7] Wrede identifies five categories of passages that involve "injunctions to keep the Messianic secret":

1. "Prohibitions addressed to demons" (1:25; 1:34; 3:12)
2. "Prohibitions following (other) miracles" (1:43-45; 5:43; 7:36; 8:26)
3. "Prohibitions after Peter's confession" (8:30; 9:9)
4. "Intentional preservation of his incognito" (7:24; 9:30ff.)
5. "A prohibition to speak which did not originate with Jesus" (10:47ff.).[8]

Along with these five categories, he discusses another category of secrecy passages, which he identifies as "cryptic speech as a mode of concealment," within which he includes Jesus' parables and the "mystery of the kingdom of God" (4:10-12).[9] He also discusses briefly the lack of understanding exhibited by the disciples.[10]

Wrede judges the secrecy passages to be historically implausible. He claims that, apart from the fact that "the supernatural view of the author" is impossible to believe,[11] no one could reasonably expect people to keep silence after Jesus had, for example, raised Jairus's daughter from the dead.[12] He also notes that Jesus frequently performs healings in full public view. Furthermore, Jesus' silence commands are often ignored.

> The facts can be put this way: since many of the miracles are public, the later prohibitions found after miraculous deeds lose their point. But they also seem pointless for another reason: those healed pay no heed to the prohibition (1.45, 7.36f.; cf. 5.19f.)—"the more he charged them, the more zealously they proclaimed it." According to Mark one would have to add that the more they spread it abroad, the more he forbade it. This has a less sensible ring about it.[13]

Wrede's explanation of the messianic secret hinges on the claim that the oldest view of Jesus' messiahship is that he became the Messiah after his death.[14] The origins of the messianic secret lie in the fact that only after the resurrection was messianic significance associated with the events of Jesus' life. Yet early Christians then had to explain why Jesus was not recognized as the Messiah during his lifetime. In pre-Markan tradition, this tension was resolved by adopting the idea that Jesus was the Messiah during his life, but that he kept his messianic identity a secret. The author of Mark's Gospel took over this understanding of Jesus' secret messiahship and incorporated it into his story. Mark 9:9 is crucial for Wrede's argument. In this passage, which immediately follows the transfiguration and God's announcement of Jesus' divine sonship, Jesus orders Peter, James, and John (the only disciples who are with him at the time) "to tell no one what they had seen, until after the Son of Man had risen from the dead." Mark, drawing on the tradition that preceded him, held that Jesus' messianic status was obscured until the resurrection, at which time it was fully revealed.

In 1907 William Sanday wrote, "The chief merit of Wrede's book consists in its independence, its originality, and the newness of the questions which it raises. I consider it to be not only very wrong but also distinctly wrong-headed."[15] To a great extent, Sanday's comment presaged much of the scholarly reaction to Wrede's work: while Wrede's overall thesis would not win the day, the set of questions that he raised would give rise to decades of scholarship. It is a testimony to the enduring nature of Wrede's works that scholarly studies that deal with the Markan concealment passages in almost all cases acknowledge the influence of *The Messianic Secret*, even more than a century after its publication. Sanday may have been right that the value of Wrede's work is in the questions that it raises, but the significance of these questions is borne out in the numerous works that have tried to answer them, including this one.

SUBSEQUENT SCHOLARSHIP: A BRIEF OVERVIEW

The history of scholarship on the passages associated with the messianic secret is long and complex. Over the years, the discussion of the messianic secret has followed the methodologies of biblical studies in becoming more complex and broader in scope. Interpretations have been offered by way of historical, form, redaction, literary, social-scientific, and reader-response criticism. Because the scholarship on this issue is so vast, it is helpful to divide the responses into a few categories:

1. interpretations that attribute secrecy to Jesus' own actions and intentions
2. interpretations that attribute the secrecy motif to Markan redaction
3. interpretations that hold that the secrecy motif is both historical and redactional
4. interpretations that explain the secrecy motif in terms of its literary features or function(s)
5. interpretations that take a social-scientific approach to secrecy

These categories often overlap one another, and some scholars offer multifaceted interpretations that fit into more than one of them. The purpose of using these categories is simply to help us understand the landscape of scholarship on the messianic secret. Over the next few pages I will discuss the different types of interpretations of the messianic secret that have been put forward since Wrede's work. For each category I will reference specific examples of scholarship that exemplify this type of interpretation. This brief survey is incomplete. Indeed, an exhaustive account of the history of interpretation of the messianic secret would be a weighty tome in itself.[16] We will, then, take a broad look at the kinds of interpretations offered by scholars in response to Wrede's work, the work of subsequent scholars, and, of course, the passages that together form the "messianic secret."

Interpretations That Attribute Secrecy to Jesus' Own Actions and Intentions

One line of interpretation holds that some aspects of the secrecy motif can be traced to the figure of Jesus. These secrecy traditions are not the product of the evangelist or of some historic community, though these may have had an influence on the ways in which the traditions were preserved. Rather, the traditions are at their core authentic and historic. For scholars who hold this position, an important task is to ascertain the reasons for Jesus' secrecy and its cultural significance.[17] Oskar Holtzmann, for example, ascribes to Jesus a concern that making public his messiahship might hinder his work.[18] Therefore, Jesus did not disclose his messiahship; rather, the disciples gradually recognized him as the Messiah. "The knowledge communicated to Jesus at his baptism by a revelation of God, that he is the Messiah (i. 11), forms the introduction to his public preaching; but he is silent about this belief until his disciples of their own accord recognise him as the Messiah (i. 25, 34, iii. 12, viii. 29 f.)."[19] Jesus, however, does not allow his disciples to call him the Messiah, "until by his entry into Jerusalem, his purification of the Temple, and his defiant answer to the emissaries of the Council, he publicly announces himself to be such—a declaration which he finally confirms again in the most solemn way in the course of the hearing before the Council..."[20]

Some scholars, such as Albert Schweitzer and James D. G. Dunn, have argued that the secrecy traditions represent an attempt by Jesus to redefine the role of the Messiah (though Dunn objects to the term "messianic secret").[21] Had he made known his messianic identity from the outset, the crowds who followed him would have understood him in terms of their traditional understandings of messiahship (often political or militaristic), rather than in the redefined manner that would be borne out in Jesus' ministry, suffering, death, and resurrection. Schweitzer, for example, held that Jesus wished to recast the messianic role in terms of suffering. For Dunn, Jesus was avoiding the temptation to become a popular messiah and specifically disavowing certain false views of messiahship. Instead, Dunn argues, Jesus wanted to show that the Messiah was one who would serve and suffer, and only after his death be exalted.

Interpretations That Attribute the Secrecy Motif to Markan Redaction

There have also been a number of scholars who have claimed that the messianic secret is not to be attributed to Jesus of Nazareth or to the pre-Markan tradition, but is mainly or entirely the product of the evangelist as he is responding to the needs of his community by reworking pre-Markan tradition. These types of arguments are many and varied. For example, some scholars, such as Ulrich Luz, have argued that the messianic secret represents a redefinition of messiahship, though not by Jesus, but by the evangelist.[22] Mark wishes to cast Jesus' messiahship in terms of the cross and resurrection. Eugene Boring holds that the evangelist is attempting to reconcile two opposing Christologies within the Markan community, one that emphasized Jesus as the powerful Son of God, and one that emphasized Jesus' suffering, cross, and resurrection.[23]

Other scholars, such as Martin Dibelius and Rudolf Bultmann, have argued that Mark's Gospel should be understood as a book of "secret epiphanies."[24] In using this term, they mean that, although continually disclosed throughout Mark's Gospel, Jesus' messiahship is hidden from all but a select few. This theme, they argue, is the product of the evangelist. Although these scholars worked prior to the emergence of redaction criticism, like Wrede they anticipated some of the important insights that redaction critics would build upon and develop, and it is appropriate to account for their contributions in connection with later redaction-critical approaches. More recently, Adela Yarbro Collins has argued for a variant of this position, arguing that the "various themes of secrecy in Mark . . . are all literary devices created or adapted by the author of the Gospel to reveal and yet conceal Jesus and to imply that, during his lifetime, his identity was similarly revealed yet concealed."[25]

Alternatively, other scholars have argued for a "history of revelation" interpretation. In this line of thought, Mark develops a schema such that Jesus' messiahship must remain hidden for a short time, but will be revealed at the appropriate time (for example, at the crucifixion or resurrection). Joel Marcus, for example, holds that in Mark's Gospel Jesus' identity cannot be truly known until his death and resurrection.[26] He proposes that "Mark is telling a story about what happened 'way back when' in Jesus' earthly ministry, when the full truth about him could not yet be revealed because the epistemological revolution created by the crucifixion and resurrection had not yet occurred. Hence the messianic secret."[27]

Still other interpreters maintain that some or all of the secrecy passages in Mark's Gospel are attempts by early Christians to explain some aspect of their faith that would be embarrassing or harmful to their cause. Wrede's interpretation falls into this category, since he holds that the messianic secret explains why no one recognized Jesus as the Messiah during his lifetime.[28] T. A. Burkill also offers an example of this type of "apologetic" interpretation.[29] He holds that, by crafting his narrative in such a way that the "true status of Jesus was a predetermined secret,"[30] Mark attempts to deal with the problem posed by Jesus' lack of success with the Jews and his crucifixion by Gentiles. "The Master was not accepted as the Messiah, and the evangelist maintains that it was an integral part of the divine purpose that he should not have been so accepted."[31]

Additionally, there are interpretations that explain some or all of the secrecy passages as having a polemical purpose. Joseph Tyson offers one such interpretation in his essay, "The Blindness of the Disciples in Mark."[32] He argues that there is a polemic in Mark's Gospel that is directed against the Jerusalem church. The evangelist was probably influenced by Paul, and his perspective may represent a form of Galilean Christianity, both factors that may have contributed to his low estimation of the disciples. Mark saw Jesus' death as having redemptive significance. This redemption was for all people, rather than only for Israel. A nationalistic, royal conception of messiahship was from Mark's perspective erroneous. The disciples, who have a narrow view of messiahship and an inflated view of their own position, and who lack understanding regarding the significance of Jesus' death, represent the Jerusalem church. Their negative portrayal shows the erroneous nature of these positions.

Heikki Räisänen likewise offers a polemical interpretation. He interprets the messianic secret within the context of a polemic against the Q tradition, which, he argues, involves a Christology much different from Mark's own. For Mark, the Q tradition reflects an inadequate understanding of the passion and the resurrection. Q's depiction of Jesus as an eschatological prophet contrasts sharply with Mark's view of Jesus as the Son of God and the Christ. By using Jesus' commands that both demons and the disciples remain silent with regard to his identity, Mark attempts to demonstrate that the advocates of the Q tradition, who appealed to the historical Jesus, had an incorrect understanding of Jesus' identity. Because of his secrecy, Jesus' identity was not known to everyone. Only privately to his disciples and fully in the resurrection was Jesus' identity truly revealed.[33]

Interpretations That Hold That the Secrecy Motif
Is Both Historical and Redactional

Some scholars have taken what James Blevins refers to as the "mediating view," which entails the idea that, while Mark's secrecy motif may have a genuine historical core, the evangelist has recorded these traditions in such a way as to shape them to his own purposes or the purposes of his community.[34] Robert H. Stein has articulated such a position in his commentary on Mark. From the "historical Jesus" perspective, he maintains that Jesus' avoidance of an open proclamation of his messiahship averted an immediate confrontation with Rome. Pilate would not have tolerated a popular leader who referred to himself by such titles as Messiah and Son of David. From the redactional perspective, Stein maintains that the evangelist wished to demonstrate that Jesus was not a political revolutionary. Jesus' reticence to reveal his identity as Messiah makes this point. The evangelist also uses the secrecy motif to highlight Jesus' greatness: Jesus' secrecy commands, coupled with frequent revelations of his authority and identity, show that the Messiah and Son of God cannot be hidden.[35]

Interpretations That Explain the Secrecy Motif
in Terms of Its Literary Features or Function(s)

Up to this point, all of the interpretations that we have considered might be grouped into three large categories: historical interpretations, theological interpretations, and those that combine these. The emergence of literary criticism offered another way of approaching the messianic secret. Some scholars began to look at these passages in terms of their function within Mark's overall narrative, the literary devices that Mark uses to advance the secrecy theme, or the ways in which it would affect readers or hearers of the Gospel. In *The Genesis of Secrecy*, for example, Frank Kermode brings his skill as a literary critic to bear on the Gospel of Mark.[36] He is attentive to the ways in which the secrecy passages affect readers and reading. His interest in the messianic secret has to do with the way secrecy functions in the narrative, the ways in which it guides the reader and interacts with other parts of the text.

Mary Ann Tolbert has a multifaceted explanation of the secrecy motif, but with regard to its literary functions she writes, "Jesus' efforts to prevent his name from becoming known throughout the first part of the Gospel are ultimately efforts to hold back the denouement, to create time where time no longer exists. In other words, *he tries to buy time for sowing the word*."[37] The messianic secret, in other words, is a narrative device that allows the plot of the story to continue. Once Jesus reveals his identity, the story proceeds quickly to the crucifixion.

Dennis MacDonald offers another literary interpretation of the secrecy motif. He argues that Mark has utilized the *Odyssey* as a model for the themes of secrecy and recognition in the Gospel narrative. MacDonald identifies a number of thematic and narrative similarities between Odysseus's attempts to conceal his plans and identity and Jesus' actions in Mark's Gospel. Like Tolbert, MacDonald holds that secrecy allows Jesus to avoid immediate and swift reprisal by the authorities. Jesus is most secretive in public, Jewish settings in which he could be seen as claiming publicly that he is the Messiah or Son of God. The reader, however, is privy to information that is concealed from many characters in the story. "Mark seems to have borrowed from Homer the motifs of disguise, testing, signs, recognitions, disclosure, and silence, and, as in the *Odyssey*, the use of these motifs permits situation irony in which the reader, knowing the identity of the stranger, enjoys the narrative at a level inaccessible to the characters themselves."[38]

Interpretations That Take a Social-Scientific Approach to Secrecy

Most relevant for this analysis are interpretations that approach the secrecy motif by way of social-scientific criticism. Gerd Theissen, for example, has argued that secrecy has a protective function. In Mark's Gospel, there is tension between secrecy and revelation, tension that reflects the lives of people within the Markan community. Secrecy is a protective measure for the Markan community, which is enduring persecution. Just as Jesus initially kept his identity a secret, these early Christians may also keep their identity a secret, therefore avoiding unnecessary hardships. Just as Jesus confessed his identity before his persecutors, however, the Markan Christians will have to confess their identity someday as well. For now, these Christians may enjoy the protection of secrecy, but it will not always be so.[39]

A number of other scholars in the social-scientific camp have made extensive use of cultural anthropology. In this line of interpretation, the ancient values of honor and shame are very important. I will say much more about these values later. Scholars such as Bruce J. Malina and John J. Pilch see the secrecy motif as a way to protect one's honor, as well as the honor of one's in-group.[40] This protective function works on a few different levels. First of all, Jesus' secrecy shows that that he was not trying to grasp at glory, praise, and reputation—in other words, honor. Ancient Mediterranean people saw such self-promotion as dishonorable behavior. There was only so much honor to go around, and intentional self-promoters were seen as trying to get more than their share. Jesus shows himself to be an honorable person precisely because he is not trying to gain honor for himself.[41] Second, if Jesus were seen as attempting to gain public praise for himself, he could expect backlash from other people in the community. In other words, secrecy has a defensive function. It allows one to avoid envy and its negative consequences. Third, secrecy divides insiders from outsiders and therefore creates social cohesion among those insiders. Only insiders are privy to certain information. In the next chapter, I will deal with these kinds of interpretations more extensively.

UNDERSTANDING THE ISSUES: THE APPROACH OF THIS WORK

The term "cultural anthropology" is generally used for "ethnographic works that are holistic in spirit, oriented to the ways in which culture affects individual experience, or aim to provide a rounded view of the knowledge, customs, and institutions of a people."[42] In other words, cultural anthropology takes a "big picture" approach, looking at broad cultural trends that affect many different aspects of life. Its breadth of scope distinguishes it from "social anthropology," which isolates and analyzes more specific systems of social relations, such as domestic life, economics, law, or politics.[43] In particular, scholars associated with the Context Group, a working group of international academics committed to the use of the social sciences in biblical interpretation, have done invaluable work in looking at the ways in which the values of honor and shame affected virtually every aspect of life in the ancient Mediterranean world. Among the leading New Testament scholars of the Context Group are Jerome H. Neyrey, Bruce J. Malina, Richard Rohrbaugh, and John J. Pilch. Other scholars not associated with the Context Group, such as Louise J. Lawrence, Mario I. Aguilar, and David A. deSilva, have also drawn fruitfully upon the insights of cultural anthropology as tools for investigating the Bible.[44]

Much social-scientific criticism of the Bible operates on two levels. On one level, this type of scholarship operates by *analogy*. Anthropological investigation of the ancient world is very different from modern anthropological research, since we cannot engage in fieldwork with these ancient people. We cannot sit at their tables, observe their festivals, listen to their stories, note their mannerisms, or ask them specific questions. If we could, the insights would surely be rich and enlightening, but we cannot. Therefore, biblical scholars working with insights of cultural anthropology must work in part by analogy. This means that they utilize models developed in modern anthropological investigations of the Mediterranean world, applying them to the lives of people in the ancient Mediterranean world.[45]

In fact, the values of honor and shame are not unique to the Mediterranean, though the cultures of this region do have their particular manifestations of these values. Rather, honor and shame tend to be important in "face-to-face" cultures, cultures in which there is a great deal of interpersonal interaction among community members. In such cultures, people do not interact with one another primarily by phone, letter, e-mail, or text message. They do not find out what is going on in the community primarily by reading about it in a newspaper or online, or watching the news on television. They interact personally, in direct, face-to-face conversation. Members of a community know one another, know one another's families, and are keenly aware of individual and family reputations. It stands to reason that in the ancient world, in which aspects of face-to-face interaction would be even more widespread than in many areas of the

Mediterranean world today, characteristics associated with honor and shame would inhere.

Social-scientific criticism of this kind, however, does not proceed simply by analogy, but also through a painstaking process of *verification* and *modification*. We have access to a vast body of literature and archaeological data from the ancient Mediterranean world. The ongoing task of social-scientific criticism is to examine our assertions about the cultural world of the ancient Mediterranean region—drawn in large part from models of modern anthropology—against data from the ancient world. To what extent do ancient writers support our assertions? To what extent must we refine, or even reject, our assertions in light of our ancient sources? Statues, temples, coins, and inscriptions can lend credence to our claims, or they can lead us to reevaluate. The work of the social historian, then, like all other kinds of historians, is never done, but remains within an ongoing process of verification, reevaluation, and refinement.

This body of social-scientific work provides new insights into those passages generally associated with the messianic secret. Scholars taking this approach have demonstrated that, for first-century Mediterranean people, issues such as fame, publicity, reputation, secrecy, kinship, group solidarity, and gift giving were governed by the values of honor and shame. Since these issues show up in many of the Markan concealment passages (as well as in passages in which Jesus is open about his identity and power), it follows that we must understand the ancient values of honor and shame if we are to understand these passages.

As I discuss many of the Markan concealment passages, I will pay special attention to the ways in which the ancient values of honor and shame come to bear on them. In the world of Mark's audience, honor was the primary value governing one's interactions with others. Yet honor meant something different to these ancient Mediterranean people than it does to people in the modern West. We tend to think of honor as an individual virtue. If I do what is right, even if it seems that everyone is against me, I have acted honorably. This conception of honor did not obtain in the world of the Bible, however. Social-scientific critics have shown that honor and shame were construed socially. Bruce Malina's influential definition is as follows: "Honor is the value of a person in his or her own eyes (that is, one's claim to worth) *plus* that person's value in the eyes of his or her social group."[46] In other words, from an ancient Mediterranean perspective, honor involves not only the way in which I think about myself, but the way in which other people think about me. Moreover, some opinions matter considerably more than others. Specifically, the opinions of my immediately family, and then other blood relatives, are of the highest importance. In general, the opinions of other people take on less significance as the relationship of those people to me becomes more distant. Exceptions to this rule were, for the most part, limited to high-ranking people who could bestow honor or shame even on people with whom they previously had only the most distant relationships.

By identifying the cultural values of ancient Mediterranean people, we can begin to look at the ways in which ancient people might have interpreted the story we read in the Gospel of Mark. When Jesus performs great deeds of power, there is potential for his honor to increase. When people spread word of his deeds, when the crowds seek after him, when he becomes known as a prophet, when Peter identifies him as the Messiah—these are all events that ancient Mediterranean people would interpret according to their system of values in which honor and shame were key components. By the same token, when Jesus makes efforts to resist becoming known, when he tries to hinder the spread of his fame, and when he silences those who know he is the Messiah, ancient Mediterranean people would again interpret these according to the honor system, though in these instances they would experience a certain disconnect: Why would Jesus behave in ways that prevented, rather than promoted, the spread of his honor broadly among the public?

There are also many passages in which Jesus seems not at all concerned to conceal his deeds, his authority, or his special relationship to God. A good example of this is the story told in 2:1-12, in which Jesus heals a paralytic. This healing occurs in the midst of a large crowd. Indeed, the house in which the healing takes place is so crowded that people cannot enter through the door. Jesus also pronounces the forgiveness of the paralytic's sins, and subsequently calls attention to this healing in his dialogue with the scribes, healing the man publicly "so that you may know that the Son of Man has authority on earth to forgive sins" (2:10). This display of healing power, along with the claim to be able to forgive sins, and thus to have authority on a par with God's authority, is anything but secretive. It is quite public, as a matter of fact, and there are a number of other such episodes in Mark as well. In fact, in some passages, such as the healing of the leper in 1:40–45, elements of concealment and publicity are woven together in the same episode. We cannot develop a clear picture of the passages in which Jesus attempts to conceal his deeds and identity without also accounting for those passages in which he makes no such attempt.

What would ancient Mediterranean people have made of this inconsistency? It is helpful to bear in mind that, while scholars sometimes dissect Mark's Gospel and closely examine it in discrete units, such was not the approach of first-century Christians. They would have engaged Mark, in fact, as a story, told from beginning to end. Much recent scholarship on the Gospel of Mark has focused on its literary aspects.[47] Narrative critics and reader-response critics have emphasized that, in approaching the Gospel of Mark as a story, we gain insights that we miss when we dissect the text or mine it for historical data. Moreover, given the general consensus that most people in the Greco-Roman world were illiterate, it stands to reason that the Markan audience was composed mainly of hearers, rather than readers. The abundance of recent scholarship on oral-aural communication in the Greco-Roman world has established clearly that such communication involves a set of dynamics much different from those which attend communication in high-literacy cultures.[48] In thinking about the passages so long associated with the messianic secret, then, it is appropriate to consider them within this oral-aural context.

It will become clear as we work through these passages that ancient Mediterranean people hearing Mark's story would have interpreted these passages much differently than modern Westerners. As noted above, the term "messianic secret" is a technical term used by scholars to talk about a group of passages in Mark, or some subset of that group. Yet if we approach these passages from the perspective of ancient Mediterranean people, the language of secrecy may influence the results of this social-scientific study before we even begin. Secrecy had rather specific functions in ancient Mediterranean culture. Jesus' behavior, however, does not look very much like secrecy from an ancient Mediterranean perspective. Nor does it seem that what he most wishes to conceal is his messianic identity. If this is the case, then assuming the presence of a theme of secrecy in Mark leads us in the wrong direction and may keep us from seeing certain possibilities for interpreting Jesus' words and deeds in Mark.

Chapter 1 of this work, then, will examine ancient conventions regarding secrecy. I will argue that ancient Mediterranean people thought about secrecy in rather different ways than modern Westerners, and therefore we are well served if we do not bind ourselves to the language of secrecy in analyzing these passages. In chapter 2, I will explore a number of passages long associated with the messianic secret in terms of the ancient Mediterranean values of honor and shame. As I will argue, the values of honor and shame, which are related to reputation, prestige, and fame, formed the backdrop against which ancient people would have understood these passages. Chapter 3 will shed more light on these passages by discussing Jesus' new vision for the kinds of actions and attitudes that should be considered honorable. Chapter 4 will take up the issue of those passages in which Jesus seems quite open about his deeds and identity. After all, if we are to identify passages in which Jesus conceals his deeds and identity, it behooves us to look just as closely at passages in which he does not. In chapter 5, I will examine the relationship of the passages discussed in chapters 2 and 3 to those in chapter 4. In other words, I will discuss the ways that the passages in which Jesus engages in specific types of countercultural behavior relate to those in which such behavior is absent. Understanding communication in cultures that retain strong elements of oral expression, as was the case in the world of Mark's audience, can shed light on the connection between these passages. We will also benefit from some of the insights of modern reader-response theory. Perhaps by looking at these much-studied texts through new lenses, we may develop a fresh perspective on those passages so long associated with Wrede's "messianic secret."

SECRECY

As noted in the introduction, the term "messianic secret" has functioned essentially as a cipher among biblical scholars. It has been a cooking pot into which scholars have poured different combinations of a select variety of ingredients, and from which they have produced a variety of interesting entrees. Another way to say this is that the "messianic secret" is a technical term in Markan scholarship. The referent of this technical term varies among scholars, but to use this term means that one is working with some subset of a broad set of issues related to Markan concealment passages (see the introduction). Exactly what scholars mean when they discuss the secrecy motif differs from case to case.

In a very broad sense, secrecy is simply intentional concealment.[1] Sissela Bok expands upon this definition, writing that to keep a secret from someone is "to block information about it or evidence of it from reaching that person and to do so intentionally: to prevent him from learning it, and thus from possessing it, making use of it, or revealing it. The word 'secrecy' refers to the resulting concealment."[2] To some extent, then, we are on safe ground in saying that Jesus keeps secrets in Mark's Gospel. Jesus does, at times, intentionally conceal some information from some people. When Jesus orders the witnesses to the raising of Jairus's daughter that no one should know what he has done (5:43), or orders the disciples to tell no one that he is the Messiah (8:30), he is concealing information. If secrecy is intentional concealment, then Jesus is practicing secrecy.

Yet secrecy will mean different things in different cultural contexts. Our concern in this chapter will be secrecy within the context of the ancient Mediterranean world. Broadly speaking, this is the context of the Markan audience, and the understanding of secrecy within this specific context should help us to evaluate whether Mark's audience would have understood Jesus' actions in terms of secrecy. As Guy G. Stroumsa has put it, "Christianity was born and first grew in a world in which esotericism, religious as well as philosophical, was rife."[3]

THE LANGUAGE OF SECRECY

The Language of Secrecy in the New Testament World

There is a broad Greek vocabulary related to secrecy. Many terms become related to secrecy by the addition of the preposition *hypo* (sometimes rendered *hyp-* or *hyph-*), which has the basic meaning of "under," rather like the prefix *sub-* in English. Hence, *histēmi* basically means "to set, place, or establish," while *hyphistēmi* means "to post secretly or wait in ambush." The word *ballō* means "to throw, put, or place," while *hypoballō* can refer to secret payments or bribes. Similarly, though less frequently, sometimes words prefixed by the preposition *para* connote secrecy, such as in the case of *parekdidōmi*, which means "give in marriage secretly," and *pareiserpō*, which means "creep in secretly."[4]

There are several other common terms for secrecy as well. The word group related to *kruptō*, which means "hide," relates to secrecy. These words, which are extremely common, do not bear specifically religious overtones.[5] Yet they are at times used in specifically religious contexts or otherwise given religious meanings. Philo, for example, uses the term *apokruphios*, which is related to *kruptos*, to speak of divine revelations that are not to be uttered aloud, but treasured in silence.[6] We also find this term in *1 Clement* in a reference to David's saying to God, "You have unveiled to me the veiled and hidden [*kruphia*] matters of your wisdom."[7] Likewise, the Wisdom of Solomon speaks of hiding (*apokruptō*) the secrets of God's wisdom (6:22). They are not, however, the more common words for secrecy when speaking of religious rites and practices.

The word *lathra* and related words are also used for secrecy. Words in this group often connote treachery, plotting, or intrigue, as in Josephus's secret instructions (*lathra*) to a certain Crispus to make the soldier guarding Crispus drunk and then to escape.[8] Deuteronomy 13:7 (LXX) refers to a secret invitation to idolatry. There are also a number of instances in which this term is used in statements that nothing can be hidden from God, as in the letter of Aristeas to Philocrates: "[E]very place is filled with His sovereignty, and...nothing done by men on earth secretly escapes his notice [*lanthanei*]."[9] Again, however, this is not a term that has specifically religious overtones.

Another term used to indicate secrecy is *arrētos,* which has among its meanings "unspoken," "that cannot be spoken," "not to be spoken," and "unutterable."[10] Forms of this word commonly describe the religious experience of the ineffable and inexplicable, experience that cannot be adequately captured in words. Plutarch uses this term to refer to mystic rites and ceremonies that are concealed from the eyes and ears of the multitude.[11] In the *Life of Apollonius*, this term is used for the rings and staffs of Indian sages, which are reportedly able to do anything and are "honored as secrets."[12] This term can also have profane usages, however, such as we see in Sirach 13:22: the rich person can say things that he should not (*aporrēta*), but he is nevertheless justified by others.

Within Greek religion, the primary term used for the keeping of secrets was *mystērion*. There were profane uses of this term, such as when Josephus describes Antipater's life as a "mystery of iniquity" because of the secrecy of his friends.[13] Yet the specifically religious uses of this term were quite common. This word could refer to religious rites available to a closed circle of initiates, including the initiation process itself. It could also refer to the secrets revealed in those rites, even when those secrets were inexpressible, along the lines of *arrētos*. One would find such rites in a variety of contexts, the most famous of which is the sanctuary of Eleusis. A "mystery" could also refer simply to a profound religious experience, or a religious truth that is beyond explanation. According to Ignatius, the virginity of Mary, her giving birth, and the death of the Lord are "mysteries."[14] In the *Epistle to Diognetus*, we read of Jesus, "Even though he was not understood by unbelievers, he told these things to his disciples, who after being considered faithful by him came to know the mysteries of the Father."[15] In the LXX, this term only appears in later works: Tobit, Judith, The Wisdom of Solomon, Sirach, Daniel, and 2 Maccabees.[16] It can refer both to secular and religious secrets. It can, for example, refer to the secret of a king (Tob 12:7), a secret plan (Jdt 2:2), the secrets of a friend (Sir 22:22; 27:16, 17, 21), or secret wartime information (2 Macc 13:21). Yet it can also refer to the "secret purposes of God" (Wis 2:22), the nature of wisdom (Wis 6:22), or to secrets that only God can reveal (Dan 2:18, 19, 27, 28, 29, 30, 47). We also find this term used for idolatrous rites (Wis 14:15, 23).

There are also a number of terms that can, but do not necessarily, express secrecy. In such cases, secrecy may be a secondary or derivative meaning. For example, *stegō* can mean "conceal or keep hidden," but refers primarily to tightly covering something to keep fluid in or out. *Keuthō* refers to the covering of an object, but also can refer to the keeping of secrets, much as we would speak of something as "veiled" in English. *Phōrios* primarily means "stolen," but it can also mean "secret" or "clandestine." *Anangeltos* means "unannounced," and therefore can connote the concealing of information. *Malē* means "armpit," but it can also refer to something done in an underhanded way. *Sigaō* and *siōpaō* both refer to keeping silence, and it is an easy move from silence to secrecy. *Skotos*, which means "dark," can relate to deeds that are concealed from other people.[17]

The Language of Secrecy in Mark

Interestingly, this rich vocabulary for secrecy rarely shows up in the Gospel of Mark. None of the words for secrecy created by prefixing *hypo-* or *para-* appears in Mark. The only possible exception to this is the use of *parerchomai*, "to pass by," in 6:48, but as we will see, "to pass by" in this context refers not to hiding, but revelation. No form of *arrētos* appears in Mark. The words *kruptos* and *apokruphos* each appear once in Mark (both in 4:22), but words related to *kruptō* are otherwise absent from the Gospel.[18] *Lanthanō* occurs in 7:24 to convey Jesus' wish that no one know he had entered a house. No other words from this word group appear in the Gospel. *Mystērion*, a word that appears rather often in the Pauline corpus, occurs only once in Mark (4:11).

The word *siōpaō*, which means "be silent," appears five times in Mark's Gospel (3:4; 4:39; 9:34; 10:48; 14:61). The use of this term in 9:34 could be seen as the disciples wishing to keep a secret from Jesus, but none of these instances refer to Jesus' keeping a secret. In fact, only once is Jesus the subject of this verb (14:61), and in the next verse Jesus admits to being "the Messiah, the Son of the Blessed One." Once in the Gospel Jesus tells a demon to be silent (1:25), but the word here is *phimaō*, which means "be muzzled," as one who silences a barking dog. If the evangelist wished to convey secrecy in this passage, he chose an unusual word to do so. This word also shows up in 4:39, in Jesus' rebuke of the sea during a storm. Clearly, secrecy is not in mind in this case.

Other terms mentioned above—*stegō, keuthō, phōrios, anangeltos, malē,* and *sigaō,* never appear in Mark. *Skotos* occurs once (15:33), but not in relationship to secrecy (darkness came over the land). In sum, the vocabulary of secrecy is exceedingly rare in Mark. In fact, with regard to the vocabulary surveyed above, there are only four instances in the sixteen chapters of the Gospel in which the language of secrecy is present (4:11, twice in 4:22; and 7:24), and three of these instances occur within eleven verses of one another.

THE FUNCTIONS OF SECRECY

The Functions of Secrecy in the New Testament World

One can, of course, refer to secrecy without using this kind of specific vocabulary. For example, one might say something like, "I went there without his knowing," or "She kept this information to herself." Alternatively, we sometimes use phrases that connote secrecy, such as when we say that a certain fact was kept "out of sight" or that a correspondence is "for your eyes only." Context, then, can be crucial to identifying secrets. Greek-speaking people of the ancient Mediterranean world also used context to express secrecy. For example, in Luke 22:6, Judas looks for an opportunity to betray Jesus "away from the crowd." In this case, secrecy is simply implied by the context.

Thus, in thinking through secrecy in Mark's Gospel, we must address both vocabulary and context. With regard to the latter, the sociologist Georg Simmel offers a helpful starting point. He discusses secrecy primarily as a protective measure. "[T]he purpose of secrecy," he writes, "is, above all, *protection*."[19] Though Simmel's interpretation does not deal specifically with ancient Mediterranean cultures, it is especially appropriate for this discussion. Scholarship on secrecy in the ancient Mediterranean world has pointed to its protective, exclusionary, or defensive functions. In some ways, the protective functions of secrecy are obvious. Knowledge of an individual or group can, in certain contexts, serve as a tool for defamation. One may therefore keep secrets as a way of maintaining one's public reputation. The Roman satirist Juvenal, for example, discusses slaves who slander their masters as retribution for beatings. The wealthy master may therefore attempt to practice secrecy in order to avoid the gossip of slaves (though Juvenal notes that this will always be unsuccessful).[20] Seneca notes that it is best to control one's anger, since other vices than anger "may be concealed and cherished in secret," but anger will show through.[21] Secrecy may also help one to avoid prosecution or persecution. If one is engaged in illicit practices, such as the practice of illegal magical acts, it is prudent to do so in secret to avoid prosecution.[22] The common admonition in the Greek magical papyri to maintain secrecy probably resulted in part from suppression, either by Roman authorities or Christian communities.[23]

The necessity of protective secrecy was exacerbated in the ancient Mediterranean context by the "high-context" nature of the culture. A high-context culture is one in which people are deeply involved in the everyday activities of those around them and in which information is widely shared.[24] Plutarch, for example, assumes that it is quite common for one's enemies to be able to pry into one's affairs, and he holds that one must live circumspectly in order to avoid the assaults of one's enemies.[25] The ancient novel *Leucippe and Clitophon* also provides commentary on the high-context culture: "Rumor and Slander are two evil sisters. Slander is sharper than a knife, stronger than fire, more plausible than the sirens; Rumor is more fluid than water, speedier than the wind, quicker than wings."[26] Within the high-context setting, secrecy would be an important and necessary means of protection.

Secrecy can also protect information that allows a group to establish social boundaries. Luther H. Martin offers an understanding of secrecy in Hellenistic religious communities that highlights this function of secrecy.[27] He argues that Hellenistic associations—clubs and *collegia*—provide examples in which we see the use of secrecy for purposes of boundary maintenance. These clubs and *collegia* were voluntary and private associations, all of which should be considered "religious."[28] He construes Hellenistic associations broadly, then, as religious communities. Martin also construes these associations as "fictive kin groups," groups that in certain ways take over the functions of the natural family, such as in responsibility for funerary obligations.[29] These associations therefore required considerable loyalty by members, who generally occupied the same social class as one another and sometimes became members through inheritance. These characteristics not only inhered among, say, associations of people who practiced the same trade, but for the mystery cults as well. Martin notes that the mystery cults were very much like other voluntary associations in a number of ways.[30]

Martin identifies secrecy as having an essential place in the lives of the members of these associations. Based upon the sociological work of Simmel, Martin argues that these associations represented a "second world" that functioned alongside of the first world, and that this second world was facilitated by means of a secret.[31] Another way of putting this is that members of these groups developed beliefs, relationships, and practices that were specific to the association, that outsiders did not share, and that were in certain ways markedly different from everyday life. As noted above, the primary term used for the keeping of secrets in Greek religion was *mystērion*, and publicizing the mysteries was a serious offense. The problem in revealing the mysteries, however, in Martin's words, "seems not to do with disclosures of concealed information, of mystery contents, which, in most cases, were either trivial or public all along."[32] Rather, by revealing the mysteries, one undermined the ritual performances, embodied particularly in funerary and initiatory rites, that marked the group members off from the rest of society. Martin notes, "The 'doing' of secrecy, in other words, is not primarily a concealing of some knowledge, but rather embodies the ritual procedures necessary for the formation and maintenance of social boundaries."[33] The rituals in which initiates received the mysteries separated insiders from outsiders. To paraphrase Simmel, one possessed more strongly what was excluded from outsiders.[34] By violating the exclusivity of the mysteries, one threatened the very existence of the group. What was important, then, was not so much the content of the mystery, but that it *was* a mystery, and that it was revealed only within particular ritual contexts. To violate the mystery was to violate the sacredness of the ritual and the group. Simmel, in fact, comments, "The striking feature in the treatment of ritual is not only the rigor of its observance but, above all, the anxiousness with which it is guarded as a secret. Its disclosure appears to be as detrimental as that of the purposes and actions, or perhaps of the very existence, of the society."[35]

This notion of secrecy creating boundaries and strengthening group cohesion may account for the exclusive nature of the Eucharist in the *Didache* (see 9:5; 10:6). The unholy are excluded from participation in the Eucharist, since their admittance would violate the nature of this gathering of the baptized and thereby profane the rite.[36] In a similar vein, Apollonius prays, "O Asclepius, the philosophy you teach is secret and congenial to yourself, in that you suffer not the wicked to come hither, not even if they pour into your lap all the wealth of India and Sardis."[37] Likewise, the *Gospel of Thomas* begins with reference

moment, secrecy is necessary in order that life may go on."[46] Pilch, however, offers no substantial analysis of Jesus' open performance of miracles. Nor does he deal sufficiently with passages such as 5:19, in which Jesus himself seems anything but secretive in his behavior.

Other scholars, however, have noted that, in Mark, Jesus does not normally engage in defensive secrecy to ward off envy. In fact, Jerome Neyrey and Richard Rohrbaugh conclude that, "except for Jesus' refusal of the compliment in Mark 10:17, he does *not* appear to have engaged in any of the classical strategies of avoiding envy."[47] They do not offer an explanation of the concealment passages in Mark's Gospel, but they do point to an important issue: whether or not the Jesus of history engaged in "defensive secrecy," the concealment traditions that Mark recounts may have a very different meaning in their narrative context than in the context of the life of Jesus of Nazareth.

Sometimes, however, secrecy had an additional function: to denote the inexpressibility of a truth. This function does not exclude the protective, exclusive, or defensive functions of secrecy. Rather, these functions could work in concert with secrecy as the establishment of social boundaries and a means for establishing group solidarity. Groups might enjoin secrecy upon their members so that the inexpressible and sacred truths of the group, communicated in ritualistic formularies, were not profaned by common usage in which the truth contained within the rituals would be lost. In such cases, ancient writers commonly used various forms of *arrētos*, which, as noted above, has among its meanings "unspoken," "that cannot be spoken," "not to be spoken," and "unutterable."[48] To quote Walter Burkert,

> Is it not true that the mysteries were "unspeakable," *arrhēta*, not just in the sense of artificial secrecy utilized to arouse curiosity, but in the sense that what was central and decisive was not accessible to verbalization? There is an "unspeakable *sympatheia*" of the souls with the rituals, Proclus states, and much older is the well-known pronouncement of Aristotle that those undergoing mysteries (*teloumenoi*) should not "learn" (*mathein*) but should "be affected," "suffer," or "experience" (*pathein*).[49]

Likewise, among groups commonly referred to as "gnostic," it was commonly the case that certain mysteries were not to be communicated to the wider public. Michael A. Williams argues that normally this did not have to do with the fact that there were particular truths that outsiders simply should not know, but that these truths were ineffable, incommunicable, or at least difficult to communicate.[50] Within the circles in which mysteries were revealed, however, the sense of social exclusiveness inhered, since the number of people within the circle was necessarily limited.

Functions of Secrecy and the Gospel of Mark

None of these functions of secrecy, however, sufficiently accounts for Jesus' concealment of his deeds and identity in Mark's Gospel. To begin with, let us consider Martin's assertion that secrecy in Greco-Roman religion normally occurred in ritualistic contexts. There is no clear ritualistic context for any of the passages associated with the messianic secret in Mark's Gospel. Admittedly, there are passages in which Jesus appears to act in ways that resemble magical practices of his day. For example, his utterance of Aramaic words in 5:41 and 7:34 could, in modest ways, be likened to the use of archaic terminology in magical acts. Likewise, in the healing of a deaf man he puts his fingers into the deaf man's ears, spits, and touches the deaf man's tongue (7:33), and in the healing of a blind man, he places spittle upon the blind man's eyes (8:23). It is important to note, however, that the intention here is not to conceal information about the specifics of the healing process. Jesus does not specifically enjoin secrecy about the words or actions he uses to heal. Rather, he seems to wish to suppress the spread of word about the healing itself. Moreover, in the only other healing story in which Jesus commands silence, the healing of the leper in 1:40-45, there are no Aramaic terms or actions such as the use of spittle. These passages bear little resemblance to secrecy enjoined within the context of rituals associated with ancient mystery cults.

Likewise, Jesus' exorcisms lack ritualistic elements, and instead emphasize his personal authority over demons. Jesus may command that the demon be silent (1:25, 34; 3:12) and come out of the possessed person (1:25; 5:8; 9:25), though he does not always do so: the exorcism of the Syrophoenician woman's daughter lacks even these elements (see 7:24-30). By contrast, we may consider Josephus's account of an exorcist who utilized incantations composed by Solomon. The exorcist employed a ring containing a specific type of root, drawing out the demon through the nostrils of the possessed man. Following this procedure, the exorcist invoked the name of Solomon in recited incantations, commanding the demon not to return into the formerly possessed man.[51]

Nor does it appear that in the passages associated with the messianic secret, Jesus is attempting to create exclusive social cohesion, establish group solidarity, or ward off envy. First of all, when Jesus does try to limit the spread of information about his deeds or identity, information is not always limited to his group of followers. In the story of Jesus' cleansing of a leper, for example (1:40-45), Jesus commands in no uncertain terms that the healed leper say nothing to anyone. There is no indication, however, that Jesus is alone in this passage. In fact, in 1:38 he invites others to join him in his proclamation in neighboring towns. His command to say nothing to anyone nevertheless applies only to the leper and not to others present. Moreover, one might expect that the method of the leper's healing would come out in conversation with the priests, which is, moreover, supposed to serve as a "witness" (*marturion*) to them (1:44).

In two of the three passages in which Jesus heals in private (7:31-37; 8:22-26), Mark in no way specifies that only Jesus' followers are with him. After healing a deaf man, Jesus orders "them" (*autois*) to tell no one (7:36). The antecedent of the pronoun, however, is unclear. In 8:23, Jesus leads a blind man out of the village before healing him. Yet exactly who is with Jesus at the time is not specified. Being out of the village does not necessarily equate to being in solitude. The episode in 5:21-24, 35-43 is rather a different story. Mark writes that Jesus took only the child's father and mother and "the ones with him," apparently Peter, James, and John (see v. 37). Nevertheless, the mourners are already wailing (v. 38), and Jesus' statement that "the child is not dead but sleeping" (v. 39) meets with contemptuous laughter (v. 40). The deed itself is not likely to remain concealed. Similarly, when Jesus silences demons, his intention does not appear to be to limit information to his closest followers. He simply silences the demons. The disciples receive no more information than anyone else.

Jesus' command to the disciples not to tell anyone that he is the Messiah after Peter identifies him as such (8:29-30) could be interpreted as an attempt to keep information strictly within the in-group for defensive purposes. If this is the case, however, we are at pains to explain why Jesus confesses that he is the Messiah before the high priest (14:62), who is most certainly not an in-group member. Similarly, in the episode of the transfiguration, Jesus' command to the disciples not to tell anyone what they have seen "until the Son of Man has risen from the dead" (9:9) could be interpreted as an attempt to keep information within the in-group. Yet this silence command has a time limit. After Jesus has risen, they may tell, but not until then. The issue, then, is not so much who knows about the transfiguration, but when it is appropriate for such information to come out.

When Jesus attempts to seek solitude and escape from the crowds in 1:35, 4:35-36, and 6:32, he is not exclusively with his circle of followers. In the first of these passages, it appears that Jesus has left his followers behind. Simon and those with him must search for Jesus (1:36). In 4:35, Jesus may take only his disciples in the boat with him (though the text does not specify). Nevertheless, Mark includes the cryptic detail "other boats were with him" (4:36). Whatever the significance of this statement may be, it militates against a sense of exclusiveness in this boat journey. When Jesus seeks solitude with his followers in 6:31-32, Mark provides a motive: Jesus and his disciples have no time for leisure, not even to eat. In none of these three passages does the motive seem to cohere with ancient social functions of secrecy.

Of the categories of passages often associated with the messianic secret, Jesus' private teaching to an inner circle of followers (4:10ff.; 4:34; 7:17-23; 9:28; 10:10; 13:3ff.) looks the most like the kinds of secrecy practiced in Hellenistic religions. Looking carefully at these passages, however, the similarities are not as clear. These teachings are not mysteries revealed only to initiates. Further, the private nature of the teachings seems to result from Jesus' followers' choice to ask him about these things in private, rather than Jesus' decision to keep them secret from the masses. The case appears to be not that either Jesus or the disciples wish to hide information from outsiders, but that Jesus' followers do not always comprehend Jesus' teachings, and try to gain clarity by approaching him for additional teaching. Consider, for example, 4:10: "When he came to be alone, those around him with the twelve asked him about the parables." In 7:17 we read, "When he had gone into the house away from the crowd, his disciples asked him about the parable." In 9:28, after Jesus' disciples are unable to cast out a demon, they approach him in a house "privately" (*kat' idian*). They ask him, "Why were we unable to cast it out?" In 13:3, Peter, James, John, and Andrew wish to know more about the destruction of the Temple about which Jesus has just spoken. The only instance of private teaching in which the text does not specify that this is at the disciples' request occurs in 4:34.

In 4:11 we have the very language of Hellenistic religious secrecy appearing in a passage about private teaching: Jesus refers to the "mystery of the kingdom of God." Indeed, if any passage in Mark looks like ancient religious secrecy, this is it. Yet this passage also presents some problems when understood in terms of secrecy. The issue here is not that Jesus and his followers are forbidden to reveal some truth to other people. Group members are not intentionally to conceal the content of Jesus' teaching. Rather, Jesus' preaching is public, and the disciples are never forbidden to talk about it. In fact, Jesus sends the twelve in 3:14 and 6:12 precisely for the purpose of proclamation.

Jesus does offer special teaching to "those around him with the twelve" (4:10), who are probably people among the crowds who have heard Jesus' teaching and responded positively to it.[52] Yet this is simply an explanation of Jesus' more public teaching, and Jesus seems taken aback by the fact that these followers do not understand from the outset. "You do not understand this parable? How then will you understand all the parables?" (4:13). Jesus' question seems to indicate that this circle of his followers should be able to understand the parable without explanation. Nevertheless, the disciples, whom Jesus attempts to make insiders, suffer from a lack of comprehension repeatedly throughout the narrative (4:13; 4:35–41; 8:31–32; 9:33–37; 10:35–45). It is important to note, though, that their lack of comprehension comes in spite of Jesus' teaching to them, rather than because he has kept secret certain crucial truths.

The reason that Mark refers to a "mystery" in 4:11 probably has to do with the fact that some people will comprehend Jesus' teaching in response to faith, some will do so only partially, and some not at all. As Joel Marcus notes in relation to Mark 4:10-12, "Human beings as human beings do not know the truth about God, Jesus, or their own condition. For them to recognize vital truth, an act of God is necessary. Knowing is connected with God's act of bringing in his kingdom."[53] We have, then, a mystery, not in the sense of secret knowledge concealed by the community for purposes of piety, but of revelation by God to the elect. This might be called secrecy, but it does not establish group boundaries or function defensively. Here we come closer to the notion of secrecy as an unspeakable truth: Mark seems to have in mind an understanding that surpasses what can be gleaned from simply hearing the teaching. Some people have "ears to hear" (e.g., 4:9), and others do not. In 4:12, Mark hearkens back to Isaiah 6:9-10 to make this point: Jesus speaks in parables *so that* the truth of Jesus' teaching will be obscured from outsiders. Only God's revelation allows one to enter another level of understanding and respond in faith to Jesus' teachings. Interestingly, however, the common Greek terms for ineffable, unspeakable truths, *arrētos* and *aporrētos*, do not appear in Mark. In fact, the only place in the New Testament in which either of these terms shows up is 2 Corinthians 12:4, in which Paul mentions *arrēta hrēmata*, "words not to be told."

CONCLUSION

In the world of the New Testament, there was a broad Greek vocabulary for secrecy. This vocabulary, however, rarely appears in Mark's Gospel. Secrecy also had specific functions in the cultural context of the New Testament, though we rarely see these functions at work in Mark's Gospel. In sum, secrecy, as understood by ancient Mediterranean people, simply does not do very much heavy lifting in Mark's Gospel. This is in no way to invalidate previous work on the messianic secret in Mark, since "messianic secret" is a technical term used by scholars to refer to some subset of a select group of passages. Yet given the understandings of secrecy prevalent in the historical context of Mark's Gospel, the language of secrecy can cause confusion. Among ancient Mediterranean people, secrecy established and preserved boundaries. It functioned defensively to preserve the reputation of a person or a group. Since in this study I am attempting to reconstruct in part the ways in which an ancient Mediterranean audience would have heard these passages associated with the messianic secret, I will avoid the language of secrecy. Instead, I will cast the argument primarily in terms of honor and shame.

Jesus Resists Honor

There is no standard definition of culture among anthropologists. Yet one definition that is commonly used comes from Daniel G. Bates and Fred Plog: "Broadly defined, culture is a system of shared beliefs, values, customs, behaviors, and artifacts that the members of a society use to cope with their world and with one another, and that are transmitted from generation to generation through learning."[1] This shared system creates certain expectations regarding issues such as speech, dress, sexual behavior, and etiquette. Normally, we take for granted the expectations of our cultural system. We tend not to notice them until someone breaks them and the contrast between that person's behavior and the cultural expectation is thrown into sharp relief. For example, most of us do not think much about eating from plates or bowls—this is simply something we do as part of our cultural programming. Yet if someone were to eat food directly off of the table, we would most certainly become aware of this convention. For the most part, we take our cultural expectations and assumptions as givens, and when someone defies these, we might experience puzzlement, surprise, or even anger.

The Jesus of Mark's Gospel often behaves in a manner that is quite unconventional according to the standards of his culture. Some of the most pointed examples of this countercultural behavior are found among the Markan concealment passages. In this chapter, I will look at the first three categories of these passages (see the introduction):

1. Jesus' commands that people whom he has healed tell no one about what he has done (1:40-45; 5:21-24, 35-43; 7:31-37; 8:22-26)
2. Jesus' healing of people in private settings (5:21-24, 35-43; 7:31-37; 8:22-26)
3. Jesus' silencing of demons, who are aware of his special status (1:23-28; 1:34; 3:12)

My intention is to show the connections of these passages with the ancient values of honor and shame, and to demonstrate that ancient Mediterranean people hearing Mark's story would have understood these passages according to these values.

Although there are silence commands after Peter's identification of Jesus as the Messiah (8:30) and the transfiguration scene (9:9), I will discuss these passages in chapter 3. Both passages are closely related to larger discussions in the narrative of Jesus' reshaping of the values of honor and shame, and both are best explained with reference to this larger narrative context.

AFFIRMATION, REPUTATION, AND HONOR IN THE ANCIENT MEDITERRANEAN CONTEXT

A letter attributed to the Cynic philosopher Diogenes claims that "popular opinion" (*doxēs*) is that "to which all, Greeks and barbarians alike, are subservient."[2] Likewise, Plutarch wrote of Alexander that "he loved his reputation more than his life or his kingdom."[3] Both Plutarch and Xenophon hold that the sweetest sound one can hear is the sound of praise.[4] Across the ancient Mediterranean world, men prized public affirmation. Women, in most cases, fit into the honor-shame system by their ability to enhance or degrade the reputation of their fathers and husbands.[5] To receive public affirmation was to receive honor, not only for oneself, but for one's family or in-group. Negative public opinion, however, meant the loss of honor.

Biblical scholars working with insights from cultural anthropology have utilized a distinction between two basic kinds of honor.[6] One kind, called *achieved* (or *acquired*) *honor*, is gained by one's own deeds, which might include military exploits, public displays of virtue, or teaching. Josephus offers an example of achieved honor in an account of Saul's military success:

> This brilliant exploit achieved by Saul spread his praises throughout all the Hebrews and procured him a marvellous renown [*doxēs*] for val-iance; for if there were some who before despised him, they were now brought round to honour him [*metestēsan epi to timan*] and to deem him the noblest of all men. For, not content with having rescued the inhabitants of Jabis, he invaded the country of the Ammanites, subdued it all, and having taken much booty, returned in glory to his own land.[7]

The second kind of honor, called *ascribed honor*, does not come first from popular appeal, and is not gained by one's merits or deeds. Rather, it is derived from a high-ranking person, either through inheritance from or bestowal by that person. As a result of this inheritance or grant, the person to whom honor has been ascribed receives an elevated social rating. We might think of a dissolute royal son who inherits the throne, or a Roman senator who is a friend of the emperor and is appointed on that basis to be the governor of a Roman province. Josephus offers an example of a royal ascription of honor in his account of a dispute between Hyrcanus and Antipater: "After hearing both speakers, Caesar pronounced Hyrcanus to be the more deserving claimant to the high-priesthood, and left Antipater free choice of office. The latter, replying that it rested with him who conferred the honour to fix the measure of the honour, was appointed viceroy of all Judea."[8] While both Hyrcanus and Antipater are granted honors in this passage, these honors derive from royal ascription, and not from popular appeal.[9]

Many passages in Mark's Gospel that have long been associated with the "messianic secret" depict events related to the giving of benefits, reciprocation, and honor. Because modern Western readers are generally not attuned to ancient Mediterranean cultural conventions related to gift giving and reciprocation, we miss the significance that such passages would have had for the Markan audience. While modern readers tend to ask something like, "Why does Jesus attempt to keep his great deeds and identity a secret?" the ancients might have asked questions such as, "Why does Jesus resist the honor that he is due?" or, "Why does Jesus not allow the recipients of his gifts to fulfill their obligations?" When one considers how deeply embedded were these concepts of gift giving, reputation, and public affirmation, Jesus' behavior in Mark's Gospel seems culturally out of place. He is clearly working against the grain of common expectations. More specifically, he is engaging in a kind of ethical revisionism. In this chapter, we will look at several examples of Jesus' countercultural behavior. First we will look at episodes in which Jesus is resistant to receiving achieved honor, and second we will look at the ways in which Jesus attempts to suppress his ascribed honor.

JESUS' RESISTANCE TO ACHIEVED HONOR

Ancient Mediterranean Gift Giving

The circumstances surrounding Jesus' provision of gifts such as healing and exorcism are illuminated by an understanding of ancient Mediterranean practices of gift and reciprocation. An important way of acquiring a good name, and thus honor, in the ancient Mediterranean context was by beneficence—the giving of goods or services that helped other people in some way.[10] Wealth, power, influence, and other marks of privilege presented significant opportunities to acquire honor.[11] In fact, *philotimia*—literally, "love of honor"—was a common term for public benefactions.[12] The concept of benefaction—beneficence toward a group of people such as those in a particular city or region—stretches back to the Homeric period and was alive and well in the first-century Mediterranean world. However, this concept changed over time. Frederick Danker notes that, in Homeric times, those people who were thought to possess exceptional merit (*aretē*) were those who had demonstrated military prowess and thus contributed significantly to the well-being of a particular land or city. Deities who worked for the preservation of those who worshiped them were thought of in much the same way. The second-century orator Aelius Aristides describes deliverance by the gods from the dangers of the sea as a benefaction.[13] Xenophon likewise writes of a conversation between Heracles and two women who are the personification of Virtue and Vice. During this conversation, Virtue says to Heracles, "[I]f you desire the love of friends, you must do good to your friends: if you covet honour from a city, you must aid that city: if you are fain to win the admiration of all Hellas for virtue, you must strive to do good to Hellas."[14] Both the warrior and the deity were perceived as benefactors or saviors, and the recognition of their acts of benefaction came to take the form of "public accolades expressed in formal civic decrees that are ordinarily incised on stone; or, in more private rhetorical statement [*sic*], sometimes of a poetic nature."[15] Such accolades and monuments would increase the fame, reputation, and therefore the honor of the warrior or deity.

Eventually, with the decreasing importance of the city-state, benefaction was recognized in other arenas, and public recognition was extended more frequently to other groups of people. Beneficent rulers, people who gave generous sums for the public good, or those who performed some exceptional deed that benefited the populace were considered benefactors, and they were honored as such. Benefactors might bankroll public buildings, sponsor games for public enjoyment, or throw banquets. The honors that the people would bestow on a benefactor who did such things were, in Dio Chrysostom's words, "bait" for the benefactor.[16] Plutarch expresses a similar sentiment in more concrete detail: "Let kings and royal stewards and those who would be foremost in their cities and hold office engage in money-getting. These are driven to it, their ambition [*philotimian*] and pretension and vainglory [*kenēn doxan*] compel them, engaged as they are in giving banquets, bestowing favour, paying court, sending presents, supporting armies, buying gladiators."[17] He describes the early days of Julius Caesar's political career as characterized by this type of ambition: "He was unsparing in his outlays of money, and was thought to be purchasing a transient and short-lived fame at a great price, though in reality he was buying things of the highest value at a small price." Caesar was therefore thirteen hundred talents in debt before he entered any public office. When he was appointed curator of the Appian Way, he spent a great deal of his own money upon it. While serving as an aedile (a magistrate and patron), "he furnished three hundred and twenty pairs of gladiators, and by lavish provision besides for theatrical performances, processions, and public banquets, he washed away all memory of the ambitious efforts of his predecessors in the office. By these means he put the people in such a humour that every man of them was seeking out new offices and new honours with which to requite him."[18]

Diogenes Laertius recounts an event in his *Life of Empedocles* that shows not only the adoration that could be bestowed upon a benefactor, but the benefactor's desire for even more adoration. He relates that there was a pestilence in Selinus caused by smells coming from the nearby river. This pestilence was causing the death of the citizens of that city, and in particular the death of women in childbirth. Empedocles, at his own expense, merged this river with two neighboring rivers, thus solving the problem of the pestilence. As the people of Selinus feasted by the river, Empedocles appeared, and the people rose up, worshiping him and praying to him as if he were a god. "It was then to confirm this belief of theirs that he leapt into the fire."[19]

What is important here is not the particular way in which beneficence was manifested, but that the beneficence was publicly acknowledged as such. One group that began to receive some degree of recognition was the philosophers, who were thought to be "benefactors of humanity" by virtue of "inward excellence and prudent counsel."[20] Like philosophers, physicians could also be honored as benefactors. The Roman historian Suetonius writes of the emperor Augustus's physician, Antonius Musa, who had overseen Augustus's recovery from a serious illness. According to Suetonius, this was seen not just as a service to Augustus, but to the populace as well. "Some householders provided in their wills that their heirs should drive victims to the Capitol to pay a thank-offering in their behalf, because Augustus had survived them, and that a placard to this effect should be carried before them." Thus a statue of Musa was set up beside one of Asclepius, the god of medicine.[21]

On a more personal level, beneficence was often manifested within the patron-client system, an institution of considerable importance in the ancient Mediterranean world. John H. Elliott describes the patron-client system as a "fundamental and pervasive form of dependency relations, involving the reciprocal exchange of goods and services between socially superior 'patrons' and their socially inferior 'clients,' [which] shaped both the public and private sectors of ancient life as well as the political and religious symbolizations of power and dependency."[22] It involved vertical, reciprocal relationships in which the patron would provide a good or service for the client, and the client would show the patron honor and loyalty. Individuals entered into such relationships voluntarily. Ideally, the relationship between a patron and client would be lifelong, though this was not always the case.[23] While patrons and clients could honorably end their reciprocal relationships with one another, continued reciprocity was the norm, and the ending of the relationship was appropriate only after some reciprocal exchange had taken place. One who mediated between a patron and a client was a broker, and a particular individual might well be patron, client, and broker all at the same time and to several parties at once.

The patron-client system functioned according to a pattern of beneficence and recognition. When a gift was given, the unspoken but clear expectation was that some type of gift would be given in return. In his work *On Benefits*, Seneca is quite clear that to return a benefit is honorable, while not to do so is shameful.[24] Yet he also points out that the giver of a gift should never ask for anything in return. It is, he says, as right to accept a return as it is wrong to demand it.[25] Therefore, the giver of a gift should forget about it, while the recipient must never do so.[26] The expectation of reciprocation was not to be spoken out loud, but it was nonetheless understood by all and considered binding. This principle was, however, like so many aspects of proper etiquette, often ignored. The more status one had, the more freedom one had to ignore it.

A continued exchange of resources was necessary for the relationship between the two parties to continue, but because the patron and
the client were not social equals, the client could not normally return
in kind the gifts of the patron. What the client could do, however,
was show the patron honor, loyalty, and trust (*pistis*). Enhancing the
reputation of the patron was an important part of the client's duties.
As Elliott states, the client

> owes the patron a variety of services (*obsequium*) and is obligated to
> enhance the prestige, reputation, and honor of his or her patron in
> public and private life. For example, the client favors the patron with
> daily early-morning salutations, supports his political campaigns, pays
> his fines, furnishes his ransom, supplies him information, does not
> testify against him in the courts, and gives constant public attestation
> and memorials of the patron's benefactions, generosity, and virtue.[27]

In the ancient Mediterranean world (and especially for people in positions of power and influence), for others to spread word of one's gen-
erosity and deeds was greatly to be desired; benefaction brought public
recognition and thus honor.[28] A common view was that the primary
reason to gain wealth was to use wealth in acquiring honor. Hence,
we read in the ancient novel *The Golden Ass*, "[T]hey not be wealthy
whose riches are unknown."[29] The reciprocal nature of the patron-
client relationship was crucial if the system was to work, although
ideally one who bestowed a favor would not act only out of a desire
for personal gain.

It was not only humans, but also divine beings, who expected
repayment for their gifts. In *The Golden Ass*, the main character,
Lucian, has been turned into a donkey, and, as one might expect, finds
life as a donkey most unpleasant. Isis agrees to turn him back into a
human being, but not without his agreement to certain demands:

> Know thou this of certainty, that the residue of thy life until the hour
> of death shall be bound and subject to me; and think it not an injury
> to be always serviceable towards me whilst thou shalt live, since as by
> my mean and benefit thou shalt return again to be a man. Thou shalt
> live blessed in this world, thou shalt live glorious by my guide and
> protection, and when after thine allotted space of life thou descendest

to hell, there thou shalt see me in that subterranean firmament shining (as thou seest me now) in the darkness of Acheron, and reigning in the deep profundity of Styx, and thou shalt worship me as one that hath been favorable to thee. And if I perceive that thou art obedient to my commandment and addict to my religion, meriting by thy constant chastity my divine grace, know thou that I alone may prolong thy days above the time that the fates have appointed and ordained.[30]

Lucian is thus bound to Isis, both in his present life and in the afterlife. His faithfulness to her will result in her ongoing patronage as long as he is alive.

While the patron-client system was quite useful, however, it could easily lead to exploitative practices. Wealthy people were expected to engage in works of patronage and benefaction. Again turning to the *Golden Ass*, we read Chryseros who, "for fear of offices and burdens in the public weal, with great pains dissimulated his estate and lived sole and solitary in a small cot (howbeit well fortified) and huddled daily in ragged and torn apparel over his bags of gold."[31] This kind of obligation could turn to resentment, and, coupled with a sense of class entitlement, could lead to deeply derisive practices on the part of the patron. One needs only to read through the satires of the Roman writer Juvenal to get a sense of the ugly side of the patron-client relationship. He asks of would-be clients, "Is a dinner worth all the insults which you have to pay for it? Is your hunger so importunate, when it might, with greater dignity, be shivering where you are, and munching dirty scraps of dog's bread?"[32] In the same work, he writes about knowing one's place and staying within one's social station: "If you ever dare to utter one word [at the patron's dinner] as though you were possessed of three names [as a free-born Roman would be], you will be dragged by the heels and thrust out of doors as Cacus was, after the drubbing he got from Hercules."[33] The patron's motives, says Juvenal, are not in the least altruistic: "You may perhaps suppose that [the patron] Virro grudges the expense; not a bit of it! His object is to give you pain. For what comedy, what mime, is so amusing as a disappointed belly? His one object, let me tell you, is to compel you to pour out your wrath in tears, and to keep gnashing your squeaking molars."[34]

Juvenal's satires are deeply bitter in tone and underscore the indignity that could accompany one who took on the role of a client.

Seneca, a man of considerable wealth, confirms this tendency among patrons to mistreat clients. His work *On Anger* aims to discourage people of high station from mistreating their subordinates, such as clients and slaves. Lucian refers to the patron-client relationship as a kind of "willing slavery," though he blames the clients as much as the patrons for perpetuating this system. The flatterers, he says, are far more destructive than the patrons, since the flatterer is the cause of the patron's arrogance. "When they admire their possessions, praise their plate, crowd their doorways in the early morning and go up and speak to them as a slave speaks to his master, how can you expect the rich to feel?" If, however, clients would agree with one another to refrain from this willing slavery, even for a short time, the tables would be turned. "The rich would come to the doors of the poor and beg them not to leave their happiness unobserved and unattested and their beautiful tables and great houses unenjoyed and unused. It is not so much being rich that they like as being congratulated on it." The splendors of riches are of no use if there is no one to admire them.[35]

Sometimes, one could perform a favor by putting a client in touch with another person who could provide important resources. One who mediated between a patron and a client was a called a broker. It might be helpful, though, to think of a broker as a particular kind of patron, one who provided connections to other people, rather than, say, money or meals. It is difficult to tell whether Mark would consider Jesus primarily as a patron or a broker. One might put the question this way: In Mark's Gospel, does Jesus act on his *own* power to perform great deeds, or does he somehow *mediate* divine power that is granted to him by God? The answer is unclear. In fact, the question may never even have occurred to the evangelist. One clue, though, occurs in Mark 3:20-29. In this passage, the scribes from Jerusalem accuse Jesus of casting out demons through Satan's power. Jesus shows them the folly of this logic ("How is Satan able to cast out Satan?," v. 23), but he also says that they have blasphemed, or slandered, the Holy Spirit (see v. 29). This may indicate that Mark sees Jesus' power as emanating from the Holy Spirit. If this is the case, Jesus functions as a broker.

To say that Jesus is a broker is not to deny a high Christology in the Gospel of Mark. John's Gospel clearly has a high, incarnational Christology, and yet in John 5:19 Jesus says, "The Son is not able to do anything on his own, but only what he sees the Father doing. For whatever he [the Father] may do, the Son does likewise." Here John seems to cast Jesus as a broker, as the one who mediates the Father's power and will to humankind.

I will, then, refer to Jesus in what follows as a broker, bearing in mind the uncertainty of this designation. Yet for the larger argument, whether or not Jesus is a broker makes little difference. The same conventions of gift giving apply. In several healing episodes, Jesus provides people with gifts of considerable value by healing and casting out demons. In contrast to the common pattern of gift and reciprocation, however, Jesus on several occasions commands that people whom he has healed tell no one about what he has done (1:40-45; 5:21-24, 35-43; 7:31-37; 8:22-26). Similarly, he sometimes heals people in private settings, rather than before a public that could witness his doings (5:21-24, 35-43; 7:24-30; 8:22-26).

Resisting the Leper's Proclamation (1:40-45)

The first attempt by Jesus to conceal his great deeds of power occurs in the episode of the healing of the leper in 1:40-45. This is also the first instance in which Mark offers an account of someone's petitioning Jesus' brokerage. The leper who comes to Jesus does so begging him to make him clean and kneeling before him, a posture typical of a client coming before a patron or broker.[36] Matthew and Luke include references to the leper's kneeling or bowing before Jesus (see Matt 8:2; Luke 5:12), although they do not duplicate Mark's wording. Their accounts suggest that they understand the leper's petition in terms of the conventions regarding the relationship between a client and a patron or broker.[37] In this Markan passage, then, Jesus functions as a potential broker, and the leper functions as a potential client.[38]

In 1:41-42, Jesus grants the leper's request: "And filled with compassion, he stretched out his hand and touched him and said to him, 'I choose [to do so]. Be made clean.' And immediately the leprosy went out from him, and he was made clean." By describing Jesus as "filled with compassion," Mark draws upon language that, to an ancient Mediterranean audience, would express "a patron's favoritism to a client"[39] (see also 6:34; 8:2; 9:22).[40] There are two aspects of Jesus' beneficence toward the leper. First, Jesus heals the leper's illness. Second, and perhaps more importantly, Jesus commands the healed leper to follow the prescribed practices for restoration into the community. Prior to his healing, the leper was forced into a state of exclusion and shame. By going before the priests in order to demonstrate that he has been healed (see Leviticus 14), the former leper may reenter normal patterns of social behavior.

The normal course of action at this point would be for the leper, who has sought Jesus' help, to respond as a faithful client should and increase Jesus' honor. Seneca states that the giver of a gift should not spread word of what he had done; rather, "Let the recipient talk."[41] A proper response to a favor would be something like, "I shall never be able to repay you my gratitude, but, at any rate, I shall not cease from declaring everywhere that I am unable to repay it."[42] Jesus' next action is therefore very peculiar: "And scolding him he immediately drove him away, and he said to him, 'See that you say nothing to anyone at all, but go and show yourself to the priest and offer for your cleansing what Moses commanded, as a testimony to them'" (1:43-44). Jesus thus attempts (unsuccessfully) to prevent the leper's response to Jesus' brokerage. Implicit in Jesus' command to the leper is that he wishes to forgo the acquired honor that would accompany the response of a client. We read in 1:45, however, that "going out, [the healed leper] began to proclaim many things and to spread the word about" (1:45).[43] To be fair to the leper, we should bear in mind how strange Jesus' admonition must have sounded. In disobeying Jesus' injunction, the leper demonstrates the standard cultural response to beneficent works, thus revealing the goal of Jesus' admonition.

In a similar episode recounted in the *Histories* of Tacitus, we read of two people—a blind man and a man "whose hand was useless"— who beg the emperor Vespasian for miracles of healing. Tacitus writes, "Vespasian at first ridiculed these appeals and treated them with scorn; then, when the men persisted, he began at one moment to fear the discredit of failure, at another to be inspired with hopes of success by the appeals of the suppliants and the flattery of courtiers." The emperor agrees to attempt these healings because "if a cure were attained, the glory would be Caesar's, but in the event of failure, ridicule would fall only on the poor suppliants." After Vespasian succeeds in this "divine service," those who are present tell of what he has done.[44] Vespasian seems to take for granted that either honor or shame will result from his attempt to heal those who beg for his services.[45] His primary motivation for granting the requests of his petitioners is that he stands to gain honor if the healings are successful.[46]

Likewise, in the *Golden Ass*, Apuleius relates the tale of an Egyptian prophet named Zatchlas, who was hired to bring back the soul of a man from hell and revive his body from the dead temporarily. Though the prophet requires financial payment, the man issuing payment must also petition the prophet with flattery to perform this deed. Underscoring the acclaim that the prophet receives, Apuleius relates that, while the prophet is performing the ritual to raise the man, the onlookers marveled greatly.[47] The flattery of the petitioner and the marveling of the crowd demonstrate the acquisition of honor by the prophet. Jesus is unlike both Vespasian and Zatchlas, then, in that he attempts to suppress the proclamation of his beneficence, and in so doing attempts to avoid the honor that he is due.[48]

A Girl Raised, Honor Resisted (5:21-24, 35-43)

The episode of the healing of Jairus's daughter offers another example of Jesus' breaking the standard patterns of gift-and-response. Like the leper in 1:40-45, Jairus comes to Jesus, falling at Jesus' feet and begging for his services in the manner of a client who is petitioning a patron or broker.[49] Because Jairus has assumed this posture before Jesus publicly (see 5:21) and makes his request to Jesus publicly, Jairus issues a "positive challenge" to Jesus. That is to say, Jesus now stands to gain or lose honor based upon his response. A positive challenge can be a compliment, a gift, a petition, or any other interaction that obligates the recipient of the challenge to reciprocate, since failure to do so would result in a loss of honor.[50] Seneca says to the giver of compliments, "You have laid more people under obligation than you think."[51] Plutarch writes of influential people who were commonly compelled against their will or better judgment to grant a petitioner's request because, were they to refuse the request, other people might speak ill of them. Their reputation was, at least to some extent, in danger because of the public nature of the petitioner's request.[52] Based on common cultural expectations, Jairus's petition presents Jesus with two options: Jesus can increase his renown by granting Jairus's request and allowing word to spread about his beneficence. Alternatively, he can lose esteem in the eyes of the public (or at best, remain at the same level) by refusing Jairus's request.

Jesus chooses neither of these options. He grants Jairus's request, but takes pains to keep his beneficence toward Jairus out of the public view. In fact, the episode of the raising of Jairus's daughter involves four instances in which Jesus attempts to prevent proclamation of the great deed that he performs for Jairus. First, although a large crowd follows Jesus and those who are with him as they head toward Jairus's house (5:24), after hearing the report that Jairus's daughter has died Jesus allows no one to continue to follow him except for Peter, James, John, and, apparently, Jairus (v. 37). Second, once Jesus reaches Jairus's house, he is confronted by a group of mourners who are "weeping and wailing loudly" (v. 38) because of the child's death. He attempts to prevent their knowing about the miracle that he will perform by telling them, "The child is not dead but sleeping" (v. 39). Third, he allows only the disciples who are with him, Jairus, and the girl's mother to accompany him into the room where the child lay (v. 40). Fourth, after Jesus raises the child, those who are with him are "overcome with amazement" (v. 42), but he strictly orders that no one should know what he has done. To an ancient Mediterranean audience, Jesus' actions would seem exceedingly odd, since patrons and brokers were expected to receive honor from their clients and the distribution of favors was a commonplace and accepted means of acquiring honor (and responding to positive challenges).

Jesus also violates the conventions of honor and shame in his interaction with the mourners at Jairus's house. These mourners issue an honor-challenge to Jesus by laughing at him when he tells them that the girl is not dead but sleeping; *katagelaō* (v. 40) means not just to laugh, but to laugh scornfully or to mock.[53] As Juvenal notes, "To condemn by a cutting laugh comes readily to us all."[54] Their laughing constitutes a "negative challenge." A negative challenge involves an action that could be perceived as damaging to the honor of another person. For example, a violent action, an insult, or some kind of affront to one's family would all be considered negative challenges. The easiest and most common types of negative challenges were verbal. As we read in the ancient novel *Leucippe and Clitophon*:

Speech is the father of [shame, grief, and anger]: like arrows aimed at a target and hitting it dead center, words pierce the soul and wound it in many places. One verbal arrow is insult, and the wound it leaves is called anger: another is exposure of one's misfortunes, and this arrow causes grief; a third is lectures on one's faults, and this wound is known as shame. One quality common to all these weapons is that they pierce deeply but draw no blood. The only remedy for them is counterattack with the same weapons. The wound caused by one sharp tongue is healed by the razor edge of another. This softens the heart's anger and assuages the soul's grief. If one is prevented by *force majeure* from uttering one's defense, the wounds silently fester. Unable to eject their foam, the waves swell up in labor, distended by the puffing breath of words within.[55]

The recipient of the challenge, then, must make satisfaction for the wrong incurred. The satisfaction should be proportional to the offense. Hence, Juvenal writes that "a man's wrath should not be hotter than is fit, nor greater than the loss sustained."[56] Jesus may either (a) respond with scorn, as if the challengers to his honor are not worthy of a riposte, or (b) issue a public riposte, which, if successful, would allow him to acquire honor from those who have issued the challenge. The alternative to these is that Jesus may choose not to respond at all, thus seemingly losing honor to his challengers. From the perspective of the mourners, Jesus chooses the third option. He does not enter into a public challenge-riposte interaction with them; he endures public scorn and loses an honor-challenge before the court of public opinion. The audience, however, along with the characters in the episode who accompany Jesus during the healing, know that the true riposte comes in Jesus' raising of the girl.[57]

Another honor-related issue is that, in the episode of the healing of Jairus's daughter, the issue of trust (*pistis*) emerges as important for the healing to take place. This is also the case with this episode's intercalated partner, which tells of Jesus' healing of a woman with a hemorrhage (5:24b-34). Normally, *pistis* refers to an ongoing, reciprocal relationship between patrons, brokers, and their clients. While "trust" is a basic definition of this term, it also involves "behavior of loyalty, commitment, and solidarity."[58] In neither of these episodes, however, does the use of *pistis* conform to concepts of reciprocation commonly associated with acts of beneficence. In the episode of the woman with a hemorrhage, *pistis* seems only manifest in her trust in Jesus' ability to heal her. Indeed, had the woman proceeded as she appears to have intended (without petitioning Jesus and with apparently no concern to reciprocate by enhancing Jesus' honor), no continuing relationship would even have been possible, other than her continued trust in Jesus' power. Jesus' approval of her actions seems to indicate that he does not offer his gifts only to those who will reciprocate according to common honor-related conventions. Rather, in contrast to the ancient Mediterranean norm, his only requirement seems to be trust in his ability to provide those gifts.

Similarly, in 5:36 Jesus says to Jairus, "Do not fear; only trust" (*Mē phobou, monon pisteue*). Yet after he has raised Jairus's daughter, Jesus commands that no one should know what he has done. Jairus, in ignoring those who say to him that his daughter is dead and that he should trouble Jesus no further, exhibits trust in Jesus' ability to restore his daughter. Jesus' silence command, however, undercuts the standard conventions of reciprocation after a gift has been given, conventions that are expressed in the *pistis* between a patron (or broker) and client. Douglas Geyer writes, "From a point of view of behavior expected of heroic saviors, Jesus makes no claim on the family or on the girl, in a strange way demanding absolutely no *quid pro quo* for the benefactions rendered."[59] A more conventional response is seen in Euripides, *Alcestis*. In this play, Heracles brings back from the dead the wife of Admetus. In response, Admetus cries: "But to the citizens and to the whole region of my four cities I now say: let there be dance and song in honor of these happy events and let the altars of the gods be fattened with the sacrifice of bulls!"[60] Admetus responds as the recipient of such incredible favor should, and people throughout the region will celebrate in honor of the gift.

As in the episode of the healing of the leper, we have the elements of a scene of brokerage, with the notable exception that Jesus attempts to avoid the honor that he is due. In Mark's schema, *pistis* is the basis of the relationship between the giver and the recipient (as was normally the case in the ancient Mediterranean world), but it is no longer associated with reciprocation by the enhancing of the giver's honor (which was counterconventional in the ancient Mediterranean world). Mark's Jesus thus subverts the conventions according to which honor was assigned in the wider culture.

In the ancient Mediterranean context, those who did not grasp at honor were thought to be all the more honorable, and thus they conformed more fully to common cultural standards.[61] Only in very particular contexts was self-praise thought appropriate. The technical term for this is *periautologia*. Plutarch, in fact, wrote an essay on this topic called *On Praising Oneself Inoffensively*. He says, for example, that self-praise is acceptable in order to defend one's good name or to answer a charge.[62] Nevertheless, as a rule, self-praise was looked down upon. Grasping at honor was considered shameful. In Lucian's comical story *The Passing of Peregrinus*, Peregrinus is cast as an object of scorn because of his unceasing grasping for honor. Lucian's story begins, "Unlucky Peregrinus, or, as he delighted to style himself, Proteus, has done exactly what Proteus in Homer did. After turning into everything for the sake of notoriety and achieving any number of transformations, here at last he has turned into fire; so great, it seems, was the love of notoriety that possessed him."[63] More plainly, Peregrinus does anything he can to achieve notoriety, including burning himself to death. Conversely, Philostratus writes of Apollonius of Tyana that "Greece was moved to near worship of him, believing him to be a divine man for this reason above all—that he did not indulge in loud boasting about any of his deeds."[64] Likewise, in Apuleius's novel *The Golden Ass*, the protagonist Lucian is set up as a patron and is rewarded with great honors. We read that his "statue or image" shall be set up in copper "for a perpetual remembrance." Lucian then resists the setting up of the statues as if he is not worthy of them, thus showing himself to be an honorable person.[65] Mark's Jesus is certainly unlike Peregrinus who will do seemingly anything for the sake of notoriety, but neither is he like Apollonius and Lucian, who gain more honor because the public perceives that they do not actively seek it. Rather, Mark's Jesus proactively attempts to avoid receiving the honor that would normally accompany his great deeds.

Another example involving Apollonius will illustrate this point more fully. Philostratus recounts an episode that offers both parallels and contrasts with the episode of the raising of Jairus's daughter. When a young girl from one of the leading families of Rome appears to have died at the very hour of her marriage,[66] Apollonius heals her by touching her and uttering secret words over her. As a reward, the relatives of the girl offer Apollonius 150,000 pieces of silver, but Apollonius returns the gift to the girl for her dowry.[67] Like Jesus, then, Apollonius heals a girl from a leading family by touching her. While Jesus' words to the girl are in Aramaic, a language that presumably would have been foreign to Mark's audience, Apollonius's words go unheard. Further, both Jesus and Apollonius refuse particular types of reciprocation. Yet Apollonius's refusal of the extravagant sum of money shows him to be virtuous and honorable by common ancient Mediterranean standards. In this ancient context, wealth was not an end in itself. Rather, it afforded one the opportunity to enhance one's honor by beneficent distributions.[68] It was not required that Apollonius refuse the money, but he gained more honor by doing so. Jesus, on the other hand, does not forgo money, but honor itself. Such behavior would have been considered aberrant by ancient Mediterranean standards.

Curbing the Tide of Proclamation (7:31-37; 8:22-26)

It is illuminating to consider the episodes of the healing of the deaf man in 7:31-37 and the healing of the blind man in 8:22-26 together. These episodes, which share a common narrative structure,[69] frame the episodes of the feeding of the four thousand (8:1-10), the Pharisees' demand for a sign (8:11-13), and an episode recounting the disciples' lack of understanding (8:14-21).

The larger narrative section in which these episodes fall (6:14—8:31; see the appendix) emphasizes, among other things, the spread of Jesus' fame. In 6:14 Mark writes that Herod had heard about Jesus and that Jesus' name had become known to him. In 6:32-33, even though Jesus and the disciples go away to a "desert place by themselves," they are followed by many people from all the cities in the region. Likewise in 6:55, people from the whole region around Gennesaret bring the sick to him and try to touch the fringe of his cloak. In 7:24 Jesus enters a house in Tyre, wishing for no one to know he is there, but he cannot remain hidden. As Jesus' fame increases, so does his acquired honor. Both of the episodes of 7:31-37 and 8:22-26 include silence commands, as well as a feature new to Mark's healing stories: Jesus' leading the person seeking his help away to a private location. These attempts to occlude his healings stand out against the backdrop of the spread of his fame.

Understanding this injunction to silence and its violation in terms of the ancient value of honor helps to make sense of the episode. The people who know about the healing say that Jesus "has done all things well; he even makes the deaf to hear and the mute to speak" (7:37). Joel Marcus rightly notes that "it is hard to imagine the Markan audience overhearing what the onlookers say in 7:37 without assenting enthusiastically."[70] Yet it is also hard to imagine the Markan audience overhearing the proclamation of Jesus' great deeds apart from the core cultural values by which great deeds and their proclamation were governed. In a cultural context in which positive appreciation by others results in honor, the public affirmation that Jesus has done all things well and expressions of amazement at his abilities would result in Jesus' acquiring honor.

Further, Jesus has apparently already become known as a healer in this region. To command silence regarding the healing of the deaf man is not an attempt to keep secret his amazing abilities. As in the episode of the healing of the leper in 1:40–45, Jesus' attempt to silence those who know what he has done is an attempt to stop the very thing that occurs in this episode: proclamation of this particular deed. Those who petition Jesus for help are obligated by the conventions of gift-and-response to act in such a way as to increase his honor. His attempts to conceal what he has done, if successful, would curb the public acclamation of him that would result from this healing. By contrast, a Greek inscription about one Harmon of Thasus recounts, "His blindness was cured by Asclepius. But, since afterwards he did not bring the thank-offerings, the god made him blind again. When he came back and slept again in the Temple, he [sc. the god] made him well."[71]

The episode of the healing of the blind man in 8:22–26 mirrors the elements of concealment in 7:31–37. Some people from Bethsaida petition Jesus, who is apparently already known as a healer, to touch a blind man. Jesus takes the blind man away from the onlookers (leading him outside the village), and after the healing has taken place he takes action to prevent this healing from becoming widely known: "[H]e sent him to his house, saying, 'Do not go into the village'" (8:26). It is noteworthy that Jesus does not command silence in this passage. Jesus does not attempt to cast a veil of secrecy over his deed, but only sends the man into his home, rather than back into the village.[72]

In the ancient Mediterranean context, the home was considered to be "private" space, the sphere of domestic activity and kinship relations. Members of an extended family would interact with one another in the home, and non-kin males sometimes associated in the home as well.[73] The market, the field, and other such open environments were considered to be the arenas of "public" male interaction. Jesus thus sends the man into the private sphere (in direct contrast with the public sphere of the "village") where his interactions with others and the evidence of the cure will be temporarily limited. Jesus and his disciples then set off for Caesarea Philippi (8:27). At least in Bethsaida, he has curbed the proclamation of this healing, and thus curbed his own acquisition of honor.

JESUS' SUPPRESSION OF HIS ASCRIBED HONOR

There are three passages in which Jesus silences demons who appear to be aware of his special relationship to God and the ascribed honor involved in that relationship (1:23-28; 1:34; 3:12).[74] Jesus' silence commands in these passages indicate that he does not wish this special relationship and the concomitant honor rating to become widely known. They also show that he wishes to avoid being beholden to the demons in any way.

Concealment of Ascribed Honor in Jesus' First Exorcism (1:23-28)

Mark 1:23-28 relates Jesus' exorcism of a man with an unclean spirit. The unclean spirit identifies Jesus as "the Holy One of God" (v. 24). Morna Hooker holds that the demon was "no doubt assumed to have supernatural knowledge" about Jesus, knowledge not available to the human characters in this episode.[75] It seems clear that Mark intends the unclean spirit's identification of Jesus to be correct (and members of the Markan audience would surely concur), even though the onlookers have no way of knowing of Jesus' identity at this point in the narrative.

The exact significance of the title "Holy One of God" (*ho hagios tou theou*) is unclear. Apart from its use in Mark 1:24, it appears in the New Testament only in Luke 4:34 and John 6:69, and in the Old Testament only in 2 Kings 4:9; Judges 16:17; and Psalm 106:16. It has been given various theological interpretations,[76] but Bruce Malina and Richard Rohrbaugh helpfully point to its social-scientific implications: "By going on to identify Jesus as the 'holy One of God,' the demon acknowledges another status for Jesus that the crowd will soon see demonstrated. As an Israelite holy man, Jesus could exorcize and heal."[77] This comment speaks to the perception of the onlookers in the story, but at this point in the narrative the Markan audience has been made privy to information about Jesus that is unavailable to characters in the world of the story: that he is the Christ and the Son of God (1:1); that his coming is foretold in prophecy (1:2-3); that he is greater than John the Baptist (1:7-8); that the Spirit has descended upon him (1:10); and that God has said to him, "You are my beloved Son; in you I am well pleased" (1:11). The use of "Holy One of God" at this point in 1:24 underscores the maximal ascribed honor to which the audience has been made privy in these early episodes of the Gospel. Jesus, however, commands the unclean spirit who calls him by this title, "Be silent, and come out of him!" He thus terminates the unclean spirit's proclamation of his ascribed-honor status.

One could argue that Jesus' command to the unclean spirit—"Be silent!" or "Be muzzled!" (*phimōthēti*)—is part of a common exorcistic formula and thus does not connote an attempt by Jesus to curtail the spirit's proclamation. The exorcist's command that a spirit "be muzzled" is found in other exorcisms, and Mark's audience may well have recognized the force of the term.[78] Graham Twelftree holds that *phimōthēti* bears the primary connotation of an "incantational restriction," and that this term "puts someone in a position where they are unable to operate."[79] Sometimes such silence commands blocked the spirit's use of the exorcist's name in its attempt to gain control over the exorcist.[80]

Yet regardless of whether Mark's audience would have initially heard *phimōthēti* as merely part of an exorcistic formula, 1:34 sheds light on the way in which the term functions in this passage: Jesus "would not permit the demons to speak, because they knew him."[81] We see a similar claim in 3:11-12. In Mark, Jesus silences demons for a specific reason: he wishes to prevent them from making known his true status. If this idea is not apparent in 1:25, it becomes clear shortly thereafter.[82] Jesus' high status is constituted by his special relationship with God. Thus, by curtailing the spread of word regarding his status—not allowing the demons to speak because they know him—Jesus curtails the public recognition of the honor that has been ascribed to him by God.

Ben Witherington represents a common line of interpretation when he states, "Jesus rebukes the demon, as he does not wish to be confessed by the powers of darkness. Though the reader knows this is a true confession, it comes from a bad source."[83] This comment is on the right track, but the unclean spirit is not so much confessing Jesus as identifying him, specifically with regard to Jesus' relationship to God.[84] Unclean spirits/demons are represented as opposed to Jesus (see 1:24; 3:22-30; 8:33), doing harm to people instead of good (see 5:1-5; 9:17-18).[85] Their attempts to identify him publicly by honorific titles (see 1:24; 3:11; 5:7) might be seen as attempts to lure Jesus into the standard conventions of honor and shame. Further, by addressing Jesus with these honorific titles, the demons would not only make known his ascribed-honor status, but obligate Jesus to reciprocate in some way. In other words, by referring to Jesus as the "Holy One of God" or the "Son of God," they issue positive challenges to Jesus. The attempt by Satan to indebt Jesus to him and Jesus' refusal to become indebted to him are more explicit in the temptation stories in Matthew 4:8-10 and Luke 4:5-8, but the same dynamic may be at work in these passages in Mark.

Aside from the demonic recognition of Jesus' true status and its implications for his ascribed honor, there is another issue to deal with: the spread of Jesus' fame as a result of his deeds and the resulting acquired honor. In 1:21-22, he enters the synagogue and teaches, and immediately people are astounded at this teaching, because he was teaching "as one having authority" (*hōs exousian echōn*). In the ancient Mediterranean context, "authority" involves the ability to exert control over others. This ability extends not just to the sheer power to do so, but the social legitimacy of one's actions. In other words, it was not enough simply to be able to compel other people. One also had to have the proper social station, or the sanction of someone with the proper social station, to do so. Further, by casting out the unclean spirit, he not only confirms the crowd's perception of his authority,[86] but shows himself to be both beneficent and powerful. Jesus' authority, the reader knows, comes from his relationship to God as Son of God and Messiah. Jesus' power is legitimate, unlike the demon that has possessed a man, or the scribes who do not teach with authority (1:22).[87]

Exorcisms, as forms of beneficence, had the potential significantly to increase the honor of the one to whom the exorcism was attributed. For example, in the *Antiquities*, Josephus writes that God granted Solomon "knowledge of the art used against demons for the benefit and healing of men. He [Solomon] also composed incantations by which illnesses are relieved, and left behind forms of exorcisms with which those possessed by demons drive them out, never to return." Josephus then recounts the tale of a Jewish exorcist named Eleazar who cast out demons from a possessed man by using an incantation that Solomon had devised. Eleazar performed the exorcism, and then,

> wishing to convince the bystanders and prove to them that he had this power, Eleazar placed a cup or foot-basin full of water a little way off and commanded the demon, as it went out of the man, to overturn it and make it known to the spectators that he had left the man. And when this was done, the understanding and wisdom of Solomon were clearly revealed, on account of which we have been induced to speak of these things, in order that all men may know the greatness of his nature and how God favoured him, that no one under the sun may be ignorant of the king's surpassing virtue of every kind.[88]

Because exorcisms and other displays of authority had such potential to increase one's honor, passages such as this episode of Jesus' first exorcism in Mark would call to mind the ancient pattern of gift-and-response that was so integral to relationships of patronage, brokerage, and benefaction. Jesus' gifts extend first to the man with the unclean spirit. As in the case of the healed leper, Jesus has restored the formerly possessed man to his rightful place in the community, not to mention the fact that the man is not possessed anymore. His gifts also extend to the people from whose midst he has removed an unclean spirit, and to those who heard his teaching. Just as philosophers were considered "benefactors of humanity," Jesus' teachings would be considered by a sympathetic audience to be a gift to his hearers.[89] Those who have witnessed and benefited from Jesus' gifts react exactly as we would expect ancient Mediterraneans to react: they spread word of what he has done. "They were all amazed, and they kept on asking one another, 'What is this? A new teaching—with authority! He commands even the unclean spirits, and they obey him.' At once his fame began to spread throughout the surrounding region of Galilee" (1:27-28). Thus, although Jesus attempts to curtail knowledge of his ascribed honor, his achieved honor increases significantly.

Interpretations that see Jesus' silence command to the unclean spirit as part of a secrecy motif must account for the fact that this exorcism is entirely public. If Jesus is successful in concealing from the public the knowledge that he is the "Holy One of God," he nevertheless shows himself to be a powerful exorcist and authoritative teacher. These issues are especially problematic for interpretations that involve Jesus' concealing his great power because he does not wish to be known as a wonder-worker. Jesus will allow himself to be known as authoritative and powerful, even as a prophet (6:4, 15; 8:28),[90] but he prevents the unclean spirit from broadcasting its knowledge of him.

Concealment of Ascribed Honor in Mass Healings (1:34; 3:12)

The episodes of 1:32-34 and 3:7-12 are generally considered "summary reports." In these passages, Jesus' healings and exorcisms are performed quite publicly, an issue that I will discuss in chapter 4. In 1:34, however, we read that "he did not allow the demons to speak, because they knew him." Jesus, then, makes no secret of his ability to heal and exorcise, but, as in 1:25, he nonetheless silences demons.[91] Similarly, in 3:11, we read that the unclean spirits cry out, "You are the Son of God!" In response, Jesus "greatly rebuked them in order that they might not make him known [*hina mē auton phaneron poiēsōsin*]" (3:12).[92] As in 1:25, Jesus' silencing of the demons in 1:34 and 3:12 relates to ancient Mediterranean conventions of honor. Were Jesus' identity as the "Holy One of God" and the "Son of God" to become widely known, Jesus' ascribed-honor rating would increase significantly. Thus, by prohibiting the demons from proclaiming his titles "Son of God" and "Holy One of God," Jesus rebuffs the honor that would accompany widespread knowledge of these titles.

Conversely, patrons and rulers often sought after titles. Some titles were honorific ("Great," "August"), while others expressed the relationship between ruler and ruled.[93] As in the case of Octavian, Apollonius, or Jesus, a title such as "son of a God" or "Son of God" conveys the relationship between the recipient of the title and a divine being. Although he is widely known as a powerful healer and exorcist, those who lack supernatural knowledge are not privy at this point in the narrative to the titles that reveal Jesus' ascribed-honor rating.[94] Later in the narrative, during the transfiguration episode, Peter, James, and John are present when God proclaims that Jesus is "my beloved Son" (9:7). They thus receive information that is unavailable to other human characters in the episode. Jesus will issue a silence command to them, however, thus curtailing the spread of information regarding what they had witnessed (9:9).

Robert Gundry holds that Jesus' silencing of the demons is a means of rebuffing the demons' *apotropaic* attempts to gain supernatural control over him—their magical control over him by utterances of special knowledge about him. As in 1:24-25, "his power crushes the attempt to gain control over his actions by uttering knowledge of him."[95] Yet in 3:12 Mark offers a reason for Jesus' silence commands toward the demons: he does not wish for them to make him known.[96] From the point of view of Mark's narrative, then, the issue is not Jesus' resistance to supernatural control by the demons, but a desire to keep them from conveying their knowledge about him to the human characters in the story. From a social-scientific perspective, however, there is a connection between Jesus' commands that the demons not make him known and his resisting demonic influence. As we have seen, by making him known the demons would issue a positive challenge to Jesus and stake a claim on him. Jesus will not allow himself to become indebted to the demons whose purposes oppose those of God. Compare, by contrast, Jesus' favorable reaction to the woman of 14:3-9 who does a "good [*kalon*] work" (v. 6) for him by anointing him for his burial (v. 8). This woman acts in accord with God's purposes, as opposed to the demons who act against them. Jesus accepts the gift that she offers while rejecting the honorific designations uttered by the demons.

CONCLUSION

Among ancient Mediterranean people, the values of honor and shame would have guided the interpretation of the passages treated in this chapter. Secrecy, as it functioned in this ancient context, seems to be a peripheral concern, if a concern at all. Mark depicts Jesus as a healer, exorcist, and teacher. In each of these capacities, Jesus provides great works of benefaction.[97] People who receive Jesus' gifts often react in ways that one would expect of ancient Mediterranean people, given their customs regarding the giving and receiving of gifts: they spread word of Jesus' great power and beneficence, enhancing his fame, reputation, and honor. In particular instances, however, Jesus attempts to break the standard pattern of gift and response by acting to curb the spread of his fame and the enhancement of his honor.

At times, Jesus is identified by messianic titles or by titles such as "Son of God," "Holy One of God," and "Son of Man." In the transfiguration scene, he is revealed as a glorious figure, God's own Son, who stands alongside Elijah and Moses. Yet with the exception of "Son of Man," which for Mark involves not only Jesus' high ascribed honor but his suffering, death, and resurrection, Jesus makes efforts to avoid being known by these honorific titles. He silences the disciples regarding his appearance at the transfiguration until after he has risen from the dead. Jesus' avoidance of honorific titles in his efforts to suppress the spread of word regarding his high ascribed honor differs markedly from normal practices of ancient rulers.

The theme of concealment, or as it has often been described, "secrecy," in Mark's Gospel does not stand on its own. The passages discussed in the present chapter are part of a larger theme in Mark, one in which Jesus attempts to reshape common conceptions of honorable actions and attitudes. Among the followers of Jesus, what most people would consider honorable is not so, and what most people would consider shameful is in fact honorable. Jesus is engaging in a revision of the honor system. It is to this topic that we now turn.

CHAPTER 3

A New Vision of Honor

In the last chapter, we looked at the ways in which Jesus resists commonplace markers of honor. Jesus resists the honor that could come to him by virtue of his beneficent works and his relationship to God. In so doing, Jesus behaves in a deeply countercultural manner. Yet his program is not entirely negative: he not only negates common standards by which honor was assigned, but replaces them with other standards. Put differently, Jesus casts a new vision for the kinds of actions and attitudes that should be considered honorable. The Markan concealment passages function in service to this new vision. They are part of a larger theme in which Jesus reshapes the criteria by which honor was assigned. In this chapter, we will look at the ways in which commonplace ancient Mediterranean standards of honor could be significantly revised within particular groups of people. We will then look at the ways in which Mark's Jesus develops a new set of standards that should inhere among his followers. The final section of this chapter will examine the failure of Jesus' disciples to adopt these new standards.

REVISING THE HONOR SYSTEM

The honor-shame value complex was very much a part of the everyday lives of men and women in the ancient Mediterranean world. People found their places in society based upon factors such as status, gender, reputation, and their networks of associations. Moreover, there was very little social mobility. People of the higher classes generally remained there for their entire lives, enjoying the privilege that came with their social rank. Likewise, those among the lower classes normally lived out their lives within the confines of their station. Yet it was possible to challenge the criteria by which people were assigned their places in society. Specific groups could, so to speak, change the rules of the honor-shame game. Within a particular group, the common markers of high honor and status might be rejected in favor of new criteria. As we will see, Mark's Jesus engages in just this kind of revisionism.

Inescapable Honor

The ways in which people thought about honor could be revised, even quite dramatically. One could not, however, altogether dispense with honor and remain a socially connected individual. The honor-shame system was too deeply woven into the cultural tapestry. In *Empire of Honour*, J. E. Lendon describes the paradox of the ancient philosophical practice of denouncing the love of honor: while it was common among philosophers to denounce the value of popular opinion, even the most unconventional of philosophers could not escape the love of

honor altogether. "[H]owever bristly his beard, however intimidat-
ing his stare, he could not escape honour. Greeks and Romans could
not take off the spectacles of honour..."[1] Perhaps this is best seen in
the case of the Epicurean Lucretius, who admits that he yearns to be
praised for a poem that he has written, "a work in which he sternly
advocates scorn for praise."[2] Compounding the irony, Lucretius could
hardly hope to win praise from those who did not share this philosophical conviction. Rather, any signs of approval would have to come
from those who, like him, denounced the love of praise.

In the group-oriented culture of the ancient Mediterranean world,
one could not altogether dispense with the public approval of others, but one could become part of an in-group that defined honorable traits in unconventional ways. The Cynic Diogenes ridiculed such
distinctions as good birth and fame,[3] and he established his own in-
group, with its own ideas of the kinds of behavior that were and were
not virtuous. In a letter written by a Cynic and attributed to Diogenes
we read, "Do not complain to my associates, Olympias, that I wear
a worn-out cloak and make the round of people begging for barley
meal. For this is not disgraceful [aischra] nor, as you claim, suspect
behavior for free men. Rather, it is noble and can be armament against
the appearances [doxōn] which war against life."[4] "Diogenes" claims
that he learned this lesson from those who have brought wisdom to
Greece, such as Homer and the tragic poets, and from heroes and
gods, such as Hera; Telephus, the son of Heracles; and Odysseus, all of
whom at one point or another assumed the appearance of a person of
low status. He then asks, "Now do my clothing and begging still seem
disgraceful to you or are they noble and admirable to kings and to be
taken up by every sensible person for frugality's sake?"[5]

Another letter describes an incident in the house of a certain
Lacydes, which was replete with the trappings of wealth, including fine couches, tables of fine wood and silver plating, and servants
standing nearby with finger bowls. "Diogenes" claims that Lacydes
had made preparation against him as an enemy would, and instructs
Lacydes to dismiss the servants and that he be allowed to recline on
the hide of oxen or a bed of straw. He also requests that Lacydes provide him with clay cups, that his drink be spring water, his food bread,
and his appetizer salt or watercress. He continues, "These things I
learned to eat and drink, while being taught at the feet of Antisthenes,

not as though they were poor fare but that they were superior to the rest and more likely to be found on the road leading to happiness, which should be regarded as the most esteemed [*timiōtatēn*] of all possessions."[6] The Cynics regarded it as a virtue to be free from "popular opinion" (*doxa*).[7] They believed that "to be enslaved to opinion [*doxē*] and disgrace [*adoxia*]...is the most irksome of all."[8] And yet they exhorted one another to adopt particular attitudes and behaviors. They did not dispense entirely with the notions of admiration and virtuous, honorable behavior. Rather, they redefined which types of behavior were admirable in ways that were contrary to the values of the wider culture. Their way of life was very much a public flouting of contemporary conventions. Perhaps the clearest example of this is that Cynics were called to break with family and possessions. In fact, Cynics believed that wealth was the greatest threat to human happiness.[9]

A similar dynamic is at work in Mark's Gospel. Jesus has at times resisted the honor that he is due by virtue of his great deeds and unique relationship to God.[10] For ancient Mediterranean people, this would imply that Jesus does not adhere to the ways in which the wider culture reckons honor. Beginning with 8:27, Jesus begins to offer a new understanding of honorable actions and attitudes. This new understanding is in many ways a reversal of common notions of the components of honor in the ancient Mediterranean world.

Jesus' Ascribed Honor and the Values of His In-Group (8:27—9:1)

The episode dealing with Peter's identification of Jesus as the Messiah and Jesus' subsequent silence command toward the disciples (8:29-30) is the linchpin for most arguments in favor of a messianic secret. As we will see, however, this passage fits into a larger Markan schema that reshapes the kinds of actions and attitudes that should be considered honorable. Beginning with 8:31, there is a shift in Mark's emphasis. While Jesus has avoided conventional markers of honor on a number of occasions prior to this point, he now begins to identify a new set of components of honor. In 8:31, Jesus refers to himself as the Son of Man, a term which, as indicated in 8:38, designates the one who will come "in the glory of his Father with the holy angels." Jesus' self-designation in Mark as the "Son of Man" has engendered no small amount of scholarly debate, and an extensive discussion of this debate is beyond the focus of this chapter. Nevertheless, a few comments are in order regarding Mark's use of this term.

Mark 8:38, 13:26, and 14:62 indicate that this Gospel's understanding of the Son of Man is informed by the imagery of Daniel 7. In this chapter of Daniel, God grants dominion, glory, and kingship—in short, honor—to the Son of Man, who symbolizes the kingdom of the "holy ones of the Most High" (Dan 7:17). Yet these holy ones, before their vindication, endure persecution and suffering (Dan 7:19ff.). Likewise, Mark's picture of the Son of Man involves not just exaltation, but rejection and suffering (cf. 8:31; 9:9 [implicitly], 12, 31; 10:33, 45; 14:21, 41, 62).[11] The paradox of the title "Son of Man" in Mark is that this same figure to whom God has ascribed such high honor is the one who will suffer and be severely shamed, only later to be vindicated in the resurrection.[12]

Jesus' questions to his disciples, "Who do people say that I am?" (8:27) and "Who do you say that I am?" (8:29), as well as the answers that the disciples provide, recall the speculation of Herod and others in 6:14-16 regarding Jesus' identity. "People" have identified Jesus in ways that would carry high honor ratings. For example, they identify him as one of the prophets, or specifically as Elijah (see 6:15 and 8:28 for both examples), and Peter identifies Jesus as the Messiah. When he does so, Jesus silences the disciples and exchanges these prophetic and messianic designations for "Son of Man" (8:30-31). This does not mean that Jesus rejects either a prophetic or messianic role, but that he wishes to shape his public persona according to the connotations of "Son of Man," rather than "Messiah." By prohibiting the disciples from telling others about him, Jesus maintains a disparity between his public persona and his in-group persona (at least temporarily).[13] By keeping his in-group persona out of the public view, Jesus avoids the widespread ascribed and acquired honor status that would accompany his being widely known as the Messiah.

Another reason for Jesus' silence command in this passage may be that, by referring to Jesus as "Messiah" in front of the other disciples, Peter issues a positive challenge to Jesus. As discussed in chapter 2, a compliment or honorific title involved a *quid pro quo*: it could lay the recipient under obligation. Those honored in such a way would be obliged to bestow favors on the ones who honored them. In this scenario, Peter's designating Jesus as the Messiah is akin to the request of James and John that Jesus do whatever they ask (10:35). By issuing a silence command to Peter and the rest of the disciples (v. 30), Jesus resists becoming obligated to Peter in some way and resists being drawn into the standard operations of honor-related exchanges.

After commanding that the disciples tell no one about him, Jesus offers an account of himself very different than the honorific title "Messiah" would indicate: "the Son of Man must undergo great suffering, and be rejected by the elders, the chief priests, and the scribes, and be killed, and after three days rise again" (8:31). Mark writes that Jesus "said all this quite openly" (v. 32), in contrast to his command that the disciples tell no one about him (v. 30). By the time we reach 8:32, then, while the title "Messiah" remains concealed, what is said "quite openly" is that Jesus is the Son of Man who will experience treatment associated with shame (rejection, suffering, execution) before his resurrection. This kind of selective disclosure represents an attempt by Jesus to cast his public persona in ways that did not cohere with commonplace standards of honor and shame.

Peter, however, rebukes Jesus for what he has said. He rejects Jesus' prophecy of suffering, rejection, death, and resurrection. Jesus in turn calls Peter "Satan" and tells him that he has his mind set "not on the things of God but on human things" (v. 33). The difference between "human things" and "the things of God" is marked out more clearly in the following verses. Jesus teaches regarding the requirements of his in-group, "If any wish to follow me, let them deny themselves and take up their cross, and let them follow me" (v. 34). In an analysis that relies heavily on the work of Bruce Malina,[14] Joanna Dewey argues that the reference to the self (*heauton*) is not a reference primarily to the individual self, as it would be in modern Western culture, but to the ancient Mediterranean understanding of the self as embedded in a particular group. In a group-oriented society, the reference to denying the self is a reference to denying the group-oriented (dyadic) self, and therefore denying the natural kinship unit. Breaking ties with one's kinship group was exceedingly aberrant behavior in the ancient Mediterranean context.[15] This would be especially the case if the values of the new group were at odds with those of the natural kinship group.

Jesus self-designation "Son of Man" involves the idea that the one who is worthy of maximal ascribed honor is the one who will go to the cross, thus suffering the "slave's punishment." The utter degradation associated with crucifixion has been well documented.[16] Seneca refers to the person who receives the death penalty as "covered with disgrace and public ignominy."[17] The cross, however, was widely considered the worst way to die, the most extreme of the three *summa supplica*, ahead of burning and decapitation. Beginning with Mark 14:43, Jesus is arrested (14:43-49); abandoned (14:50-52); put on trial (14:53-64; 15:1-5); spit upon by his accusers (14:65); beaten by the temple guards (15:65); denied by his disciple Peter (14:66-72); condemned by the crowds (15:6-14); flogged (15:15); mocked, beaten, and spit upon by Roman soldiers (15:16-19); crucified (15:24); and then mocked further while he hung upon the cross (15:29-32), even by the two other criminals who were crucified alongside him (15:32). It is hard to imagine a clearer case of public humiliation.

It was not simply the physical torture of crucifixion, then, that made this death so despised. Rather, the public humiliation that went along with it made it all the more loathsome. Crucifixion played upon widely held ideals of masculinity. In the ancient context of Mark's Gospel, it was thought appropriate and necessary for adult males to demonstrate prowess. Demonstrations of prowess could take any number of forms, such as the conferral of benefits;[18] teaching,[19] rhetoric,[20] the writing of poetry;[21] military victory;[22] or avenging some type of insult or injury.[23] Overly reserved men gave the appearance of being effeminate. Suetonius, for example, recounts that Vergil was so "modest in speech and thought" that he was called "the maiden."[24] It follows, then, that to be rendered unable to demonstrate prowess, to be made powerless, was shameful for a man. To be beaten, to be unable to repulse an attacker, was degrading because it was the inverse of the masculine ideal.[25] In the *Alexander Romance*, Alexander frees captive soldiers with mutilated feet, ears, and noses, but they ask not to be returned to their families because "in their present condition they would bring embarrassment upon their relatives."[26] Crucifixion, a very public act of brutal physical abuse, represented the loss of prowess and power in the extreme.

Status had a direct bearing on the likelihood that one might die by crucifixion. It was a punishment for the lower classes, a fact that increased its power to degrade. Cicero writes that "the executioner, the veiling of the head, and the very word 'cross' should be far removed not only from the person of a Roman citizen but from his thoughts, his eyes and his ears. For it is not only the actual occurrence of these things or the endurance of them, but liability to them, the expectation, nay, the mere mention of them, that is unworthy of a Roman citizen and a free man."[27] Among the upper classes, then, the cross was an obscenity, best not to be spoken of in polite company. For the lower classes, and especially slaves, it was a very real threat and a shocking manifestation of the violence that could be inflicted when the more powerful members of society felt threatened by their social subordinates.

Joel Marcus discusses crucifixion as a death that was generally reserved for people who had "gotten above themselves."[28] Slaves who revolted against their masters or people who engaged in rebellion against the government would be good candidates for this punishment. Irony, Marcus argues, was the very intention of such a death: "this strangely 'exalting' mode of execution was designed to mimic, parody, and puncture the pretensions of insubordinate transgressors by displaying a deliberately horrible mirror of their self-elevation."[29] The "elevation" of crucifixion, the "enthronement" upon the cross, was a way of mocking those who had acted above their proper social station.

The deterrent force of the cross also relied upon the group-oriented personality of the ancient world. People were embedded in groups, which consisted not just of families, but friends, patron-client relationships, and other types of voluntary associations such as *collegia*, religious groups, or philosophical groups. What happened to one member of the group reflected upon the group itself. In *The Golden Ass*, a certain Aristomenes finds his friend Socrates sitting in squalor like a common beggar. Aristomenes says to his friend, "And dost thou live here as a ghost or beggar to *our* great shame and ignominy?"[30] In his current state, Socrates brings shame not just to himself, but to his friends. Likewise, Plutarch states that it is impossible for a friend not to share his friend's wrongs or disrepute or disfavor.[31] Certain people were more important for a group's collective honor than others. For example, the father was the most visible representative of a family's honor. The head of a philosophical group, such as Epicurus, was the most significant member of that group in the eyes of the public. Crucifying the head of a group, then, would bring considerable shame on all of the members of the group. The cross did not simply punish one person, but shamed all people associated with that person. It could serve as a group punishment inflicted upon a visible member of that group.

In Mark's story, the issue of denying oneself and taking up the cross has to do with remaining loyal to Jesus' group and the values that it represents. There is no way of getting around the fact of Jesus' crucifixion. To be loyal to Jesus means to be loyal to a crucified person—one who has endured the most shameful and demeaning of all punishments. Loyalty to Jesus will therefore place one in conflict with other groups, such as one's family, that hold more conventional values. Unless one denies one's current group associations and affiliates with the group that is centered on the one who went to the cross, then one cannot be a follower of Jesus. In 8:38, Jesus teaches, "Those who are ashamed of me and of my words in this adulterous and sinful generation, of them the Son of Man will also be ashamed when he comes in the glory of his Father with the holy angels." Those who are ashamed of Jesus are those who do not share the new in-group values and are concerned to receive affirmation from the wider society instead. As Bruce Malina and Richard Rohrbaugh put it, "To be ashamed of a person is to dissociate oneself from that person, to not recognize that person's claims to honor, to distance oneself from that person's honor rating. When the Son of Man comes with power, he will in like fashion be ashamed of 'this generation.'"[32]

We should not underestimate the power of shame in this context. Shame was an effective means of social control.[33] The desire to avoid shame compelled people to behave in certain ways. Seneca, for example, writes that one who errs in conduct should be reproved, first privately and then, if the behavior continues, publicly. If one is so far advanced in vice "that words can no longer bring you to your sense, then you shall be held in check by public disgrace."[34]

Thus, Jesus effectively states that the people who are ashamed of him are dishonorable and will be publicly shamed by the coming Son of Man. This is a reversal of standard conventions regarding honor: those who associate with the "shameful" cross are those who are in Jesus' in-group and are therefore the most honorable. Those who are ashamed of Jesus—that is, those who affirm the commons values of

the ancient Mediterranean culture—are part of an adulterous and sinful generation and deserve to be shamed.

What we see in Mark 8:27—9:1 is a call to accept a new in-group,
which would involve a new set of honor values and a new court of
public opinion. Jesus begins by suppressing proclamation of a title
that, if widely known, would bring him widespread acclaim (8:30).
He then teaches a new way of understanding who is and who is not
honorable, a way that is specific to his in-group and scandalous and
dishonorable to those who are not part of it. To set one's mind on
"human things" is to reject the cross because of its associations with
shame and suffering, whereas to set one's mind on the things of God
is to follow Jesus and thus join the in-group that affirms that the cross
is the way to glory and honor.

One common interpretation of Jesus' silence command in 8:30
holds that Mark is redefining traditional notions of messiahship. Jesus
silences the disciples because they hold incorrect notions of the role of
the Messiah. Similar lines of interpretation can be extended to other
silence commands. For example, some scholars have held that Mark's
Jesus does not wish to be known as a wonder-worker, or that Mark is
countering a "divine man" Christology. Messiahship is to be defined
by the cross, and Jesus is to be seen as a suffering messiah. Yet if the
silence commands primarily convey a reinterpretation of messiahship,
we are left with the question of why Mark's Gospel is almost entirely
devoid of teaching regarding the nature of messiahship.[35]

In the cultural worldview assumed by Mark's Gospel, messiahship is not the primary issue in this passage. The main function of
the silence commands, including the one that occurs in 8:30, is to
demonstrate Jesus' renunciation of traditional components of honor.
He does not deny that he is the Messiah, but he renounces the honor
associated with public proclamation of this title. He then offers a new
understanding of the ways in which members of his in-group should
conceive of honorable behavior. In support of this way of interpreting
the silence commands are teachings related to glory, precedence, and
prestige—and thus honor—in chapters 8, 9, and 10. (The teachings
in chapters 9 and 10 are discussed below.) An ancient audience would
not have heard the episode in 8:27—9:1 primarily as a redefinition of
messiahship, but as a refashioning of the components of honor, within
a specific in-group, through the actions of the Messiah.

Jesus' Ascribed Honor Fully Revealed and Temporarily Concealed (9:9-13)

The episode of the transfiguration is as perplexing as any in Mark's Gospel. Theories abound with regard to the significance of the presence of Elijah and Moses, as well as Jesus' white clothes and Peter's rationale for wishing to build tents and remain on the mountain. The silence command in 9:9 is equally curious, in part because it is the only silence command in Mark that has a time limit: Jesus commands that the disciples say nothing "until the Son of Man [has] risen from the dead." It does seem clear, however, that various aspects of the transfiguration episode testify to Jesus' high status. Jesus' dazzlingly white clothes may allude to the attire of the Ancient One in Daniel 7:9, in which case Jesus is shown as clothed in God's heavenly glory. In Revelation 3:4; 4:4; 6:11; 7:9; and 7:13, white clothes symbolize righteousness and heavenly existence. In general, white clothes signified one who was set apart from the ordinary or somehow connected with the divine, and they were often worn by elites such as priests and kings.[36] Jerome Neyrey associates Jesus' white clothing with "the heavenly world of angels, elders, faithful martyrs, and God."[37] Jesus is further marked off from the ordinary by the appearance of two great figures from Israel's past, and then given elevated status over them by the voice from heaven.

Given that honor must be acknowledged by others, Peter's assessment that "it is good for us to be here" appears to indicate an intention to acknowledge Jesus' great honor that is revealed in this episode (even before God's proclamation of Jesus' divine sonship). Mary Ann Tolbert points out that Peter's reaction to seeing the transfigured Jesus alongside Elijah and Moses contrasts with Peter's recent rebuke of Jesus after Jesus has foretold his suffering, death, and resurrection (8:32). Peter's "desire is clearly to commemorate and honor the occasion in some material way. In contrast to his utter rejection of Jesus the Messiah's words about the inevitability of suffering (8:31-33), this glorified Jesus in company with Elijah and Moses wins his approval ('it is well that we are here') and his esteem. He wants to honor what he has seen."[38]

Yet Peter's approval of and desire to honor this vision of Jesus in traditional trappings of honor shows that he still has his mind set on "human things." His understanding of honorable actions and attitudes is still quite conventional. The author underscores Peter's traditional views of honor by linking them with fear: "He did not know what to say, for they [the disciples] were terrified [*ekphoboi*]" (9:6). Fear, while not considered virtuous, was a common response to a person of high honor. For example, in the *Life of Apollonius*, Indians are said to fear certain highly venerated sages even more than they fear their own king.[39] Peter and the other disciples who are with him perceive that Jesus is a high-honor person, but they do not comprehend the way of the cross which he began to teach in chapter 8.

Subsequently, there are words from heaven that further confirm Jesus' high-honor status: "This is my Son, the Beloved; listen to him!" (9:7). God, then, reveals a unique father-son relationship between God and Jesus. Thus, God declares Jesus both "beloved" and "Son," "informing the world that he enjoys unique honor, status, and even role ascribed by God."[40] Just as the favored son of a king has high ascribed honor by virtue of his relationship to the king, Jesus has high ascribed honor by virtue of his relationship to God.

In the story of the transfiguration, then, Jesus' glory is revealed: he stands alongside Elijah and Moses, he is clothed in heavenly attire, and his divine sonship is proclaimed by God, who commands that the disciples listen to Jesus. These elements demonstrate Jesus' maximal ascribed-honor status. Peter and the other disciples who are with him rightly perceive that Jesus is a person of significant honor. Yet combined with his rejection of Jesus' suffering in 8:32, Peter's reaction in 9:5-6 exemplifies a misunderstanding of the new in-group honor values. Jesus' maximal ascribed honor, as well as his considerable acquired honor, cannot be separated from the aspects of following Jesus that would bring dishonor in the wider culture, and Peter has rejected those. All the more significant, then, is God's admonition to listen to Jesus (9:7). The episode is thick with irony: Peter has not listened to Jesus, has not heard him redefine honor, and this deafness to Jesus' teachings will continue not just with Peter, but with the other disciples as well. In contrast to Jesus, the disciples offer examples of the *wrong* ways of regarding honor, glory, and reputation.

It is for this reason that Jesus commands that the disciples who are with him tell no one what they have seen "until the Son of Man [has] risen from the dead" (9:9). Jesus' death—shaming by conventional standards—has been given new honor value by his foretelling of his death and resurrection (8:31) and his words about the way of the cross (8:34—9:1).

Note the use of "Son of Man" here, evoking the pattern of high ascribed honor, persecution, and vindication. The new honor value that Jesus gives to his death on the cross will be validated by God in his resurrection. It will be appropriate for the disciples to proclaim all that they know of Jesus' great honor and glory, but only after the honor value of his apparently shameful death on the cross has been confirmed by the resurrection. For Mark, to be regarded favorably in God's eyes necessarily involves being regarded unfavorably, and thus dishonorably, in the eyes of the wider culture. Thus, the clearest sign of God's favor comes only after Jesus has been severely shamed before the general public. The disciples, however, do not understand the role of the resurrection in validating the honor of Jesus' death, and they debate among themselves regarding "what this rising from the dead could mean" (9:10).

The disciples then pose a question to Jesus regarding a particular scribal tradition: "Why do the scribes say that Elijah must come first?" (9:11).[41] Like the question itself, Jesus' response is ambiguous and continues to engender scholarly debate.[42] For our purposes, however, it is important not so much to decipher this question and its response completely as to identify a few issues in 9:12-13 related to honor and shame. Primarily, it is noteworthy that in these verses, both Jesus and John the Baptist (represented as Elijah) are held up as figures who, though righteous and favored by God, are treated shamefully. Jesus speaks of the Son of Man's being "treated with contempt" (v. 12). The verb that we translate as "treated with contempt" is *exoudeneō*, which connotes scorn and worthlessness.[43] Thus, despite all of the marks of honor and glory displayed in the transfiguration that witness to Jesus' special favor with God, Jesus will receive scornful and contemptuous treatment.

"Elijah" in 9:12-13 refers to John the Baptist.[44] John, like Elijah, was God's prophet. John was the one who proclaimed Jesus' coming (1:2-8) and baptized Jesus (1:9-11). In 6:20 we read that Herod "feared John, knowing that he was a righteous and holy man." Yet it is this figure to whom "they did whatever they wished [*ēthelon*]" (9:13); in other words, they treated him as if he had no status or honor. Robert Gundry points out that forms of *thelō*—"I wish"—occur several times in the episode of the death of John the Baptist (6:19, 22, 25, 26) to refer to the wishes of Herod, Herodias, and Herodias's daughter.[45] To do "whatever they wished" in this case involved a particularly shameful means of execution: beheading. To be struck in the head was disgraceful[46]; to be beheaded and killed, with no chance to gain satisfaction, was shameful in the extreme. For example, in 1 Maccabees, the beheading of Nicanor and display of his head and right hand are meant as a repudiation of his arrogance, a shaming that negates his claims to honor (1 Macc 7:47). Jesus and John the Baptist therefore provide two examples of righteous people who enjoy special relationships with God (Jesus as God's Son, John as God's prophet), yet suffer shamefully because of their righteousness.

In the episode of 9:2–13, then, the extent of Jesus' ascribed honor becomes manifest to three of the disciples, but he commands that the disciples be silent about what they have seen until he has risen from the dead. Mark then turns the narrative toward a discussion of figures who have high honor through their special relationships with God but are treated shamefully by other people. A similar pattern appears in 8:27—9:1: Peter reveals Jesus' identity, Jesus issues a silence command, and Jesus then teaches that he and those who follow him will endure suffering and shame before "the Son of Man . . . comes in the glory of his father with the holy angels" (8:38). This pattern differs significantly from ancient Mediterranean conventions regarding ascribed honor: those with high ascribed honor were normally to be recognized as having such, and these highly honored people would avoid at all costs shame such as was associated with the cross. Mark's Jesus inverts the standard conventions: the one most worthy of honor prevents the proclamation of this honor and will endure shame. Jesus' "shameful" death on the cross will be honored by God through the resurrection, and the resurrected Jesus will shame those who adhere to conventional notions of honor.

THE DISCIPLES' FAILURE TO UNDERSTAND

Mark 9:33–37 and 10:35–45 follow a pattern similar to that of 8:32—9:1. Each of these passages immediately follows Jesus' foretelling of his suffering, death, and resurrection. Further, in each of these passages

Jesus' teaching is intended to correct misunderstandings on the part of the disciples (or, in 8:32, Peter), and each of these three passages is closely tied to issues of honor and shame.[47]

A Misunderstanding of Greatness (9:33-37)

The episode recounted in 9:33-37 offers a concrete picture of the disciples' failure to understand what Jesus has taught them about the requirements of his new in-group. Jesus, whom Peter has recently identified as the Messiah, who has just been revealed in his full glory in the transfiguration, and whom God has declared to be "my Son, the Beloved," has chosen to conceal his high status rather than to broadcast it. He has recently taught that those who wish to be his followers must take up the cross, thus associating themselves with an object of shame (8:34). Yet in 9:34 we learn that the disciples have been arguing with one another over which of them is the greater (*meizōn*). They have this argument despite the fact that they have just failed in an attempt to cast a demon out of a boy (9:14-29). The contrast is clear: Jesus, who is truly worthy of maximal ascribed and acquired honor, rejects the way in which the wider culture reckons honor. The disciples, who have not demonstrated their worthiness of honor, squabble over issues of precedence. The disciples thus show themselves still adhering to the values of the wider culture despite Jesus' teaching and example. William Lane summarizes this passage concisely: "In Mark . . . the dispute over greatness indicates the degree to which the disciples had failed to understand Jesus' solemn affirmation concerning his abandonment to the will of men (Ch. 9:31f.). It also shows how impregnated they were with the temper of their own culture where questions of precedence and rank were constantly arising."[48] In response, Jesus teaches his disciples, "Whoever wants to be first [*prōtos*] will be last [*eschatos*] of all and servant [*diakonos*] of all" (9:35).

Mark then writes that Jesus "took a little child and put it among them; and taking it in his arms, he said to them, 'Whoever welcomes one such child in my name welcomes me, and whoever welcomes me welcomes not me but the one who sent me'" (9:36-37). Morna Hooker holds that "the saying about receiving a child does not really suit the present context, which is concerned with the humility which ought to characterize a disciple, not with receiving those who are humble."[49] If we see both passages as reversing common honor-related expectations, however, the appropriateness of verse 37 becomes apparent. Jesus first reverses traditional honor-related expectations by saying that whoever will become first of all must become a servant, and then he likens himself to a child.[50] In the ancient Mediterranean world, children were not the proper recipients of honor. They did not compete for esteem or display prowess. Aristotle writes that "children and animals" are "those for whom men feel great contempt," and to whose respect or esteem these men pay no heed, "or, if they do, it is not for the sake of their esteem, but for some other reason."[51] In the *Alexander Romance*, King Darius insults Alexander by calling him a child. Alexander clearly understands that this is a joke at his expense.[52]

A related issue is that the term *pais*, or "child," was a common term for a slave, which was a way of reinforcing the slave's powerlessness and passivity.[53] For Jesus to equate himself, and even God, with a *paidion* (a little child), and to describe entrance into God's kingdom in terms of being like a *paidion*, would be a challenge to any person who had been culturally formed within the honor-shame value complex.

To welcome this Messiah, a great healer, exorcist, and teacher, is to show hospitality to one who is worthy of great honor. To welcome a child is to welcome one who is generally considered empty of either ascribed or acquired honor. Yet to receive a child in Jesus' name is in fact to receive Jesus (who has maximal ascribed honor and significant acquired honor), and to receive Jesus is to receive God (who is maximally worthy to ascribe honor).

To summarize, in 9:33-37 Jesus represents the appropriate perspective of his in-group, and the disciples represent the perspective of the wider culture. Jesus reverses conventional expectations related to the components of honor, thus creating a contrast between the values of the wider culture and the values of his in-group. The disciples, on the other hand, continue to manifest understandings of honor centered on precedence and competition.

A Grab for Honor by James and John (10:35-45)

In 10:35-45 this contrast of values continues. James and John request of Jesus, "Grant us to sit, one at your right hand and one at your left, in your glory" (10:37), and the remaining ten disciples become angry with them. James and John are seeking precedence, recalling the disciples' squabbling in 9:34. A number of commentators correctly suggest that the other disciples' anger stems from their own desire to have the position of privilege that James and John request, or at least a desire to avoid being pushed into a position of lesser privilege.[54] In the ancient Mediterranean context, such a desire to gain positions of privilege and to keep others from gaining them emerged from a limited-good understanding of honor.[55] Seneca speaks from this position when he writes, "An over-confident demeanor, a voice too loud, boldness of speech, foppishness in dress, a pretentious show of patronage, popularity with the public—these inflame anger."[56] He also notes that, among the common folk, "no one makes gain save by another's loss."[57] Oratorical competitions among the Hellenistic educated elite, however, show that the upper classes also shared in this perspective. Plutarch also describes a limited-good perspective when he writes, "[T]hose with an inordinate and unrelieved appetite for fame disparage fame to others, their rivals as it were in love, in order to secure it without competition."[58] He also writes of "love of contention, love of fame, the desire to be first and greatest, which is a disease most prolific of envy, jealousy, and discord."[59] All goods, including components of honor such as reputation, fame, and precedence, were seen as being in limited supply. From this perspective, any honor ascribed to James and John by Jesus would not be available to the other disciples. Therefore, the other disciples experience indignation and envy toward James and John. They react in keeping with the values of the wider culture. The fact that the disciples apply common standards of honor within their in-group shows that they have not comprehended Jesus' teaching.

After each of the three passion predictions, the disciples fail to respond appropriately.[60] In 10:33, the third of these, Jesus has just predicted that he will be condemned to death, handed over to the Gentiles, mocked, spit on, flogged, and killed (10:33-34), and yet James and John are still focused on acquiring precedence and status. His response to James and John indicates that the disciples hold incorrect notions of what it means to follow him. His statement, "You do not know what you ask," and his question, "Are you able to drink the cup which I drink or be baptized with the baptism with which I am baptized?" (v. 38) allude to the shame, suffering, and death that he has just predicted, though James and John seem not to realize the full implications of Jesus' references to the baptism and cup. They are focused upon precedence, and not upon the way of the cross.

In the verses that follow, Jesus expands upon his teaching regarding honor, glory, and precedence: "You know that the ones who are supposed to rule over the Gentiles lord it over them, and their great ones [hoi megaloi] exercise authority over them. But it is not so among you; but whoever wishes to become great [megas] among you will be your servant [diakonos], and whoever wishes to be first [prōtos] among you will be slave [doulos] of all. For [gar] even [kai] the Son of Man came not to be served but to serve [diakonēsai], and to give his life as a ransom for many" (10:42-45). This passage, like 9:35, contains specifically honor-related Greek terms. The words megas—"great"—and the related words megaloi and meizōn are terms of prestige (see 6:21). When applied to persons, megas has connotations of renown and status. It is a term used of kings, heroes, and deities. In its superlative form (megistos), it is used in ceremonial court proceedings as a title of honor.[61] Likewise, prōtos—"first"—also has honor-related meanings since, when used of persons, it can mean "the most eminent, important."[62] Josephus uses this term to describe "the leading men of a tribe, the people, the priesthood, etc."[63]

On the other hand, diakonos—"servant"—and doulos—"slave"—naturally connote low status and servitude. John N. Collins argues that diakonos was used at times to denote a "go-between" in matters of commerce, a messenger, or a diplomat,[64] yet he holds that, in this passage in Mark, "the term is merely a synonym of words meaning 'slave' or 'last.'"[65] The word eschatos can mean "the last in rank, usually to denote what is mean and poor."[66] In Luke 14:9, this term is used specifically to refer to the least honorable place at the table. Positions of servitude and low rank obviously did not carry high-honor ratings. Plato tells us that ruling, rather than serving, is proper to a man, and Seneca writes, "By freedom the spirit grows, by servitude it is crushed."[67] Yet Jesus holds up such positions as virtuous, and thus honorable. Jesus uses conventional honor-related terminology in ways that subvert the meanings that these terms usually bear.[68]

Moreover, Jesus contrasts what should occur among the twelve with what does occur among the Gentiles (10:42). Essentially, this is a contrast between the values of Jesus' in-group and the values of the wider culture of the ancient Mediterranean world. Among the "Gentiles," assertions of power and authority by rulers, which would relate to the honor of the rulers, are commonplace. In Jesus' in-group, however, servants and "the last" are exalted: those who are servants and do not seek precedence over others are the ones who are truly great, who are "first" according to the values of Jesus' in-group.

The ability to exercise rule and authority was seen to be in limited supply in the ancient Mediterranean world and was widely desirable since rule and authority were closely connected with honor. For example, Xenophon recounts that Cyrus "used to reward with gifts and positions of authority and seats of honour and all sorts of preferment others whom he saw devoting themselves most eagerly to the attainment of excellence; and thus he inspired in all an earnest ambition [philotimian], each striving to appear as deserving as he could in the eyes of Cyrus."[69] Jesus, however, challenges the disciples' conventional attitudes toward authority and precedence. Though the desire to wield and demonstrate authority may be widespread, he then says to them, "[I]t will not be so among you" (10:43). The disciples should not seek after these conventional markers of status and honor. As Jesus defines it, greatness is to be found in the positions of servant and slave. Unlike the exercise of authority over others, service of others does not diminish them or rob them of honor. While there was a limited supply of positions in which one could rule over others, there was no such limited supply of positions of servitude. Thus, the relationship to others that Jesus holds up as virtuous implies no competition for honor or jockeying for position among his followers.

Of note is the word for (gar) in 10:45, which provides a rationale for abiding by Jesus' teachings regarding greatness and priority (and thus honor) in 10:43-44.[70] The one who wishes to become great must become a servant, and the one who wishes to be first must be slave of all, "for even the Son of Man came not to be served but to serve, and to give his life as a ransom for many." The word even (the adverbial kai) in verse 45 emphasizes the solidarity of the Son of Man with those to whom Jesus has just directed his teaching. Even one so great as the Son of Man—who has authority to forgive sins, is Lord of the Sabbath, and will come in the glory of his Father with the holy angels—comes to serve and to give his life as a ransom. Thus, as in 8:31—9:1 and 9:33-37, Jesus serves as the model of behavior for those who wish to be a part of his in-group.

Also noteworthy is Mark's use of *thelō*—"wish"—in the section extending from 9:35 through 10:52. In 9:35 Jesus states, "If anyone wishes [*thelei*] to be first, he will be last of all and servant of all." Yet shortly thereafter, in 10:35-36, Mark writes, "And James and John the sons of Zebedee approached him, saying to him, 'Teacher, we wish [*thelomen*] that whatever we may ask you, you may do for us.' And he said to them, 'What do you wish [*thelete*] that I do for you?'" Their wish to sit at Jesus' right and left in his glory expresses an understanding of honor quite different from the understanding that Jesus has expressed in 9:35, according to which the first must be last of all and servants of all.[71] Jesus' corrective to James and John as well as the other ten disciples reiterates the understanding of honor in 9:35: "Whoever wishes [*thelē*] to become great among you will be your servant, and whoever wishes [*thelē*] among you to be first will be slave of all" (10:43-44).

In the episode relating the healing of Bartimaeus (10:46-52), Mark offers a contrast to the episode in which James and John express their wish to be great. Like James and John (10:35), Bartimaeus petitions Jesus (10:47-48). Echoing the language with which he inquired regarding the petition of James and John (10:36), Jesus asks Bartimaeus in 10:51, "What do you wish me to do for you? [*Ti soi theleis poiēsō*]."[72] Yet, unlike James and John, Bartimaeus does not request precedence. Rather, he requests that Jesus give him sight. Mark links faith and sight in 8:14-21, and the Bartimaeus episode forms a frame with the episode of the healing of the blind man in 8:22-26 (see the appendix), within which the disciples exhibit on several occasions their "blindness" to Jesus' teachings (8:32; 9:10, 18-19, 32, 33-34, 38; 10:13, 24, 35-45).[73] Moreover, after he has been healed, Bartimaeus follows Jesus "on the way." The audience is already aware that Jesus is on the way to Jerusalem (10:32), the place where he will suffer shamefully and die (8:31; 9:31; 10:33-34). Bartimaeus's act of following Jesus into Jerusalem thus contrasts sharply with the disciples' bickering over greatness, request for precedence, and envy.

In sum, these passages that demonstrate the disciples' lack of understanding and have sometimes been associated with the messianic secret are best seen in terms of the reversal of conventions regarding the components of honor that Mark expresses through Jesus' teachings. In these passages, the disciples serve as examples of the traditional understanding of honor and the behavior that comports with it, in contrast to Jesus, who exemplifies a concept of honor that values service and rewards suffering. As Plutarch notes, proper living is a useful way of showing others the virtuous way to live.[74] Jesus, then, is the positive example, and the disciples are a foil. As Tolbert puts it, "Understanding the disciples' desire for glory and renown as a foil to Jesus' actions suggests a different construction for secrecy [than one which sees his secrecy as related to his messianic identity]: Jesus' commands for silence and his attempts to stay hidden define his steadfast rejection of personal renown and glory."[75]

The use of negative examples as a teaching technique is common in oral cultures, and Mark often makes use of this technique by contrasting Jesus with examples of negative actions and attitudes (such as those of Jesus' opponents or the disciples).[76] Presumably, the negative portrayal of the disciples will cause the hearer or reader to dissociate from the disciples and to see them as exemplifying the ways in which one should *not* act. Jouette Bassler offers a helpful analysis of the reader's dissociation from the disciples in Mark. She writes that, after each of the three passion predictions in Mark, there is a clear indicator of the disciples' inability to understand or accept what Jesus has told them. The reader of Mark, however, is alerted several times through the course of the narrative to the importance of overcoming the kind of misunderstanding that the disciples demonstrate. "At each point in the narrative where Jesus' insistence on the necessity of suffering is met with the same fear and lack of understanding that characterized the boat scenes (9:32; 10:32), the reader, by acquiring the understanding so elusive to the disciples, can attain some distance from them."[77] Yet Mark does not leave the reader with no one with whom to identify. Bartimaeus, who receives his sight and follows Jesus along the way, offers a contrast to the disciples, who remain "blind" to Jesus' message. "[T]he newly enlightened reader can now identify with the newly sighted Bartimaeus and has, like him, the potential of following Jesus."[78] From a social-scientific perspective, we can say that

Jesus' in-group within the story largely fails to adopt the understanding of honor that Jesus sets forth. The Markan audience, however, forms an in-group outside of the story, one that has dissociated from the disciples and can adopt Jesus' new understanding of honor. In fact, as I will discuss in the conclusion of this work, this understanding of honor would be highly appropriate for the Markan audience.

CONCLUSION

Jesus' resistance to the honor that he is due, discussed in chapter 2, is a deeply countercultural way of behaving. Yet we might think of it as an enactment of the teaching that begins in Mark's eighth chapter. Jesus teaches that true greatness consists in servitude and putting others before oneself. One should not seek the high place in the pecking order, but become last of all and servant of all. The rulers of the Gentiles may lord over their subjects, but Jesus' followers are to reject such ambitions. Jesus likens himself to a child in a context in which children are not the proper recipients of honor. Moreover, he instructs his followers that they, too, must become like children. The wider culture may conceive of honor in terms of precedence and authority tempered with humility, but Jesus rejects these conventional standards. Among Jesus' group, honor is reckoned differently.

In chapter 8, Jesus offers a choice: one can assent to the values of Jesus' in-group, or one can assent to other values that will make one ashamed of Jesus, scandalized by the cross. Mark's Jesus challenges characters within the Gospel and the Gospel's audience to join Jesus' in-group and "take up" the cross, an object of shame in the wider culture, but a symbol of honor and virtue within Jesus' group. The issue for those who would be Jesus' followers is one of allegiance: one may adhere to the values of the wider culture that rejects the cross, or to the values of Jesus' group in which the cross is considered honorable, but not to both. Those who choose to embrace the way of self-denial—leaving behind their old in-groups and joining Jesus' group—will be vindicated in the future, just as Jesus was vindicated in the resurrection.

Many have agreed with William Wrede's assertion that "the gospel of Mark belongs to the history of dogma,"[79] and this assertion has formed the backbone of much scholarship on the messianic secret, especially redaction-critical scholarship. Yet while Mark's Gospel can be interpreted in theological terms, we get closer to its impact on Mark's audience by attending to the sociocultural issues imbedded in the narrative. Seen within the cultural context of the ancient Mediterranean world, many of the Markan concealment passages have more to do with honor, shame, and communal identity than with "dogmatic" issues such as whether Jesus was the Messiah or the nature of his messianic role. Thus, while much of the debate in the history of scholarship on the messianic secret has focused on the Markan concealment passages as a product of theological reflection (either by the evangelist or by the Markan community), it is reasonable to hold that, for the Markan audience, the passages in which Jesus is concealing find their major significance neither in history nor theology, but in the fears, pressures, and concerns of everyday living. Being a Christian had serious honor-related implications, and Mark's Jesus provides a model of the ways in which honor is rightly to be demonstrated and understood within the group of which he is the head.

CHAPTER 4

HONOR IN THE PUBLIC EYE

Many scholars have noted the presence of passages in Mark's Gospel in which Jesus does not attempt to conceal his deeds and/or identity. William Wrede himself noted, "If Jesus repeatedly commands sick people ... to keep the fact of their healing secret, he nevertheless frequently performs his miracles in the full glare of publicity."[1] Regarding what he termed "contradictions in the narrative," Wrede wrote, "The public nature of the miracles does not accord with the command to keep silence about certain miracles."[2] He attempted to explain these contradictions in a few ways. First, he said, there are passages in Mark's Gospel in which the evangelist has simply taken over traditional materials in which the secrecy motif was not present (for example, Jesus' entry into Jerusalem). Second, for Mark to write a story of Jesus that depicted Jesus as the Messiah and Son of God, Jesus sometimes had to engage in "messianic activity and speech to those among whom he had lived."[3] Third, the evangelist did not perceive the implications of depicting Jesus as commanding something (secrecy) that did not come to pass. Wrede argued that the frustration of Jesus' intention could not be what the evangelist wished to convey. Rather, Mark's intention was to demonstrate Jesus' glory by showing that "he wanted to remain hidden yet is at once confessed."[4]

These passages, however, have received far less attention than Markan concealment passages. In chapter 2 I argued that several Markan concealment passages demonstrate Jesus' resisting and reshaping traditional ancient Mediterranean concepts of honor. In light of those arguments, it is necessary now to examine the "conventional" episodes, ones in which Jesus is open about his deeds and identity. There is no single "emic" term—one from the cultural world of Mark's audience—that describes the form and function of all of these passages. Further, these passages do not contribute to a single theme in the Gospel by which we might identify them. The term *conventional* is a helpful way to describe them, though we should not take this term to mean that Jesus' behavior (of healing and exorcism, for example) was typical of an ancient Mediterranean person. Rather, this term indicates that in these passages Jesus does not engage in the countercultural behavior of concealment. Jesus may violate other conventions in many of these passages, but our concern here is with the relationship of these passages to the passages in which Jesus is concealing.

In this chapter, I will explore a number of the episodes in which Jesus makes no attempt at concealment, paying special attention to the ways in which these episodes function alongside the concealment episodes discussed in chapter 2. My concern here is not with every instance in which Jesus is open about his deeds or identity, but with those that occur in the same sections of the Gospel as the concealment episodes. Most scholars hold that Mark's eleventh chapter begins a new section of the Gospel: Jesus enters into Jerusalem, the conflict between Jesus and his opponents escalates, and the story moves quickly toward the crucifixion. Clear attempts by Jesus to conceal his deeds or identity are absent in this section of the Gospel. I will therefore focus primarily on episodes in the first ten chapters of Mark.

The passages in table 4.1 depict Jesus in ways that seem inconsistent with his countercultural behavior discussed in chapter 2. I have

Honor Displayed Before Onlookers

1:21-28	Jesus' first exorcism.
1:32-34	Jesus heals a multitude at Simon's house.
2:1-12	Jesus heals the paralytic before a great crowd and claims authority to forgive sins.
2:28	Jesus claims to be Lord of the Sabbath.
3:1-6	Jesus heals a man with a withered hand on the Sabbath.
3:7-12	Jesus performs a mass healing and exorcism.
5:1-20	Jesus exorcises the Gerasene demoniac. Not only does he issue no silence command, but he tells the former demoniac to broadcast what God has done for him.
5:24b-34	In the midst of a large crowd, Jesus heals a woman with a hemorrhage.
6:30-44	Jesus feeds five thousand people.
6:53-56	At Gennesaret, Jesus performs a mass healing. His fame has preceded him to this region.
8:1-9	Jesus feeds four thousand.
9:14-28	Before a crowd, Jesus casts out an unclean spirit from a boy.
9:38-41	An exorcist is casting out demons in Jesus' name, and Jesus indicates his approval of this.
10:46-52	Jesus heals blind Bartimaeus.

Honor Displayed in Private or Secluded Spaces

1:29-31	Jesus heals Peter's mother-in-law and issues no silence command afterward.
4:35-41	Jesus causes a storm to cease but issues no silence command afterward.
6:45-52	Jesus walks on water and stills a storm, with no silence command afterward.
7:24-30	Jesus heals a Syrophoenician woman's daughter and issues no silence command afterward.

TABLE 4.1

divided these passages into two broad categories: honor displayed before onlookers, and honor displayed in private or secluded spaces.

HONOR AND ONLOOKERS

Insofar as Jesus successfully displays his power, authority, and ascribed-honor status before onlookers, we should also expect his honor rating to rise proportionately. Joseph H. Hellerman writes that Jesus' teaching, healings, and exorcisms are "undeniable demonstrations of divine authority" which result in a steady increase of his honor rating. "For Mark, the public verdict of affirmation of Jesus' honor comes again and again, as the 'crowd' (*ho ochlos*) responds to Jesus' authoritative teaching and marvelous deeds."[5] An example of this comes early in the Gospel, in 1:21-28. Hellerman also writes that it is only at the end of his life and ministry, during the incident of the "Temple cleansing" found in Mark 11:15-18, that Jesus "openly asserts his claim to honor in a most straightforward, indisputable way."[6] The Temple cleansing may be Jesus' *most* straightforward claim to honor, but as we will see, there are several earlier instances in which he makes relatively straightforward claims.

Mark 1:21-28

In this exorcism story, Jesus does attempt to stop the proclamation of his *ascribed*-honor status, but word spreads of his exorcism and teaching, thus increasing his *achieved*-honor rating. Put differently, Jesus does not let everyone know who he is, but he does let everyone see what he does. In 1:21-22, Jesus enters the synagogue and teaches, and immediately people are astounded at this teaching, because he was teaching "as one having authority" (*hōs exousian echōn*). In the ancient Mediterranean context, "authority" involves the ability to exert control over others. This ability extends not just to the sheer power to do so, but the social legitimacy of one's actions. In other words, it was not enough simply to be able to compel other people. One also had to have the proper social station, or the sanction of someone with the proper social station, to do so. Further, by casting out the unclean spirit, he not only confirms the crowd's perception of his authority,[7] but shows himself to be both beneficent and powerful. Jesus' authority, the reader knows, comes from his relationship to God as Son of God and Messiah. Jesus' power is legitimate, unlike the demon that has possessed a man, or the scribes who do not teach with authority (1:22).[8] The characters in the story, however, are not privy to this information, but only see the manifestation of Jesus' authority.

Exorcisms, as forms of beneficence, had the potential significantly to increase the honor of the one to whom the exorcism was attributed. For example, in the *Antiquities*, Josephus writes that God granted Solomon "knowledge of the art used against demons for the benefit and healing of men. He [Solomon] also composed incantations by which illnesses are relieved, and left behind forms of exorcisms with which those possessed by demons drive them out, never to return." Josephus then recounts the tale of a Jewish exorcist named Eleazar who cast out demons from a possessed man by using an incantation that Solomon had devised. Eleazar performed the exorcism, and then,

> wishing to convince the bystanders and prove to them that he had this power, Eleazar placed a cup or foot-basin full of water a little way off and commanded the demon, as it went out of the man, to overturn it and make it known to the spectators that he had left the man. And when this was done, the understanding and wisdom of Solomon were clearly revealed, on account of which we have been induced to speak of these things, in order that all men may know the greatness of his nature and how God favoured him, that no one under the sun may be ignorant of the king's surpassing virtue of every kind.[9]

Because exorcisms and other displays of authority had such potential to increase one's honor, passages such as this episode of Jesus' first exorcism in Mark would call to mind the ancient pattern of gift-and-response that was so integral to relationships of patronage, brokerage, and benefaction. Jesus' gifts extend first to the man with the unclean spirit. As in the case of the healed leper, Jesus has restored the formerly possessed man to his rightful place in the community, not to mention the fact that the man is not possessed anymore. His gifts also extend to the people from whose midst he has removed an unclean spirit, and to those who heard his teaching. Just as philosophers were considered "benefactors of humanity," Jesus' teachings would be considered by a sympathetic audience to be a gift to his hearers.[10] Those who have witnessed and benefited from Jesus' gifts react exactly as we would expect ancient Mediterranean people to react: they spread word of what he has done. "They were all amazed, and they kept on asking one another, 'What is this? A new teaching—with authority! He commands even the unclean spirits, and they obey him.' At once his fame began to spread throughout the surrounding region of Galilee" (1:27-28). Thus, although Jesus attempts to curtail knowledge of his ascribed honor, his achieved honor increases significantly.

Mark 1:32-34; 3:7-12

The "summary reports" of Mark 1:32-34 and 3:7-12 illustrate the extent of Jesus' ability to heal, his great authority, and his power to cast out demons. Jesus performs works of beneficence for all the sick and possessed in Capernaum (1:33), and then for people from regions that encompass the full extent of the united kingdom of Israel (3:7-8). He thus functions as a broker on a very large scale.[11] Although he does issue silence commands to unclean spirits (discussed in chapter 2), Jesus issues no silence command to those whom he has healed. Such a command would be pointless, given that he heals so many people and that the whole town has gathered to seek healing and exorcism. In the first episode, "they brought to him all the sick and possessed" (1:32), apparently because of the spread of Jesus' fame of which we read in 1:28. "They" in this passage probably refers to the people of Capernaum who are gathered at the door of Simon's house (1:33). This passage, like its chiastic partner in 1:40-45 (see appendix), illustrates the spread of Jesus' fame. By the time we get to 3:7-12, Jesus' fame has spread well beyond Galilee. People come to him from "Judea, Jerusalem, Idumea, beyond the Jordan, and the region around Tyre and Sidon... hearing all that he was doing" (3:8).

Mark 2:1-12

An individual healing and a claim to authority, both of which many people witness, occur in the story of Jesus' healing of the paralytic in Capernaum. Mark writes that Jesus was in a house, and "many were gathered together, so that there was no longer room, not even in front of the door" (2:2). In fact, the crowd is so great that those who wish to bring a paralytic to Jesus must dig through the roof of the house and lower the paralytic through the opening. In front of the entire crowd, Jesus says to the paralytic, "Son, your sins are forgiven." Such an action would obviously be seen as a claim to honor and authority far beyond the station of a peasant carpenter, or any human being, for that matter. Thus, some of the scribes who are present question "in their hearts" (2:6). They believe that Jesus has placed himself on a par with God and claimed authority that is only rightly God's, thereby slandering God. Hence, they accuse Jesus of blasphemy, the base meaning of which denotes slander. According to Morna Hooker, Jesus is claiming that he has the authority to forgive sins, rather than assuring the paralytic of God's forgiveness,[12] while Joel Marcus argues that God "has delegated his power of absolution to a 'Son of Man' who carries out his gracious will in the earthly sphere."[13] Marcus's position coheres with ideas expressed by Bruce Malina and Richard Rohrbaugh: "Nowhere in the Gospels does Jesus say, 'I forgive you.' Instead, as in 2:5, Mark is careful to show that God does the forgiving and that Jesus is acting as a broker on behalf of the forgiving Patron. Patrons were often absent and designated brokers to distribute favors on their behalf. What is being questioned in the challenge to Jesus, then, and what he demonstrates in his careful response, is his authorization to act as God's designated broker."[14] The broker of a very powerful figure could indeed have a great deal of authority, and here it appears that Jesus does claim and exercise authority attendant with his role as God's broker.

Such would be consistent not only with widespread ancient Mediterranean notions of brokerage, but with specifically Jewish notions of agency. In Peder Borgen's study of the Jewish concept of agency in the Fourth Gospel, he focuses on the rabbinic principle that "an agent is like the one who sent him."[15] This principle applied regardless of the identity of the sender. The agent and the sender were not social equals; rather, the agent was subordinate to the sender, and it was assumed

that an agent (such as a messenger) would carry out a mission in obedience to the sender. Yet agents could wield authority, including legal
authority, on behalf of their senders. Jesus' claim to have authority
to forgive sins extends from his agency—which in this case takes the
form of brokerage—on God's behalf.

It is before a crowd that the actual healing of the paralytic takes
place. Moreover, Jesus commands the paralytic to "take up your mat
and go to your house" (2:11) so that "you [the scribes] might know
that the Son of Man has authority to forgive sins on the earth" (2:10).
The response of the onlookers to this healing is that "all were aston-
ished and glorified God, saying, 'We never saw anything like this
before!'" Clearly there is no concealment in this episode, nor does
Jesus make any attempt to resist acquiring honor. Although this story
is about a healing that Jesus performs, it also serves a larger purpose in
the story by depicting one of a number of challenges to Jesus' authority, challenges that will culminate in his crucifixion.

There are interpreters who see verse 10a, "so that you may know
that the Son of Man has authority to forgive sins on earth," as an aside
to the Markan audience, rather than as a statement of Jesus which
could be heard by characters in the story.[16] If this line of interpretation
is correct, then Jesus does not openly claim the authority to forgive
sins on earth in this episode. This would leave us with the issue of
Jesus' performance of a public healing, but would eliminate the issue
of Jesus' claim of authority on a par with God's authority. Jesus' words
in Mark 2:8-9 are clearly addressed to the scribes, however, and in
the absence of some type of compelling indicator that the evangelist
has switched midsentence from Jesus' addressing the scribes to the
narrator's direct, second-person address to the reader, one should not
assume such change.[17]

What are the honor-related implications of the Son of Man title,
which is introduced here? Jack Dean Kingsbury argues that "Son of
God" in Mark represents God's point of view (see 1:11; 9:7) and is
therefore a normative title for Jesus in Mark.[18] "Son of Man," however,
also indicates an important aspect of Jesus' relationship to God. This
title, which alludes to Daniel 7, gives expression to a patron–client
relationship between God and Jesus: Jesus is the one who will suffer
in obedience to his divine patron, and his divine patron will vindi-
cate Jesus after he has suffered shamefully. In other words, "Son of

Man" expresses a mutual commitment between God and Jesus, and in the ancient Mediterranean world one's network of commitments was largely indicative of one's identity.[19]

By this point in the narrative, Jesus has already attempted to deflect honor from himself (see 1:25; 1:34; 1:40-45). Here, though, Jesus is seen not only claiming the honor of the Son of Man but also acquiring honor at the expense of his enemies. This is conveyed most forcefully by the form of the exchange between Jesus and the scribes. This passage is the first of five challenge-riposte scenarios in the form of "responsive *chreiai*." A *chreia* was a short reminiscence of an action or saying of some person, and a responsive *chreia* was one in which the character (often a sage) was required to respond to some question or situation.[20] It is not the case that Jesus' opponents verbally question him in each of these episodes (for example, they do not in 2:1-12 and 3:1-6). At times they question "in their hearts" (2:6) or look for some pretext by which to accuse him (3:2). For the audience of the story, such questions and pretexts for accusations are challenges to Jesus' authority and the legitimacy of his actions. Questions were often perceived as honor challenges, and accusations most certainly were. These *chreiai* advance the theme of conflict between Jesus and his opponents and, because Jesus always prevails in the verbal exchanges, they advance his honor at the expense of his opponents. In each of these *chreiai* the challenge to Jesus is the result of a claim to authority that he makes implicitly or explicitly. The story of the healing of the paralytic does not advance the theme of Jesus' resistance to the traditional components of honor, but it does advance other important honor-related themes, including Jesus' authority, the widespread acknowledgment of his power and authority, his acquisition of honor, and the rising opposition to him.[21]

Mark 2:28

In the responsive *chreia* that includes Mark 2:28, Jesus bests his opponents in a challenge-riposte interaction, thus acquiring honor at their expense. He also claims to be Lord of the Sabbath, a significant claim to authority.[22] As with 2:10a, "Son of Man" is here connected with this claim to authority. We have seen that in Mark, "Son of Man" alludes to the figure of Daniel 7 and is a term that carries a high honor rating. To be "Lord of the Sabbath" is an even loftier claim. The title *kurios* ("lord"), which is in the emphatic position in this clause, designates Jesus as a person of high ascribed honor. It is also a title that one might use to designate a patron or broker.[23] The phrase *kurios tou sabbatou* would have called to mind a claim to authority on a par with that of Yahweh (see Exod 16:25, 20:10, 31:13; Lev 19:3, 30; Deut 5:14; Ezek 20:12-13), authority that comes from Jesus' role as God's broker.[24] R. T. France argues that the use of this phrase "represents yet another escalation of the unique *exousia* [authority] exercised by Jesus."[25]

Mark 3:1-6

The episode in which Jesus heals a man with a withered hand offers another example of a healing that takes place in front of witnesses and after which there is no silence command. This episode is set in a synagogue, a public area in which male interaction would take place. Mark specifically notes the presence of onlookers (3:2) who wish to see if Jesus will violate the law by healing on the Sabbath. Mark does not indicate that the healed man reciprocated Jesus' beneficence by promoting Jesus' honor, nor does the story relate the astonishment of the onlookers.[26] Yet ancient Mediterraneans would expect that word of the healing would spread quickly.

This passage presents particular problems for positions such as that advanced by Mary Ann Tolbert, who claims that Jesus is trying to delay the crucifixion, or, in her words, "*buy time for sowing the word.*"[27] In 3:6 the evangelist specifies the identity of at least some of the onlookers as the Pharisees.[28] Jesus' opponents are thus present and aware of his actions, and Mark even indicates that the reason that they look on is to see whether Jesus will heal on the Sabbath and incriminate himself (3:2). This episode represents a responsive *chreia*, with Jesus' words in verse 4 and his healing of the man in verse 5 representing a riposte to the implicit challenge of those who wish to accuse Jesus. In the context of the ancient Mediterranean world, any action by Jesus that results in his acquiring honor will be taken by his opponents as an affront to their honor. When Jesus performs this healing in front of onlookers, his opponents experience envy, and the common recourse at this point would be for them to attempt to deprive Jesus of the honor that he had acquired. Indeed, this is exactly what they try to do: the result of the healing is a conspiracy between the Pharisees and the Herodians to "destroy" Jesus (3:6). The issue is not simply that Jesus violates the law. Rather, it is that, in connection with 2:23-28, the episode of 3:1-6 shows Jesus claiming authority on a par with God's. Therefore, his opponents see him as encroaching on God's territory, claiming honor outside of his station, and, through his riposte, causing an affront to their honor. That Jesus has (in the eyes of his opponents) violated the Sabbath law provides a pretext for plans to destroy him. If Mark wishes to depict Jesus as trying to avoid retributive action by his opponents and prolong the length of his ministry, it is difficult to explain why this passage comes so early in the narrative.

This episode is the last in a series of responsive *chreiai* (2:1—3:6), and it is the chiastic partner of 2:1-12 (see appendix). It is also juxtaposed with another *chreia* relating a Sabbath controversy (2:23-28), and both 2:23-28 and 3:1-6 underscore a claim of authority and honor by Jesus: "The Son of Man is lord even of the sabbath" (2:28). As noted above, the *chreiai* in this section convey Jesus' authority, his acquisition of honor through challenge-riposte interactions, and the opposition to him on the part of the scribes and Pharisees (2:1—3:6). Mark 3:1-6 functions primarily to advance these themes. Like 2:1-12, it is a story about a healing, but it also demonstrates the rising opposition to Jesus. It helps to lay the groundwork for the crucifixion by relating not only the plot by Jesus' opponents to destroy him, but (implicitly) their envy of him. Because Mark has repetitively portrayed Jesus' acquisition of honor from his opponents in these responsive *chreiai*, the audience is prepared when in 15:10 Mark writes that the chief priests hand Jesus over out of envy.

Mark 5:1-20

Unlike some of the other exorcism stories in Mark's Gospel (1:23-28; 1:32-34; 3:7-12), the exorcism of the Gerasene demoniac involves no silence command to the demoniac, despite the fact that the demonic identifies Jesus as "Son of the Most High God" (5:7). The text is not entirely clear as to whether anyone witnesses the encounter between Jesus and the demoniac. Against Kingsbury, who argues that there are no witnesses to the encounter,[29] Robert Gundry holds that the presence of the swineherds should be assumed from the mention of the swine in verse 11, although there is no mention of them until verse 14. He also maintains that *ekei*—"there," or "in that place"—in verse 11 indicates that the mountain on which the pigs are feeding is nearby, and he notes that Mark describes the demoniac's shout as "loud" (*phōnē megalē*, v. 7). Therefore, "the herdsmen's hearing and seeing what happened so as to tell others coheres with the earlier part of the story."[30] J. Duncan M. Derrett notes that swine require four times as many keepers as do sheep,[31] and Mark indicates that there are about two thousand swine. While we cannot be sure, it is reasonable to postulate that there is an implicit understanding in the story that the swineherds overheard Jesus' dialogue with the demoniac.

Some scholars, including Wrede, have seen Jesus' command to "go to your house, to your people" (*hupage eis ton oikon sou pros tous sous*) as an instance of Jesus' "secrecy."[32] Gerd Theissen writes that Mark 5:19ff. "does not contain a command to silence, though Mark will have taken it as doing so. The cured man is sent 'home'—for Mark often a place of secrecy (7:17; 7:24; 9:28; 10:10)—but proclaims the news in the Decapolis."[33] Each of the passages (apart from 5:19) that Theissen cites does provide an example of the house as a place of *privacy*, though not necessarily *secrecy*. Yet we have seen that while the house represents "private" space, it still involves interactions with other people. Wrede himself concedes that the house is not always a place of "secrecy,"[34] and Marcus notes that, up to this point in Mark's narrative, the house has been a place in which Jesus' power and authority have been made known, rather than hidden (1:29-34; 2:1-2, 15; 3:20).[35] Continuing this trend, the reference to the house in 5:19 does not involve the idea that Jesus is trying to suppress knowledge of his exorcism.[36] Thus, it is reasonable to hold that Jesus sends the man to his house not to suppress information, but so that the man can tell (*apangeilon*) his family all that the Lord has done for him. The verb *apangellō* is the same verb used in 5:14 to describe the swineherds' spreading word of what they witnessed. John Donahue and Daniel Harrington note that it is also "part of the mission vocabulary of the early church (Acts 15:27; 26:20)."[37] Jesus' command that the man go to his house simply stands in contradistinction to the man's request to go with Jesus (5:18) (hence the adversative *alla* in 5:19), but is not equivalent to an attempt to keep the exorcism a secret.

An interesting aspect of this episode is that it is the only one of Jesus' healings or exorcisms in which Jesus instructs someone to go and tell what has happened. He instructs the man to proclaim what "the Lord" has done for him. In all likelihood, "the Lord" in this passage refers to God, the true source and patron of the man's healing.[38] Luke reads the story in this way, replacing Mark's term *kurios* (Lord) with *theos* (God) (8:39). Such would also be consistent with the LXX use of *kurios*. In only one instance in Mark (11:3) does Jesus use *kurios* with an article unambiguously to refer to himself, and this occurs well after the last clear instance of Jesus' concealment (9:9). Thus, Jesus does not issue a straightforward command that word of his brokerage not be made known. Rather, he attempts to steer the proclamation toward God.[39] He wishes for the recipient of his brokerage to spread word of God's patronage among those of his house (in other words, his extended family), especially since the people of the village have rejected Jesus and asked him to leave (5:17). However, the client who has been healed responds in a way that is not in keeping with Jesus' wishes:[40] he proclaims all that *Jesus* has done for him (5:20). The client does not acknowledge the true source of Jesus' power, and thus mistakes the broker for the patron. Yet this is far from a command that the man tell no one what Jesus has done.

Mark 5:24b-34

In the story of the healing of the woman with a hemorrhage (5:24b-34), the woman apparently has no intention of approaching Jesus openly. In contrast to many other recipients of Jesus' beneficence, she does not petition Jesus' services, but tries to benefit from his power without his consent. Mark writes in 5:27 that the woman had heard about Jesus; her actions are properly seen as a response to his fame and indicate that he has already acquired a reputation as a healer in this region. Mark also relates that she "came up behind [Jesus] in the crowd and touched his cloak, for she said, 'If I but touch his clothes, I will be made well'" (5:28). It is she, rather than Jesus, who attempts to conceal this healing, and it is Jesus who calls attention to the fact that the healing has taken place when he attempts to find out who touched him:[41] "Immediately aware that power had gone forth from him, Jesus turned about in the crowd and said, 'Who touched my clothes?' And his disciples said to him, 'You see the crowd pressing in on you; how can you say, "Who touched me?" '"[42] He looked all around to see who had done it" (5:30-33). The use of the imperfect *perieblepeto* ("he looked around"), especially since it is juxtaposed with the aorist *hēpsato* in verse 31, indicates an ongoing action on Jesus' part.[43] The healing that had occurred was nothing that Jesus was trying to hide. This action precipitates the woman's coming forward publicly, falling down before him, and confessing her deed.

Some scholars have argued that, despite the crowd around Jesus when the healing takes place, it is best to see the interaction between Jesus and the woman as a private affair that the others around do not overhear.[44] It is true that no one is specifically said to overhear the dialogue between Jesus and the woman, though this does not mean that ancient hearers would infer that none of the people in the crowd heard this dialogue. The ancient Mediterranean culture was a "high-context" culture, one in which people were deeply involved in the everyday activities of those around them and in which information was widely shared.[45] A modern, Western understanding of privacy did not obtain in this context. One of the key mechanisms in this sharing of information was the "gossip network." Gossip, a common feature of ancient Mediterranean life, could function positively or negatively.[46] For example, it might function as a means of enhancing the reputation of honorable individuals, as we read in one of the satires of Persius: "it is a fine thing to have a finger pointed at one, and to hear people say, 'That's the man.' "[47] Conversely, it could function as a way of defaming those who were seen as dishonorable. It could, in fact, serve as a means of social control.[48] Seneca writes that one who errs should be reproved, first privately and then, if the behavior continues, publicly. If one is so far advanced in vice "that words can no longer bring you to your sense, then you shall be held in check by public disgrace."[49]

We should expect an ancient audience to understand the goings-on in Mark's Gospel according to the ways that things normally work for ancient Mediterraneans. Unless there is some indication to the contrary, we should assume that the natural conventions related to interpersonal relationship were at work. People did not simply "mind their own business" (as they would in a "low-context," individualized culture), but were very much involved in the lives of the other people around them.

Concealment on Jesus' part simply would not fit into this story: the great crowd, the woman's uncleanliness among so many other people, her attempt to touch Jesus' clothes and then slip away, Jesus' looking for the person who touched him, and the woman's coming forward in fear preclude a private venue. For the Markan audience, this story would not demonstrate Jesus' resistance to traditional concepts of honor, but would advance other ideas, such as the importance of having faith and overcoming fear.[50] The public nature of the healing indicates that, for Mark, it is simply not necessary for Jesus always to conceal the spread of information regarding his healings. Sometimes other themes are more important.

Mark 6:30-44; 8:1-9

The feeding miracles in 6:30-44 and 8:1-9 depict Jesus as a broker on a very broad scale. Regarding the first of these stories (6:30-34) Douglas Geyer writes, "The Greek inscriptions remind us that giving of free bread was a well-known institution, typically taken as display of the *charis* (grace) of the benefactor who, especially if he is a king, is expected to be publicly accessible to his people and to solve problems that range from adjudication of cases to provision of necessities for those who are without. It would seem in Mark that, even though there is no actual royal title attributed to Jesus, we have all the ingredients for a scene of royal benefaction."[51] In the feeding stories, Mark relates that Jesus had "compassion" (*splanchnizomai*, 6:34 and 8:2) on the crowds, just as he had upon the leper earlier in the story (1:41). As we have seen, the references to Jesus' compassion call to mind the favor of a patron toward a client (or, in this case, a great multitude of clients). Further, Jesus sees the crowd as "sheep without a shepherd" (6:34). In the ancient Mediterranean world, the image of a shepherd was a very common metaphor for both divine and human kings.[52] Jesus' assuming the role of the shepherd and feeding the crowd places him in a kingly role as the distributor of gifts and mediator of divine benefaction.

Yet Geyer also holds that, in the feeding of the five thousand, Jesus makes efforts *not* to be seen as the benefactor. Rather, the disciples are told to act as the benefactors while Jesus stands in the background. "We have here a backwards benefaction, in which the benefactor remains occluded and his virtue unrevealed. It is a very paradoxical depiction, given the kinds and types of benefactions that populated everybody's expectations at the time Mark was written."[53] If this interpretation were correct, this episode would function as an example of Jesus' suppression of widespread knowledge of his beneficence and would advance nicely the themes discussed in chapter 3. Geyer's conclusion, however, is questionable. Given the large number of people to whom the food must be distributed, we might expect the disciples to function as attendants, or subbrokers. The Roman emperors maintained a corn distribution that was allocated monthly to 200,000 people who held tickets (*tesserae*). Yet the distribution was not supervised by the emperor himself, but by two senators known as the Prefects of the Corn Distribution, who presumably oversaw other employees or slaves.[54] Similarly, the same people who held tickets for the corn distribution also occasionally received distributions of cash (*congiaria*), normally on special occasions. The emperor presided at these distributions, but coins issued to mark these occasions show the emperor presiding while a functionary hands out coins to the people.[55] Likewise, the disciples assist Jesus, but there is nothing compelling in the feeding stories to indicate that the disciples are understood as the benefactors (to use Geyer's terminology). In both of Mark's feeding stories, Jesus' widespread brokerage is available for all to see, rather than occluded.

Mark 6:53-56

Like the episodes of 1:32-34 and 3:7-12, the episode of 6:53-56 is a summary report, and like the other summary reports, it recounts Jesus' widespread beneficence and the spread of his fame. In 6:54-56, Mark relates that the gossip network is in full force. As soon as Jesus and the disciples get out of the boat at Gennesaret, people immediately recognize him and "rushed about that whole region and began to bring the sick upon mats to where they heard that he was. And wherever he went, into villages or cities or farms, they laid the sick in the markets [*tais agorais*] and begged him in order than they might even touch the fringe of his garment. And all who touched him were healed." As Philo specifically notes, the market was one of the arenas of male public interaction.[56] Jesus' healings in the markets are public events. Unlike the two previous summary reports, this episode does not specifically mention exorcisms or demons who have special knowledge regarding Jesus' identity. Thus, whereas the two previous summary reports at least related Jesus' silencing of demons, this episode involves no silence commands whatsoever.

Moreover, it is significant that this passage takes place within a larger section dealing with discipleship (6:14—9:1). The crowds react to Jesus positively with great enthusiasm, and this reaction contrasts with the increasing blindness of the disciples (6:45-52; 7:17ff.; 8:4, 14-21, 33) and the continued rejection of Jesus by the scribes and Pharisees (7:1-14; 8:11-13). It may be that at this point in the Gospel, the evangelist has simply laid aside the theme of Jesus' rejection of the honor that he is due. Mark 6:53-56 is the third of four consecutive instances in which Jesus makes no attempt to hide his deeds or identity (see 6:30-44; 6:45-52; 7:34-30). Themes other than the rejection and reshaping of the traditional components of honor dominate this part of the narrative.

Mark 9:14-28

In Mark 9:14-28, Jesus performs an exorcism for a boy who is possessed by a spirit that makes the boy unable to speak. In the first verse of this episode, Mark relates that a "great crowd" was present on the scene before Jesus arrived. Mark notes that the people who make up the crowd are "amazed" (*exethambēthēsan*). Some scholars have suggested that Jesus' appearance is still in some way transformed from the transfiguration episode.[57] Such would be reminiscent of Moses coming down from the mountain and still reflecting the glory of God from his face, thus causing the people to be afraid (Exodus 34).[58] Other scholars have suggested that the evangelist uses *exethambēthēsan* "to denote the powerful impression which Jesus' personal presence by now created,"[59] or to express "an authority that emanates from him even before he speaks or acts."[60] Hooker correctly points out that the reference to amazement in this passage seems out of place.[61] Amazement and fear commonly come after Jesus has performed great deeds, rather than beforehand (see 1:27; 2:12; 5:15; 6:51; 7:37).[62] Yet if Jesus' personal presence somehow invoked amazement in people, the reference to amazement at the beginning of this episode would not be so unusual. The text does not allow for a definitive solution to the problem posed by the amazement of the crowd, but given the reference to Moses in the transfiguration episode, the location of Jesus on a mountain (like Moses), the fact that upon descending the mountain both Jesus and Moses encounter large groups of people, and the juxtaposition of this passage and the transfiguration episode, it is reasonable to hold that Mark's audience would have understood the amazement of the crowd to come from Jesus' appearance (affected by the transfiguration) and to parallel the events in the story of Moses. Further, while Mark relates that Moses and Elijah disappear after God speaks (9:8), Mark provides no information regarding whether Jesus' appearance has returned to normal.[63] It is thus possible that Mark intended to portray Jesus as still bearing some of the glory of the transfiguration while not making known the full extent of his ascribed honor.

Puzzlingly, we read in verse 25 that Jesus rebukes the demon when he sees a crowd running together. Hooker remarks, "The reference to a crowd gathering is odd after the earlier setting in vv. 14-17, and a possible indication that two narratives have been joined together. Nor is the relevance of the remark to the story clear—unless the original account described a healing which was performed as privately as possible."[64] In the form in which Mark has related this episode, however, this exorcism does not clearly come across as one that Jesus is trying to hide from the onlookers. The hearer or reader already knows that a crowd is present, there is no mention of Jesus' taking the possessed boy to a private location, and Jesus issues no silence command after the exorcism. Like Jesus' other exorcisms in Mark, this one is carried out openly.

Unlike some other episodes involving exorcisms (1:21-28; 1:32-34; 3:7-12), however, this one involves no verbal exchange in which the demoniac identifies Jesus by some honorific title. Mark describes the spirit as *alalon*, or "speechless" (5:17), and thus the hearer or reader should expect no such exchange.[65] Gundry comments, "Though the spirit will let out a shriek toward the end of the story, that shriek will signal the end of the spirit's dominion over the son."[66] This is a violent spirit (5:18), but a silent one. Thus, the silence commands that appear in other exorcism stories are absent from this one. There is no need to silence a silent spirit.

Mark 9:38-41

The episode of Mark 9:38-41 is another in which Jesus makes no attempt to suppress information about himself. In this episode, John reports to Jesus the disciples' attempt to stop an exorcist who is casting out demons in Jesus' name, but who is not "following us" (9:38). John's report provides a context for the sayings of Jesus in verses 39-41, sayings which demonstrate that the disciples' response—forbidding the exorcist's use of Jesus' name—was not in keeping with Jesus' wishes. This episode follows the larger pattern of 9:30-50, in which the disciples' misunderstanding provides the occasion for teaching that clarifies what it means to be a part of the group of people who follow Jesus.[67]

There are numerous interpretations of this episode.[68] For the purposes of this chapter, however, it is sufficient to point out that, while the spread of Jesus' fame and the increase of his honor and reputation are not the main foci of this story, they are implicit in the use of Jesus' name to cast out demons. One's name and one's honor were inseparable. Regarding this issue, Jerome Neyrey writes that in a limited-good context, one's honor would be diminished insofar as unauthorized people make use of one's name and power, as in Acts 19:13-17.

> When the disciples report to Jesus that an unauthorized person was "casting out demons in your name, and we forbade him, because he was not following us" (Mark 9:38//Luke 9:49-50), Jesus does not view this as an encroachment on his honor; rather, he interprets this as further broadcasting his name and thus adding to his reputation (9:39). But "coming in the name of" and "acting in the name of" both claim that honor resides in the person whose name is used.[69]

Thus, in this episode, Jesus attempts neither to conceal the great power associated with his name nor to suppress the spread of his reputation and increase of his honor.

Mark 10:46-52

In the story of the healing of Bartimaeus, Mark recounts that, along with his disciples, a great crowd (*ochlos hikanos*) is present with Jesus (10:46). It is before this crowd that Bartimaeus addresses Jesus by the honorific title "Son of David," which carried messianic significance for early Christians, and which called to mind the figure of Solomon, shown in the Old Testament to be a generous benefactor and known in Jewish tradition to have healing powers.[70] Yet Jesus does not silence Bartimaeus as he does Peter or the demons. Further, when Jesus heals Bartimaeus there is no mention of his leading Bartimaeus away from the crowd (as there is in 7:33 and 8:22), and there is no silence command after the healing (as there is in 7:36 and implicitly in 8:26). Bystanders do attempt to silence Bartimaeus, although the narrative purpose of their attempts is to highlight the faith Bartimaeus displays in his resistance to them,[71] and their attempts to silence him are unrelated to Jesus' silence commands which occur at other points in the Gospel.[72] After the healing, Bartimaeus follows Jesus "on the way" as his client, thus bringing honor to Jesus as living proof of Jesus' beneficence and healing prowess.

Not surprisingly, scholars assuming a "secrecy motif" have found this passage puzzling. J. H. Charlesworth does not offer a positive proposal to solve the problem of this supposed break in the secrecy motif, but remarks, "If [Mark] thought about the exhortation of Bartimaeus as a messianic confession, then his handling of this tradition departs from his usual tendency and the so-called Messianic Secret."[73] If we understand Mark to be reshaping common understandings of honor, however, the puzzlement of this passage diminishes somewhat.

Unlike the story of the woman with the hemorrhage (5:24b-34), the elements of this story do not preclude Jesus' healing in private or issuing a silence command afterward. Yet if the silence commands are attempts to resist and reshape traditional components of honor, by this point in the narrative such attempts would be superfluous. In

10:32 the audience learns that Jesus and the disciples are on the road to Jerusalem. Mark has already mentioned that Jesus' opponents are from Jerusalem (3:22 and 7:1), and in 10:33 Jesus speaks of Jerusalem as the place where "the Son of Man will be handed over to the chief priests and the scribes, and they will condemn him to death and hand him over to the Gentiles, and they will mock him, and spit on him, and scourge him, and kill him, and after three days he will rise" (10:33-34). Further, it is reasonable to think that Mark's audience was familiar with Jerusalem as the place of Jesus' crucifixion. Jericho lies only about fifteen miles from Jerusalem, and by mentioning Jericho in 10:46, Mark signals that Jesus has drawn very near to the city in which the events of the prophecies of 8:31, 9:31, and 10:33-34 will take place. As the action in the narrative draws ever closer to the crucifixion, Mark need not show Jesus issuing a silence command and thus resisting traditional components of honor: Jesus is going into the holy city to die a death that was widely regarded as maximally shaming. The story itself is redefining of the nature of true honor.

The episode of the healing of Bartimaeus presages the acclaim that Jesus will receive (and does not shun) as he enters Jerusalem (11:1-11). Donahue and Harrington refer to this episode as a "bridge to the next phases in Mark's story of Jesus' public ministry."[74] Whereas Bartimaeus refers to Jesus as "Son of David," the crowds along the road as he enters Jerusalem shout, "Blessed is the one who comes in the name of the Lord! Blessed is the coming kingdom of our ancestor, David!" (11:9b-10). Because the Son of David rides into Jerusalem to suffer shamefully and die, the title "Son of David" does not conform (in Mark) to standard conventions of honor, and thus there is no need to reject it. Or, to put the matter very simply, there is no point in a silence command here since it is clear that Jesus is going into the city where he will be crucified.

For this reason, Jesus allows Bartimaeus to follow him as a client. By following Jesus "on the way" (10:52) into Jerusalem, Bartimaeus embodies the way of the cross about which Jesus spoke in 8:34ff. and offers a sharp contrast to the disciples. The Bartimaeus episode forms a frame with the episode of the healing of the blind man in 8:22-26 (see the appendix). Within this frame of two episodes that relate the giving of sight, there are a number of passages in which the disciples exhibit blindness and incompetence (see, for example,

8:31-33; 9:10, 14-29, 32, 33-37, 38-41; 10:13-16, 35-45). Bartimaeus, who would normally gain honor by his association with such a powerful figure as Jesus, follows Jesus on the way of the shameful cross. Jesus, who should gain honor through Bartimaeus's *pistis* (trust, faith), demonstrated by his following Jesus, walks into a situation in which he will suffer total disgrace in the eyes of the wider public. In this way, Mark's narrative continues to overturn the ancient Mediterranean conventions regarding the ways in which honor and shame were assigned.

Honor Displayed in Private or Secluded Spaces

In some instances, Jesus' great deeds take place in private or in secluded locations. At times the locale of these deeds results from Jesus' own preference (and these instances are discussed in chapter 2), but at other times Jesus encounters people who are already in private or secluded locations. Yet the fact that a particular work of beneficence occurs in such a location does not necessarily mean that Jesus is trying to conceal the favors that he bestows. In the ancient Mediterranean context, "private" does not equate to "hidden." Rather, "private" space (such as within a house) could refer to the sphere of women and domestic activity or to the sphere of male interaction with kin or friends.[75]

Mark 1:29-31 and 7:24-30

Mark 1:29-31 and 7:24-30 offer two episodes in which Jesus encounters women within houses, and in both episodes Jesus performs some work of beneficence. Insofar as Jesus interacts with non-kin women, we should expect that he would do so within a house, as in the story of the healing of Jairus's daughter (see 5:40-43).[76] As the silence command to those who witness the healing of Jairus's daughter suggests, however, a "private" location in and of itself does not necessarily imply any kind of information control. Nevertheless, a private location *can* imply control. When Jesus heals the blind man in 8:22-26, he sends him to his house as a way of preventing the spread of information regarding the healing, but in that episode the house is specifically set in contrast to the public space of the village (8:26), where the healed man would interact with non-kin males and be observed doing so.

It is therefore significant that in neither 1:29-31 nor 7:24-30 is there any positive action on Jesus' part to prevent the healings from becoming widely known. In the first of these episodes, Mark's audience has already been informed that Jesus' fame has spread throughout Galilee (1:27-28), and Jesus makes no attempt to prevent the continued spread of gossip regarding his healing of Simon's mother-in-law. He issues a silence command neither to Simon's mother-in-law nor to the four disciples who are with him. Apparently, after the first of these episodes word of Jesus' skill as a healer gets out, since Mark writes in 1:32 that on the same evening, it was not simply the demon-possessed who were brought to him, but the ill (*tous kakōs echontas*), and Jesus has performed no other healings prior to this point in the Gospel.[77]

In the episode in which Jesus casts out a demon from the Syrophoenician woman's daughter, the gossip network has preceded Jesus, and he has already become known in the region of Tyre (see 3:8).[78] The fact that the woman comes to Jesus for healing after "hearing about him" (7:25) also testifies to the workings of the gossip network in making Jesus known as a healer and exorcist in this region.

Mark writes that Jesus went into a house, and though he wished that no one might know where he was, he could not remain hidden (7:24). According to Wrede, Jesus' wish to remain hidden in the house in Tyre is part of the messianic secret.[79] However, the evangelist gives no indication that Jesus is attempting to hide his identity or word of the deeds that he has done. The fact that Jesus has already become known in this region weighs heavily against Wrede's interpretation. Marcus holds that "the hiding motif here primarily serves to demonstrate his charismatic power, which *cannot* be hidden—a point that will quickly be reiterated in 7:36."[80] Whether or not this interpretation is correct, it leaves open the question of Jesus' reasons for entering the house in the first place. David Rhoads suggests that Jesus' attempt to seek privacy is a stylistic technique intended to increase the tension in the story when the woman seeks him out: "Jesus is trying to hide, and a Gentile requests healing. What will happen?"[81] However, he also rightly notes that Jesus' reasons for retreating into privacy are unclear.[82]

In 1:45 and 6:31, Mark specifically notes that Jesus seeks solitude because his fame has become so great,[83] and in another instance we read that the crowd around Jesus (and the disciples?) was so great that "they could not even eat" (3:20). Perhaps in 7:24, in which Jesus enters the private sphere in which his interactions with others will be more limited, Jesus is again seeking a respite from the crowd.[84] It is plausible, however, that the Markan audience might perceive the following scenario: Jesus' fame preceded him in the region of Tyre, and as a result he was offered hospitality upon his arrival. He then accepted this hospitality because of his desire to escape the great crowds. This scenario, while somewhat speculative, is culturally appropriate and much more satisfying than to claim that Jesus is trying to keep his identity a secret in this region in which he is already well known.

At no point in Mark's Gospel does Jesus issue a silence command to prevent the spread of word regarding an exorcism that he performed. However, we have seen that in three different instances Mark relates that Jesus silences demons who know of his identity (1:25; 1:34; 3:12). Such a command is not fitting in this episode, however, because Jesus casts out the demon from a distance. As in 9:14–29, there is no verbal exchange between Jesus and the demon, and therefore there is no opportunity for a silence command.

Mark 4:35-41 and 6:45-52

The stories in 4:35–41 (in which Jesus stills a storm) and 6:45–52 (in which Jesus stills a storm and walks on water) are generally categorized separately from the healing and exorcism stories.[85] Rudolf Bultmann referred to these as "nature miracles."[86] Nevertheless, like the episodes relating healings and exorcisms, these stories reflect Jesus' role as the broker of God's patronage. When Jesus' friends are in trouble, he draws upon the power of his divine patron in order to assist them.

More significant than Jesus' ability to provide brokerage, however, are the maximal status, honor, and authority that he displays in these episodes.[87] Kingsbury holds that the disciples do not comprehend

Jesus' identity after he stills the storm (4:41).[88] On one level, of course, they do: they know that this is Jesus of Nazareth, the leader of their group, a teacher, healer, and exorcist. Their question, however, relates to Jesus' authority. In the background of this Markan story are Old Testament stories of God's power over the forces of nature. Clearly the creation narrative of Genesis 1:1—2:3 comes to mind, as well as passages exalting God's work in creation such as Psalms 8, 19, 33, and 104, and Sirach 42:15—43:33. Job 40:15—41:34 relates God's victory over Behemoth and Leviathan, representatives of the chaotic forces of nature (see also 2 Esd 6:49-52). Sirach depicts the forces of nature as taking delight in doing God's bidding (Sir 39:28-31). Control over the forces of nature is also manifested by agents of God's authority, such as we see in the story of Moses, who stretches his hand out over the sea, thereby invoking the power of God to part the waters (Exodus 14). In the Wisdom of Solomon, it is Wisdom who led the people through the sea and drowned their enemies (Wis 10:18-19). Another example is Elijah's prophecy of a drought that God would bring upon the land (1 Kgs 17:1-7). From the Gentile world, we find these words of Isis in one of the hymns of Isodorus (ca. 50 B.C.E.): "I am Mistress of rivers, and winds and sea. . . . I calm and swell the sea. . . . I am the Mistress of sailing. . . . I render navigable things unnavigable when it might be to my glory."[89] In sum, control of nature is the prerogative of the divine. How is it, then, that Jesus can control the wind and the sea? The question is an inquiry into Jesus' status vis-à-vis the divine.

In the episode of 6:45-52 in which Jesus walks on the sea, it is possible to interpret the statement "He intended to pass by [*parelthein*] them" (6:48) as an instance of Jesus' self-concealment.[90] However, John Paul Heil has argued convincingly that Jesus' "passing by" connotes not concealment or secrecy, but revelation. He holds that the background of this passage is Exodus 33:18—34:6. In this passage, Yahweh's passing by Moses involves appearing to Moses, rather than hiding or withdrawing.[91] Further, Heil notes that in both the Exodus theophany and Mark's story of Jesus' walking on the sea, the appearance is followed by a proclamation of identity (or, in social-scientific terms, an acknowledgment of his honor status).[92] Other Old Testament instances of the use of this term for God's appearing include Genesis 32:31-32 (with reference to Jacob's having seen God face to face) and 1 Kings 19:11 (God's "passing by" Elijah). In Daniel 12:1 this term is used to describe the action of the angel Michael. The LXX rendering of each of these passages uses some form of *parerchomai*, the lexical form of the word *parelthein* used in Mark 6:48. Thus, Heil holds that, in many passages in the Old Testament, "to pass by" is "practically a 'technical term' for the appearance of a divine being, in the sense of his drawing near and showing himself before human eyes."[93] If these passages are in the background of Mark's story of Jesus' walking on the sea, his "passing by" the disciples connotes not concealment, but an epiphany, along the lines of the transfiguration episode (9:2-8). Yet, unlike the transfiguration episode, in this story Jesus issues no silence command after the epiphany.

However, in neither 4:35-41 nor 6:45-52 is a silence command necessary. Though Jesus extends his beneficence to those present and in so doing makes an honor-claim, their lack of understanding makes proclamation unlikely. They do recognize that Jesus is a person of great power and worthy of great honor, as is indicated by the references to their "awe" of him (*phobeō*) in 4:41 and their being "astounded" (*exhistēmi*) in 6:51. They do not, however, recognize Jesus as the beneficent broker of God's power, nor do they trust in Jesus' ability to provide for them in their times of need. Mark specifically notes in the first episode that the disciples lack trust (*pistis*) (4:40), and in the second that "their hearts were hardened" (6:52). Thus, the disciples will not engage in the practice of reciprocating Jesus' brokerage by enhancing his reputation, since they are without understanding with regard to the source of his power and what he is able to do for them. Rather than proclaiming what Jesus has done, the disciples cower in incomprehension. They cannot react to Jesus' brokerage with the exuberance of those who, despite his admonitions, spread word of his beneficence according to the conventions of faithful clients. A silence command in these episodes would be the equivalent of a refusal of thanks from someone who is not grateful.

CONCLUSION

In treating the story of the Gerasene demoniac, Donald Juel writes, "The secrecy theme, so common in Mark, is conspicuous here by its absence."[94] Likewise, Scott Gambrill Sinclair refers to "gaps" in the "messianic secret," anomalies that stand out against a standard practice of secrecy on Jesus' part.[95] Such interpretations are not uncommon, yet in light of the substantial number of passages surveyed above, it is difficult to sustain the position that the "messianic secret" is a rule to which there are occasional exceptions. Hooker notes this issue when she writes,

> In contrast to these commands for secrecy we have frequent references to the fact that men and women talked freely about what Jesus was doing (1.28, 45; 2.12), that Jesus made no secret of his healing (5.19, 30), and that crowds flocked to him as a result (3.10; 6.54ff.). The exorcisms themselves are common knowledge (3.20-30). The secret is thus only one side of the story; just as important is Mark's insistence that everyone in Palestine knew about Jesus' teaching and healing and was marvelling at it.[96]

Sometimes there is a clear narrative reason for the open nature of Jesus' healings and proclamations. Jesus' resisting and reshaping of conventional components of honor is indeed a Markan theme, and an important one. Yet it is not the only Markan theme, and quite often it gives way to other ideas that develop through the progression of the narrative.[97] At other times, however, no such reason is readily apparent. Yet, regardless of whether one can clearly identify elements of a particular episode that preclude Jesus' attempts to suppress information about himself, the fact remains that Mark's story simply does not present Jesus' concealing behavior as consistent or pervasive in the first ten chapters of the Gospel, after which it disappears entirely.

Simply put, there are many passages in which Mark's Jesus enjoins nothing like concealment or secrecy. He heals openly, performs mass exorcisms, shows his ability to control nature, feeds the thousands of people, and refers to himself as having authority to forgive sins and as

Lord of the Sabbath. Such passages have often been seen as exceptions to the general rule of secrecy in Mark's Gospel. Yet these passages are too numerous to be considered mere exceptions. They have their own purposes in the narrative, purposes that may be overlooked, or at least minimized in significance, if we consider them primarily as violations of a dominant theme of secrecy in the narrative.

In sum, it is important to realize that the passages which have been associated with the "publicity motif," which I refer to as "conventional episodes," do not all support the same theme in the narrative. Rather, they support a variety of themes that may be no less important than the theme of Jesus' resistance to honor demonstrated by the Markan concealment passages. Put differently, it is not the case that in Mark's Gospel there is a publicity theme that competes with a concealment theme. Rather, there is a theme of Jesus' revision of honor-shame conventions that interacts dynamically with a number of other themes in this Gospel. This interaction is the subject of the next chapter.

CHAPTER 5

MAKING THE PARTS INTO A WHOLE

How might Mark's audience have reacted to the very countercultural passages that we have reviewed thus far? Moreover, how might they have reconciled these with the conventional passages in which Jesus does not manifest the same type of countercultural behavior? To answer these questions, it will be necessary to take a different approach than in the last three chapters. Our concern will not be primarily with the ancient honor-shame value complex, but with the way in which people encounter narratives. The first part of this chapter will look at some of the elements of oral communication. I will also draw upon some common theories of "reader response," a field of inquiry that examines, among other topics, the ways in which people "make sense" out of stories in the process of reading them. By examining elements of oral communication and the reading process, I hope to demonstrate the ways in which the conventional episodes relate to the concealment episodes in Mark's narrative. In the third part of this chapter, I will offer a brief comparison of Mark's Gospel with the ancient novel *Life of Aesop*, pointing out similarities regarding the ways in which these two works are structured and the ways in which they communicate important ideas.

Mark's Gospel and Oral Communication

It is crucial to keep in mind that Mark's Gospel is a narrative written in a culture in which most people could not read, or at least not very well, and important ideas were communicated normally through oral, rather than written, expression. In antiquity, reading was generally a vocalized activity. As Rosiland Thomas puts it, "practically all ancient literature, however compressed in style (e.g. even Pindar or Thycydides), would have been heard and not read silently."[1] In general, written texts were used to facilitate oral communication, and they often bore certain characteristics of oral expression. Thus, they are called "oral-derived texts."[2] In other words, these written texts are structured as if they were composed to be spoken aloud and heard, rather than read silently. They are "stand-ins" for the spoken word.

Oral performances could take place in a variety of settings. Paul Achtemeier writes that "authors gave public performances of their works with some regularity, and one of the characteristics of public games was poets reading aloud from their writings. Such reading was also typical, it would seem, of early Christian gatherings."[3] In less public settings, a reader might read aloud privately or a person of means might have a slave read to him or her; the latter of these was the preferred method but was obviously limited to the wealthy.[4]

In part, the fact that reading was generally vocalized can be attributed to low literacy in the Greco-Roman world.[5] Although written texts were not rare in antiquity,[6] literacy was. In his landmark work on ancient literacy, William V. Harris discusses the extent of literacy in the Roman Empire. He argues that within this context, a few people used writing quite proficiently, but no more than 10 percent of the population of the Greco-Roman world was literate beyond the most basic of levels.[7] Harry Y. Gamble offers a comparable estimate, arguing that, at most, 10 to 15 percent of ancient Christians were literate, and that the percentage of literate people in the larger society was probably smaller.[8] Other scholars have estimated that the number would have been as low as 2 to 4 percent.[9]

Of course, there are various levels of literacy. Carolyn Osiek observes that the "ability to sign one's name to a legal document, to scribble a graffito on a wall, or to keep a list of business records is not the same as the ability to compose literary works or to think habitually in ways associated with literacy."[10] Our concern, however, is with the ability to read and comprehend sufficiently the Gospel of Mark, which would require a fairly high level of literacy. It is likely that most people among the Markan audience lacked the skill to read Mark's Gospel.[11]

Characteristics of Oral Expression

Given the context in which it was written, it stands to reason that Mark's story was meant to be heard, rather than read.[12] Mark's Gospel bears some of the distinctive marks of oral expression.[13] In other words, it is an oral-derived text. A sermon text that is meant to be preached on Sunday morning will likely differ in structure from a theological reflection written for a magazine. The preacher knows that because the congregation is going to hear the sermon rather than read it, he or she will need to repeat certain points, that too much detail will likely be forgotten, and that catchwords, rhymes, and other memorable phrasing will help the congregation members to retain what they have heard. Likewise, in cultures in which most communication is spoken aloud (oral), communication is structured differently than in high-literacy cultures. The work of Walter J. Ong has been central to the discussion of these differences.[14] Three of these characteristics are especially important for our discussion: oral expression is *additive*, *aggregative*, and *redundant* (copious).

Additive expression joins one sentence or clause to another by simple conjunctions or other connecting words. In Mark's Gospel, one episode does not always flow naturally into the next. In fact, the transitions between episodes can be quite abrupt. Mark often joins together episodes with the words, "and immediately..." Moreover, it is sometimes difficult for modern readers to see the importance of the sequence of the various episodes. From our perspective, one episode in the narrative does not always connect well to the preceding and following episodes. Joanna Dewey notes that Mark "consists of independent, often repetitive, episodes loosely connected without the linear climactic plot development we are accustomed to from modern novels and short stories."[15]

Oral expression is also *aggregative*, proceeding in a formulaic manner in which particular words or types of phrases are consistently found together. Ong offers several short, formulaic expressions as examples, such as "the brave soldier," "the beautiful princess," and "the glorious revolution."[16] A variant of this aggregate quality is seen in the formulaic structures of pericopes that have been brought to our attention by form critics. For example, Rudolf Bultmann's identification of "Miracles of Healing," "Nature Miracles," and "Exorcisms of Demons" is based largely on particular features that are consistently found together in passages of Scripture.[17] In other words, healing stories tend to follow a certain pattern, as do nature miracles and exorcism stories. Mark's use of common patterns, such as we see in the healing stories, exemplifies this aggregative quality.[18]

Redundancy is another characteristic feature of oral expression. In an oral performance a speaker may repeat the same idea or phrase again and again.[19] Though repetition can be burdensome in a written text, it is necessary in oral communication. Unlike readers, hearers of a story cannot review what has already been expressed except as they mentally retain various components of the story. Repetition facilitates this retention.[20] As Werner Kelber puts it, "repetition is the oral substitute for the eye's privilege to revisit words."[21] We see this in Mark's Gospel, for example, in Mark's treatment of the disciples. Mark does not simply tell us once, "The disciples did not comprehend Jesus' teaching," and let it go at that. Rather, Mark tells and shows us repetitively the disciples' failure to understand and abide by Jesus' teaching.

In sum, oral narratives simply have a different structure than narratives in high-literacy cultures. The additive, aggregative, and redundant style of oral and oral-derived narratives means that these types of

stories do not have the kind of climactic, linear storyline that generally characterizes narratives that derive from high-literacy cultures.
Frank Kermode speaks from the perspective of a literary critic when
he observes that Mark's narrative "moves erratically, and not always
forward; one thing follows another for no very evident reason."[22]
Indeed, there is no very evident reason for the structure of Mark's
narrative—from the perspective of modern print culture.[23] Yet Mark's
Gospel was written for the ear, rather than the eye. Dewey summarizes the implications of this fact when she writes,

> This additive, aggregative style creates its effect not through analytic
> or linear reasoning, but through repetition of similar, but not identical,
> episodes. The picture of Jesus as healer is created by telling one healing
> after another, but varying scenes showing the healing of a particular
> individual with scenes portraying crowds being healed. The emphasis
> on Jesus' coming death is created by the repetition of passion predic-
> tions. Furthermore, the logic of this additive style is an inclusive both/
> and logic: Jesus is both this *and* that rather than the more analytic print
> understanding of Jesus is this but *not* that.[24]

Fitting the Pieces of the Story Together

The evangelist has not explicitly stated the reason for Jesus' concealing behavior. Rather, the audience is left to supply this missing information. Moreover, Jesus is sometimes concealing in regard to who
he is or what he has done, but as we have seen he sometimes heals
and exorcizes openly, and he sometimes makes or allows open claims
regarding his great status and authority. Mark does not explain how
the "concealing" episodes relate to these "conventional" ones. Again,
it is the audience who must make sense of this seemingly inconsistent
behavior.

Wolfgang Iser, who has written extensively on the ways in which
readers engage texts, observes that "literary texts are full of unexpected twists and turns, and frustration of expectations. Even in the
simplest story there are bound to be some kind of blockages, if only
because no tale can ever be told in its entirety."[25] There are places in
every story in which certain information is left out, where we are

forced to make connections between one part of the text and another. Iser refers to these as "gaps" or "blanks."[26] Readers try, normally without even realizing it, to fit pieces of the narrative together, to make a story out of them. A story that tried to tell us everything, that tried to leave no gaps, would be exceedingly boring, not only because it would be cumbersome and unnecessarily long, but because there would be so much less for the reader to do as he or she progressed through the story. When we encounter gaps in a text, we undertake the set of mental operations necessary to create some type of consistency in the narrative. Put differently, readers fill in these gaps as they make their way through a story. Readers unconsciously build consistency—"make sense"—out of the various parts of the story. In this sense, hearing a story is no different than reading a story. We have to put the parts together, make sense out of, a story we hear, just as in the case of stories we read.

Iser's insights are applicable not just to the process of reading a story, but to hearing one as well. Whether we encounter a story by reading it or hearing it spoken aloud, we have to make sense out of the text. Because oral-derived texts tend to be less detail oriented than narratives in high literacy cultures, the reader of an oral-derived text must do even more work to put the pieces together and make sense out of the story. In Iser's terms, there are more gaps to fill in. The fewer the details, the more work the hearer or reader must do.

Since Mark does not provide much information regarding the purpose of Jesus' concealment, the concealment passages result in narrative gaps, especially when read or heard alongside passages in which Jesus is open about his deeds and/or identity. Scholarship on the "messianic secret" might be thought of as a series of attempts to fill these gaps, to provide the missing information that will make sense of the concealment passages. In discerning the ways in which Mark's audience would have filled in these gaps and built consistency within Mark's story, it is important to consider not only the ways in which information is conveyed in oral-derived texts, but the values that governed the types of behavior and interactions described in the relevant passages. When the ancients filled in gaps and built consistency, they would have done so by drawing upon their own values, assumptions, and experiences. As we have seen, honor and shame were central to their assumed value system.

One feature of oral expression is that it tends also to stay "close to the human lifeworld."[27] In other words, knowledge communicated in oral cultures is expressed with reference to the familiar, concrete life situation of human beings. Learning in oral cultures tends to take place in empathetic and participatory ways rather than through "objective" or detached contemplation as in high-literacy cultures. Think, for example, of cultures in which the history of a people is passed down in song and poetry, rather than in history books. As another example, think of a novice carpenter who learns the craft by working alongside a master, rather than from "how-to" manuals or attending classes. As an oral-derived text, Mark tells a story that is close to the everyday experiences of the Markan audience. In fact, this has been an implicit assumption of much redaction-critical work on the Gospels, as scholars have sought the circumstances of the various communities of the Gospels and the ways in which those circumstances might have influenced the writing of the Gospels.

Modern Western readers of Mark, who do not share the ancient Mediterranean value system centered on honor and shame, will find few clues regarding the reason for Jesus' silence commands and other examples of concealing behavior. Our values are in many ways different from those of ancient Mediterranean people. As we have seen, fame, reputation, special status, the giving and receiving of gifts, and related issues were governed by honor and shame, core values in the world of Mark's audience. The fact that the story does not specify that the Markan concealment passages relate to the values of honor and shame is entirely reasonable, since honor and shame would naturally have formed the backdrop against which ancient Mediterraneans would have interpreted these passages. One does not generally state what is blatantly obvious.[28] The *Rhetorica ad Herennium*, an ancient manual for the composition of public speeches, indicates that the ancients did recognize that hearers could fill in missing information. Its anonymous author writes that one may present the outcome of a particular account "in such a way that the facts that have preceded can also be known, although we have not spoken of them. For example, if I should say that I have returned from the province, it would also be understood that I had gone to the province."[29]

It is quite reasonable, then, that Mark would assume that the audience would know that honor and shame were involved in much of his depiction of Jesus, and that he would not need to spell this out in the text. Yet, despite the fact that within the ancient Mediterranean context these passages were clearly related to honor and shame, the particular ways in which these passages were related to such values are a bit more complex. Given ancient Mediterranean honor-related conventions, Jesus' behavior of resisting and reshaping the traditional components of honor would have been quite striking to Mark's audience. The passages that help to reshape the components of honor would have provided a number of unexpected twists and turns. This is especially true for the passages that come earlier in the Gospel, since, in the progression of the narrative, the hearer who has encountered some of these passages already will be less surprised when others arrive.[30] Yet, regardless of where one of these passages is found in the narrative, the behavior that Jesus exhibits in these passages does not match the common ancient Mediterranean cultural expectations for someone who had the status and authority consistent with his being the broker of God's power and wisdom.

In hearing these passages that frustrated certain widespread cultural expectations, the Markan audience would have been compelled to fill in missing information. In other words, the audience would have experienced narrative gaps.[31] "Why was Jesus behaving in this way?" they would ask. Honor and shame were givens, but what might Mark's audience have made of Jesus' behavior when it was inconsistent with the ways in which honor and shame were traditionally assigned? The audience members are presented with a set of paradoxes related to the head of their in-group and the ways in which they understand honor in their own lives. The one who was most deserving of widespread acquired honor resisted it. The one who could legitimately claim maximal ascribed honor did not do so. The one whom crowds proclaimed as a king embraced the cross and demanded that his followers do the same. Those who wish to follow Jesus, the one most worthy of honor, must give up striving for honor conventionally understood. Robert Tannehill comments helpfully, "Paradox, a conflict in language, reminds the reader that the positive alternative indicated by the author persistently conflicts with what people assume is right and reasonable. So the positive alternative remains a mystery and a challenge."[32] The positive alternative that Jesus displays in Mark's

Gospel did indeed conflict with common expectations of what was right and reasonable in the ancient Mediterranean context. The mystery and challenge for the audience would be to appropriate into its communal norms the ethos that Jesus demonstrates. By filling in the narrative gaps created by Jesus' countercultural behavior, the audience, in concert with the text, creates an exemplar of honor-related behavior, behavior that involves a set of standards much different from those that were widely held in the ancient Mediterranean world.

Frustrated Expectations (Again and Again)

As noted above, Mark's story does not have the type of linear plotline that typifies modern narratives. Mark's Gospel exhibits additive expression: it consists of episodes that are sometimes only very loosely connected to one another, and the transition between episodes can be quite abrupt. Mark's style is also aggregative, using formulaic structures for particular types of stories. Further, Mark's story is often redundant, communicating important ideas through repetition. For the purposes of the discussion in this chapter, the most significant of these characteristics of oral expression is redundancy.

One example of Mark's use of redundancy to convey a particular idea occurs in the way in which Mark communicates the idea of Jesus' authority. For instance, the idea of Jesus' authority develops progressively as one encounters his first exorcism at Capernaum (1:21-28), his healing of the paralytic (2:1-12), his controversy with the Pharisees regarding the Sabbath (2:23-28), and his sending of the twelve (6:7-13). Mark does not communicate Jesus' authority simply by telling the audience that Jesus is authoritative or by building up to a point at which Jesus' authority is revealed. Rather, the evangelist repetitively portrays Jesus as authoritative. Likewise, Mark demonstrates Jesus' great ability and willingness to provide large-scale works of beneficence by repetitively portraying him as a willing broker (see, for example, 1:21-28; 1:32-34; 3:7-12; 6:30-44; 8:1-9). The repetition of these passages has a cumulative effect in which each repeated episode contributes to some aspect of the picture of Jesus that develops over the course of the narrative.

A number of scholars have dealt with variation within the repetition of episodes that are formally similar to one another.[33] David
Rhoads describes this phenomenon as follows:

> In each familiar recurrence of the type-scene, the basic pattern remains
> the same but the details of the episode—time, place, characters, mal-
> ady, manner of healing, and so on—differ markedly. In addition to
> variations in the details, there are variations in the form and features
> of the type-scene: the emphasis falls on different features; the order of
> the features varies; some features do not appear; or the functions of the
> features differ.[34]

Clearly, we do see in Mark instances of concealment that represent
variations of particular "type-scenes." For example, in healing episodes that exhibit the typical "form" of such, sometimes Jesus attempts
to conceal his healings (see 5:21-24, 35-43; 7:31-37; 8:22-26) and at
other times he does not (see 2:1-12; 3:1-6; 5:24b-34; 10:46-52).

Regarding Mark's healing stories, Kelber comments, "Despite an
essential uniformity in composition, these stories display a remark-
able variability in the use of commonplaces. Compositional restraints
do not manifest themselves as iron grids upon the material. There is
ample room for narrative maneuvering, and no single story is quite
like any other."[35] Likewise, in the exorcism stories, he notes "defin-
ing and stabilizing constituents," although the "stable constructs offer
seemingly inexhaustible narrative license. What is essentially one and
the same story can be told in a multitude of different ways."[36] In a
number of instances, Mark brings Jesus' reshaping of honor to the
forefront of the audience's attention by telling stories that are structur-
ally similar to one another, but contain the important variant of an
attempt by Jesus to conceal his deeds or identity.

Tannehill has written on the "echo effect" in Acts 3–5, which in
many ways parallels the repetition of similar episodes in Mark's Gospel.
He states, "Characters and events in this section of Acts echo characters
and events already presented in the Gospel, and recall of these earlier
characters and events suggests a complex set of similarities, differences,
and fulfillments which contribute to the significance of the story.
Therefore, the text takes on resonance.... The echo adds emphasis,
helping to specify and ensure communication of central meanings."[37]

In this way, repetition has a persuasive effect.[38] It reinforces particular important ideas. However, Tannehill also notes that the similarity between particular stories may lie "less in the healing itself than in the function of these scenes in the larger narrative."[39] In other words, the narrative may advance a particular theme or idea through repetition, although not necessarily through *formal* repetition (their structure and wording). Rather, the repetition may inhere in the narrative *functions* of these episodes (their contributions to the overall story). This is what Ong would call "backlooping," the repetition of an idea that has been communicated earlier in the narrative.[40] Mark's various healing stories, exorcism stories, nature miracles, and authoritative pronouncements do share certain similarities of vocabulary and structure within the particular forms that they represent. Yet in the passages in which Mark reshapes traditional concepts of honor, repetition is also found in their narrative function, the ways in which these episodes frustrate expectations and convey ideas that run counter to particular ancient Mediterranean conventions related to honor and shame.

To be more specific, Mark repetitively portrays Jesus as either resisting or reshaping traditional ways in which honor was assigned and recognized. Examples of his doing so appear in several different types of episodes: healing stories after which Jesus issues a silence command (1:40-45; 5:21-24, 35-43; 7:31-37; 8:22-26); the story of Peter's identification of Jesus, after which Jesus issues a silence command (8:27-30); the transfiguration episode, after which Jesus issues a silence command (9:2-9); exorcism stories in which Jesus silences demons (1:23-28; 1:34; 3:12); and teaching episodes in which Jesus redefines the components of honor (8:27—9:1; 9:33-37; 10:35-45). The audience encounters these episodes, and in the progression of the narrative the hearer's expectations begin to change. Hearers remember what they have heard earlier in the narrative, and they are especially likely to remember an idea that has been communicated several times already. Thus, the set of expectations that the audience has for Jesus will change over the course of the story, particularly the way in which the audience expects Jesus to regard honor and shame.

By the time the audience reaches Jesus' teachings in 8:27ff. about a new basis for honor, it has already been prepared, at least to a certain extent, by what has come before: Jesus' repeated rejection of honor from his beneficence. The audience has been confronted again and again with Jesus' countercultural behavior. Naturally, the audience would question Jesus' repeated attempts to *refuse* honor that is rightly his. Beginning with Jesus' first passion prediction (8:31), however, Jesus begins to *reshape* the ways in which honor was normally reckoned (see, for example, 8:34—9:1; 9:30-31; 9:33-37; 10:13-16; 10:23-27; 10:32-34; 10:35-45).[41] For example, after Peter confesses him as the Messiah, Jesus teaches that the Son of Man must suffer shamefully and die before being vindicated by God (8:31), and he reiterates this point on two other occasions (9:31; 10:33-34). Moreover, Jesus teaches his disciples that those who will be his followers—those who wish to be a part of the in-group centered on God's own Son—must take up the cross (8:34) as well. Those who are shamed by their association with Jesus will be shamed by Jesus when "the Son of Man... comes in the glory of his Father with the holy angels" (8:38). Jesus teaches that the "first must be last of all and servant of all" (9:35), and later that the "first" must be "slave of all." Likewise, the "great" one must be a "servant" (10:43). Correlatively, the rich (who generally did not serve but were served) cannot enter the kingdom (10:25). Yet Jesus, to whom God has granted maximal ascribed honor, has come not to be served but to serve (10:45). Further, he likens himself to a child (9:37) and claims that it is to "such as these [children] that the kingdom of God belongs" (10:14), even though children were considered empty of honor. Further, those who wish to "receive the kingdom of God" must do so as a little child (10:15). Again and again, Jesus upends the conventional markers of honor. This reshaping of honor culminates in the crucifixion and resurrection, when the one who is maximally worthy of honor submits to what was widely considered a maximally shaming death, and then is vindicated by God, an act that gives new honor value to the crucifixion.

Inconsistency

Another set of narrative gaps emerges from the fact that Jesus is not consistent in his concealing behavior. As noted earlier in this chapter, while he sometimes attempts to conceal his deeds and status, at other times he seems not at all concerned to do so. Strangely enough, passages in which Jesus issues silence commands or otherwise attempts to conceal his status or deeds are often located in the text immediately adjacent to passages in which Jesus exhibits no such concern. Jesus' healing of the man with a withered hand, after which Jesus issues a silence command (1:40-45), immediately precedes his healing of the paralytic (2:1-12), which is performed in full public view. Jesus' healing of Jairus's daughter (5:21-24, 35-43), which he attempts to conceal, is intercalated with the story of the healing of the woman with a hemorrhage (5:25-34), which is performed in the midst of a large crowd. Jesus issues no silence command in the story of the healing of the Syrophoenician woman's daughter (7:24-30), and yet in the next episode, the healing of the deaf man (7:31-37), he takes the man to a more secluded location and does issue a silence command. Alternatively, the same episode may have elements of both concealing and conventional behavior: each time we are told that Jesus issues a silence command in the course of an exorcism, the exorcism itself is performed before onlookers (1:21-28; 1:32-34; 3:7-12).

Mark does not explain how the concealment passages relate to the conventional passages. The hearer or reader is left to make sense of the elements of the story. Iser notes that the meaning of the text begins to form only when the reader begins to connect its various, disparate parts. The process of filling in the narrative gaps—supplying the information that is not in the text—gets this operation underway.[42] Yet how can these Markan concealment passages relate to the conventional passages? Modern scholars have dealt with this issue in a variety of ways. William Wrede holds that Mark simply did not carry through this motif consistently, further evidence for him that the secret cannot be historical.[43] Jack Dean Kingsbury takes a more extreme approach, maintaining that Jesus does not actually violate the secret in Mark's Gospel, that Jesus obscures his identity by referring to himself as the Son of Man, and that the crowds are unable to perceive the truth about Jesus that is manifest in his great deeds and some of his sayings.[44] Heikki Räisänen takes still a different approach, stating that the "secrecy motif" is simply not very important for Mark, and therefore violations of the secret are to be expected: "Mark was not concerned to carry through consistently the idea that Jesus' identity was kept a close secret."[45]

Räisänen also points out that there are a number of other themes in Mark, and that sometimes these themes supersede the secrecy theme in importance. He writes, "It seems reasonable to conclude that, although the secrecy idea was clearly important for the evangelist, it was not *so* important for him that his work was determined by this motif through and through. The secrecy motif (or rather, the secrecy motifs) is only *one* motif in Mark's theology. It should not be made absolute."[46] If I have argued correctly in chapters 1, 2, and 3, from an ancient Mediterranean perspective secrecy is not the primary issue in the Markan concealment passages. Nevertheless, there is much to be said for Räisänen's claim that the theme developed by the concealment passages is at times overridden by other concerns. If we do not insist that a motif of secrecy or concealment must be an overriding, dominant motif in Mark's Gospel, it follows that, at times, Mark wishes to highlight other themes, even if it means abandoning the concealment motif temporarily. It is often the case that particular aspects of a given episode in Mark preclude Jesus' behaving in such a way as to conceal his deeds or identity.

Then there is the question of whether the hearers of Mark's Gospel would have even noted the inconsistency. Jack Goody, for example, argues that "[i]nconsistency, even contradiction, tends to get swallowed up in the flow of speech (*parole*), the spate of words, the flood of argument, from which it is virtually impossible for even the most acute mind to make his mental card-index of different usages and then compare them with one another."[47] This is a reasonable claim, but it does not mean that ancient hearers would be unaffected by formal and narrative variations that they encountered in a story. The ancients did understand contradictions and inconsistencies, although these were not always thought of in a negative light.[48] In fact, some Latin literature of the first centuries B.C.E. and C.E. makes use of the technique known as *ritratto paradossale*, a means of character portrayal in which the same character is portrayed as exhibiting apparently contradictory traits (usually particular virtues and particular vices). This model may in fact have already been in use in the Greek literature of earlier centuries.[49] According to the *Rhetorica ad Herennium*, inconsistency was an expected and favorable trait in a narrative that was about a person. Such a narrative "should present a lively style and diverse traits of character, such as austerity and gentleness, hope and fear, distrust and desire, hypocrisy and compassion, and the vicissitudes of life, such as reversal of fortune, unexpected disaster, sudden joy, and a happy outcome."[50] Mark, then, follows an approved convention when he portrays Jesus as acting in different ways at different times.

It is important to distinguish between (1) noticing and focusing on contradictions as such and (2) being moved by variation in the encounter with a story. While the former of these expresses the experience of many modern scholars who have carefully scrutinized Mark's Gospel, it is reasonable to suggest that the latter much more accurately expresses the experience of the Markan audience. I maintain that the concealment and conventional episodes work *together* in the narrative in important ways. Robert Fowler has written on what he calls Mark's "rhetoric of indirection." Those places in the text that are relatively clear, in which we feel as if we are on stable footing, are examples of "direction." Conversely, indirection, as Fowler states, "beckons the reader to step off of the clear pathway, to ponder puzzles. Direction, although sometimes subtle or implicit, is largely determinate. Indirection is more indeterminate and open-ended; some indirection can be puzzled over and resolved, but much remains permanently obscure or uncertain."[51] Fowler identifies the messianic secret as an example of Markan indirection, arguing that, in talking about a "messianic secret," scholars are responding to Mark's "narrative rhetoric, which they encountered in the act of reading."[52] The general consensus has been that the solution to the problem of the messianic secret is to be found in careful scrutiny of the text. However, as Fowler points out, "The harder we look, the more elusive the solution, because the Messianic Secret is not in the text itself but in the experience of reading the text."[53]

Fowler's comments are directed toward modern scholars of Mark's Gospel, but ancient hearers, like modern scholars, would also have been puzzled by Jesus' behavior. A major difference, however, is that while scholars of the post-Wrede era have tried to explain why Jesus would have cast a veil of secrecy over his messiahship, ancient hearers would have puzzled over Jesus' reasons for acting so strangely with regard to the honor code of their culture. Nevertheless, ancient people, like modern ones, would have encountered both direction and indirection in the progression of Mark's narrative. Put differently, they would have encountered places in the text where they felt they knew what was going on, where they felt they were on stable footing. At other times, however, they might feel puzzled and unsure of what was going on in the narrative. Jesus does not always act so strangely; as we have seen, he often heals, performs exorcisms, performs other types of wonders, or speaks without the kind of countercultural behavior that he exhibits in those passages examined in chapter 3. These passages provide direction, the "stable footing" that helps to contextualize Jesus within the conventions of honor and shame, and especially the patron-broker-client relationship. Ironically, these "conventional" passages contribute to the undermining of standard honor-related conventions.

Meir Sternberg writes that within narratives, "the making of sense hinges on the postulation of constancies—laws, rules, regularities, continuities, or, in short, norms—if for no other purpose than to make divergence perceptible and meaningful."[54] The parts of the narrative that easily make sense to us help us to interpret the parts that do not. In the cultural world of Mark's audience, the conventions of honor and shame provided one such set of "constancies." Instances in which these constancies are manifest in the actions of Jesus provide a familiar backdrop (direction) against which Jesus' countercultural behavior stands out (indirection). It is left to the audience to construct a workable relationship between the passages that provide direction and those that provide indirection. Or, to put the matter differently, the audience must fill in the narrative gaps that are created when Jesus deviates from widespread cultural conventions regarding honor and shame. Though the Markan concealment passages and the conventional passages may appear to be incompatible when taken out of their narrative contexts, in fact they function in tandem with one another within their narrative context. In so doing, they produce a picture of Jesus as authoritative and deserving of honor (conventionally understood) even as he reshapes the way that honor was conventionally assigned.

By Comparison: The *Life of Aesop*

A brief comparison with another ancient work, the *Life of Aesop*, will help to illuminate some of the important points in this chapter.

Though there are abundant differences between the *Life of Aesop* and the Gospel of Mark, the two works are similar to one another in important ways. These texts date from roughly the same historical period: most scholars date Mark's Gospel around 70 C.E., and while it is more difficult to date the written text of the *Life of Aesop*, it probably comes from the first or second century C.E.[55] Both are anonymous narratives, probably composed from oral and written traditions, and both narratives are made up of a series of relatively short episodes. Both may be considered aretalogical, novelistic biographies.[56] There are also several thematic similarities between the two narratives, such as the death of the protagonist through the connivance of his foes.[57] For some time neither work was thought to contain any purposeful arrangement of its episodes, though this is no longer the case with regard to either.[58] Neither text represents the literature of the educated elite; in all likelihood these stories would appeal to audiences made up of people from the lower strata of society.[59]

Upending Expectations

In the *Life of Aesop*, the slave Aesop subverts one set of values (those of the educated upper classes and slave owners) in favor of the values of a less privileged group (the lower classes, and particularly those who lack formal education but find wisdom in sources other than those of the school philosophers). One encounters in this narrative a more or less stable set of "constancies" of the ancient Mediterranean world. Among these are slave ownership and the cruelty that it entailed; an educated and wealthy elite; the supposed superiority of the wealthy and educated over the poor, slaves, and the uneducated; and the conventions of honor and shame.[60]

Aesop is the very opposite of the ideal Greek male. He is, first of all, physically unattractive by Greek ideals. In the Hellenistic world, physiognomics—the idea that one could discern the character of an individual by his or her physical appearance—was a part of the cultural milieux. In the *Physiognomics*, Pseudo-Aristotle writes that a single physiognomic sign is not a good indicator of the character of an individual, but a number of signs together make a much stronger case.[61] Aesop has quite a few negative physiognomic signs: he is described as "loathsome of aspect...potbellied, misshapen of head, snub-nosed, swarthy, dwarfish, bandy-legged, short-armed, squint-eyed," and "liver-lipped" (1). He is also compared to a turnip (14), a goose egg (14), "a frog, a hedgehog, or a potbellied jar, or a captain of monkeys," and "a dog in a basket" (87).[62] According to the *Physiognomics*, the "little-minded" (*mikropsychos*) person is "small-limbed, small and round, dry, with small eyes and a small face."[63] A "snub-nosed" (*simēn*) person, moreover, is thought to be salacious;[64] a person who is too swarthy (*agan melanes*) is likely to be cowardly;[65] the "ill-proportioned" (*asymmetroi*) are thought to be scoundrels.[66] These characteristics correspond to Aesop's short arms, small stature, large belly, squinty eyes, "snub nose" (*simos*), and swarthy (*melas*) complexion. The Hellenistic audience of the *Life of Aesop* should therefore expect him to be untrustworthy and of base character.

Additionally, Aesop is a slave. As noted in chapter 3, the most common terms for slaves were *sōma* and *pais*—"body" and "child"—indicating that slaves were powerless and were expected to be passive toward their masters.[67] The function of the slave, it was thought, was to carry out the master's will as a "living tool."[68] Yet even among slaves Aesop's status is very low. He is not a household slave, a role that would have accorded him a bit more standing, but a field slave. On top of all this, he is a Phrygian, a designation of provenance that was also often used as a synonym for "slave" in the Roman era.[69]

Perhaps worst of all, Aesop cannot speak. The possession of language was seen in the Hellenistic world as a trait, like upright posture, reason, and morality, that separated human beings from animals.[70] It was also a key component in the acquisition of honor among males. Among the educated elite, who routinely engaged in rhetorical contests, such verbal agonistic interaction reached perhaps its most developed form. Yet less formalized agonistic interaction inhered in relationships between males across the social strata.[71] *Philotimia*—love of honor, or ambition—inhered not only among the upper classes, but among males of all social groups, including slaves. Because Aesop lacks the power of speech, he lacks the critical means to achieve the small amount of honor potentially available to him among social equals.

Yet this inversion of the ideal Greek male is granted wit, wisdom, and verbal skill by Isis and the Muses. By virtue of these gifts, he is able repeatedly to outwit people of higher social strata, most often his master, the philosopher Xanthus. Not only does he consistently show himself to be Xanthus's intellectual superior, but he repeatedly dishonors his master. Richard Pervo comments that "Aesop is, when all is said and done, a *loyal* slave who repeatedly helps his master when he appears, in the eyes of modern readers, to have no moral obligation to do so."[72] Yet this assessment of Aesop does not account adequately for the deep dishonor that Xanthus endures from Aesop. He scoffs at this master and embarrasses him (35-37). More than once he humiliates Xanthus before dinner guests (39-43, 51-55), and he also embarrasses Xanthus's friends (77b). He has intercourse with his master's wife ten times (75). He disgraces both Xanthus and his wife by exposing her rear end to Xanthus's students while she is sleeping. Afterwards Xanthus scolds Aesop, saying, "You runaway, you've embarrassed me many a time, but you've never done a more embarrassing thing than this, disgracing me and your mistress" (77a). In a context in which slave owners (who had some degree of wealth) and philosophers were thought to occupy higher stations of honor than uneducated slaves, the *Life of Aesop* shows the slave as his master's superior. Aesop is wittier and wiser than Xanthus. He cuckolds Xanthus and manipulates him into giving him his freedom (89-90). He can interpret portents that Xanthus cannot, and it is he, rather than the philosopher, who is honored as a true prophet (91-93).

Thus, like the Jesus of Mark's Gospel, Aesop undermines traditional notions of those who are, and are not, honorable. Aesop resists the confinement of his station as a slave, whereas Jesus resists the honor that he is rightly due. While Aesop the slave shows himself to be the superior of his master, Jesus holds up slaves and servants, children, "the last," and other unlikely candidates (from an ancient Mediterranean perspective) as deserving of honor. In both stories, the stable backdrop of common cultural expectations and conventions allows the behavior that defies those expectations and conventions to stand out. Aesop's behavior is irreverent and frequently comical precisely because he defies conventions: the uneducated slave bests his master, the philosopher. Jesus' behavior is countercultural because he is worthy of honor yet often attempts to avoid it and regularly assigns honor to those who are least likely to receive it in the wider culture.

Inconsistency

Unquestionably, an ancient audience (especially one made up of lower-class individuals) would take away from the *Life of Aesop* a sense of Aesop's superiority to his master and to other members of the upper class and intellectual elite. Yet Aesop does not outwit his master in every instance. Xanthus commonly exerts his authority over Aesop, sometimes violently so. At one point Aesop loses a contest with his master and is beaten as a result (56-58). Only on his second try is Aesop able to defeat his master in this contest and avoid the consequences that Xanthus threatens: "I'll put you on the rack and break you" (58). In another episode, Xanthus sends Aesop to look for a specific good omen: a pair of crows in front of the door. Aesop sees just such a pair of crows at the door and reports this to Xanthus. By the time Xanthus goes to the door to see for himself, one of the crows has flown away, and Aesop is beaten for reporting incorrectly to his master. Aesop is able to convince his master that he is unjustly punishing him, but not before receiving a thorough beating (77). Such episodes keep the story rooted in the stable backdrop of conventions of slavery in the ancient Mediterranean world.

There are other apparent inconsistencies in the story, as well: at one point, Aesop appears intentionally to cause strife between Xanthus and his wife; he then takes action to reconcile the two of them (44-50); and later he ends up in bed with her (75). At another point Aesop pledges faithfulness to his master (64), claiming that Xanthus will find no reason for complaint (64). Immediately thereafter, however, Aesop deliberately tricks his master, who does in fact complain (65-66). Aesop then insults his master, essentially calling him witless (67). In another episode, Aesop convinces Xanthus that the interpretation of omens is an idle business (77), but he later gains fame by interpreting an omen (91-93). At the end of the story, Aesop, who has shown such resourcefulness since his blessing by Isis and the Muses, dies because his resourcefulness fails him.[73] In fact, he makes the simplest of mistakes: he insults the people of Delphi, seemingly unaware that they will wish to gain satisfaction (124-126). In turn, they trick him by placing a golden cup from the temple in his bag and then accusing him of thievery. When accused of having stolen the golden cup, Aesop steps into their trap utterly unawares, saying, "I am ready to die if I am found guilty of such a thing" (128). They do find him guilty, and he does die.

One can find many other examples of such inconsistency in Greco-Roman literature. For example, in Suetonius's description of Vergil, we read that in oration Vergil spoke very slowly, "almost like an uneducated man." Yet Suetonius says of the poet shortly thereafter that Vergil's delivery in reading was "sweet and wonderfully effective. In fact, Seneca says that the poet Julius Montanus used to declare that he would have purloined some of Vergil's work, if he could also have stolen his voice, expression, and dramatic power; for the same verses sounded well when Vergil read them, which on another's lips were flat and toneless."[74]

Similarly, in Lucian's *Demonax* we see tension between the claim on the one hand that the philosopher Demonax was loved by all, and on the other that he made enemies because of supposed religious crimes. Lucian writes that because Demonax conducted himself in such a virtuous way, "all Athens, high and low, admired him enormously and always viewed him as a superior being." Shortly thereafter, however, he writes that the philosopher made enemies because of his "freedom of speech and action" and was charged with religious crimes: "he had never been known to sacrifice and was the only man in the community uninitiated in the Eleusinian mysteries."[75] Later we read, "He lived for almost a hundred years, without illness or pain, bothering nobody and asking nothing of anyone, helping his friends and never making an enemy."[76] This remark, however, comes after pages of episodes recounting the philosopher's insults toward other people.

What is one to make of these apparent inconsistencies? Not much. Ancients, who were hearing rather than reading these accounts, would not engage in this kind of careful analysis. Like audiences today watching action movies, apparent inconsistencies and breakdowns in the plot might be noticed but would be quickly subsumed within the larger story. Aesop's concern for his master's marriage at one moment and disregard for it at another do not demonstrate entirely consistent behavior, but they do demonstrate his cleverness. Likewise, the failure of Aesop's resourcefulness at the end of the story may seem inconsistent with earlier demonstrations of his abilities, but his death at Delphi may represent a different theme: the consequence of offending the gods.[77] The point is not to create an entirely coherent narrative, but to tell a story with which the audience can resonate. One could imagine slaves and other members of the lower strata of society hearing the stories of Aesop, laughing and cheering Aesop's triumphs over Xanthus, and jeering the hostile crowd at Delphi. Like Mark's Gospel, the *Life of Aesop* appears to combine traditions, "not all of which are in concord,"[78] but all of which do contribute to some overarching ideas in the story, ideas that interact to challenge particular well-established values.

CONCLUSION

Mark does not offer a specific reason for Jesus' attempts to conceal who he is or what he has done. To complicate things further, Jesus does not consistently attempt to do so. It is left to the audience to put together the pieces of the narrative, to fill in the gaps and make sense of this inconsistent concealing behavior. Because ancient Mediterraneans understood such issues as fame, reputation, beneficence, and name in terms of the values of honor and shame, these values would naturally have formed the backdrop against which the audience would understand the passages in which Jesus attempts to conceal who he is or what he has done. Through repetition, but not consistency, Mark develops a picture of Jesus as one who rejects and reshapes traditional concepts of the ways in which honor was assigned.

A number of scholars have struggled with the issue of the inconsistency with which Jesus conceals his deeds and identity. Yet the concern with consistency, while not unknown among the ancients, is much more of a modern preoccupation. Those who encountered Mark's story aurally rather than visually would simply not have the opportunity to analyze Mark's text, to check for inconsistencies and coherence. Rather, they would "make sense" of the story, just as readers do, but with a lesser degree of scrutiny of the text. Those passages in which Jesus is open about who he is or what he has done help to provide a stable backdrop of "direction" against which the counter-cultural passages act as "indirection." We see a similar scenario in the *Life of Aesop*. Indirection beckons the audience to ponder puzzles, to think through the ways in which the text frustrates conventional expectations. Both the concealment passages and the conventional passages are important, then. Both are essential for Mark's Jesus to act in a way that overturns the ways in which honor and shame were commonly assigned. Over the course of the narrative, the audience comes to see Jesus as having honor, claiming honor, and gaining honor, yet exhibiting a way of assigning honor that undermines conventional norms.

CONCLUSION

Why This *Story, Told in* This *Way?*

In previous chapters I have argued that particular passages that have long been associated with the messianic secret are best understood in terms of ancient Mediterranean conventions related to the values of honor and shame. Mark portrays Jesus first as periodically resisting honor that he is rightly due, and then as offering a new understanding of the ways in which honor and shame should be assigned. Yet Mark's Jesus does not always forgo the honor that he is due. At times he is quite open about who he is or about great deeds that he has performed. At times he actively acquires honor at the expense of his opponents. Regarding this issue, I have argued that in oral-derived texts one would expect important ideas to be conveyed repetitively, but not necessarily consistently. Additionally, instances in which Jesus acts according to common conventions provide a stable backdrop against which instances in which he defies these conventions stand out. By the end of the story, an ancient audience would perceive Jesus as one who is worthy to receive maximal ascribed and acquired honor, but who demonstrates a way of thinking about honor and shame that differs greatly from the ways in which many ancient Mediterraneans thought about these values. Servants, children, and the last are exalted, rather than the rich and powerful and those with great authority. Indeed, the one with authority on a par with God's chose not to lord it over others, not to be served, but to serve and to go willingly to the cross, a symbol of shame in the ancient Mediterranean world. Mark's Jesus does not dispense with honor; rather, he turns it on its head.

CHRISTIANS AGAINST CULTURE

A question that scholars have often asked, however, is, "For whom would such a story be written?" We can make assertions about the Markan audience with varying degrees of specificity. A guiding assumption of this book (and a very safe one) is that the members of the Markan audience were ancient Mediterranean people, and as such they would interpret Mark's story in light of ancient Mediterranean values, especially those of honor and shame. Using ancient sources and modern resources of cultural anthropology, we can identify the contours of the honor-shame value complex. We can therefore make informed judgments about the ways in which ancient people would have understood passages in Mark's story that relate directly to the conventions of honor and shame.

Particular assertions about the Markan audience—its identity as a community, the characteristics that bound it together as a community as such, characteristics that distinguished it from the broader culture in which it was embedded—are a different story. What we have in Mark is a narrative, a story about Jesus' ministry and death, followed by a brief account of the empty tomb. Since the story tells us nothing about its intended audience and because we lack any outside sources that reveal to us information about the audience, our only option is to extract the characteristics of the Markan audience from the story. To extract from a story a particular audience, such as a "Markan community," is necessarily a speculative undertaking.[1]

The idea, however, that the Markan audience in some way lived out the modified honor-shame values conveyed in Mark's story is an intriguing one. Was there a "Markan community" that in some way embodied these values? Were there churches in which the distinctions of status and honor were inverted, so that serving, rather than ruling, was most honored? Oral expression tends to stay close to the human life-world. Werner Kelber's "law of social identification," according to which traditions that survive are those that have concrete relevance for the group that maintains them, indicates that Mark's Gospel probably reflects many of the concerns of the audience for which it was written.[2] One way, albeit speculative, to approach this issue is by positing that Mark's audience constituted a subculture within the larger honor-oriented culture of the ancient Mediterranean world. Anthropologist Kirk Dombrowski describes subcultures as

> those groups that have found the culture they live within—the ways, that is, in which meanings are created and meaningful lives lived—to be unsatisfying, unfair, or most often, unattainable. Their response, however, has not been to overturn the culture entirely, but rather to co-opt and redefine elements of the dominant culture and to make these elements into alternative systems of meaning, or alternative ways of living meaningful lives. The notion of subculture captures the fact that most people find ways to live differently within, and even against, a set of meanings and institutions they find impossible to live with—and that they do so without actually leaving entirely (or even mostly) those same meanings and institutions.[3]

This sounds like a reasonable assessment of what a community of Christians who internalized the values of Mark's story might look like. There is no reason to postulate that Mark's audience was a sectarian community. Were they truly sectarians like the Qumran community, the esteem of the wider world vis-à-vis specifically Christian understandings of honor and shame probably would not have been such a considerable issue in Mark's story. If these Markan Christians continued to live in the midst of a culture in which they were a very small minority, however, the Markan emphasis on these teachings is understandable. In this scenario, Mark's story spends so much time undermining conventional understandings of honor and shame because honor-related pressures are bearing down upon the people for whom this Gospel was written.

Whatever reasons the philosophers may have had for denouncing popular opinion, it is not difficult to imagine why early Christians might do so. It is quite likely that one of the major concerns of this audience was a sense of social dislocation. At the time of the writing of Mark's Gospel, Christians were not held in high regard. Abraham Malherbe writes, "It is well known that Christianity was regarded as a lower class movement and that Christians were viewed as uneducated and socially insignificant, if not downright irresponsible or dangerous."[4] He notes that the actual social situation of early Christians was more complex than this and that a description such as this one was often used as a "standard polemic."[5] Nevertheless, it seems reasonably clear that early Christianity was, for the most part, a movement that drew from the lower classes of society. Paul writes to the Corinthian congregation that "not many of you were wise by human standards, not many were powerful, not many were of noble birth" (1 Cor 1:26). Richard Rohrbaugh has argued forcefully that the Markan Christians came from the lower social strata.[6] While it seems clear that there were also early Christians who did come from the higher social strata, one should also keep in mind that one's in-group was largely determinate of one's honor rating. If Christians as a group were perceived as a lower-class movement, the low-honor rating that would accompany such a perception would reflect on the individual members of this group as well.

Further, Christians were seen to be socially disruptive. They did not worship the pantheon of gods who were thought to support the empire, nor did they participate in the emperor cult. These refusals were taken as a sign of disloyalty, and the fact that Christians proclaimed a crucified savior contributed to the suspicion that was directed toward Christians. Paul admits that the cross is "a stumbling block to Jews and foolishness to Gentiles" (1 Cor 1:23). Moreover, the Greco-Roman disdain for innovation and "newness" in religion did not help Christians. Roman upper classes tended to direct scorn toward foreign religious groups, and groups whose members were thought to be doing something new, something that upset the established social order, were seen as dishonorable.[7] Yet Christians were seen as doing exactly this; hence the claim in Acts that Christians were "turning the world upside down" (17:6).

In a well-known passage, Tacitus writes that a high level of public suspicion arose that Nero was responsible for the fire that ravaged much of Rome in 64 C.E.

> Therefore, to scotch the rumor, Nero substituted as culprits, and punished with the utmost refinements of cruelty, a class of men loathed for their vices, whom the crowd styled Christians. Christus, the founder of the name, had undergone the death penalty in the reign of Tiberius, by sentence of the procurator Pontius Pilatus, and the pernicious superstition was checked for a moment, only to break out once more, not merely in Judaea, the home of the disease, but in the capital itself, where all things horrible or shameful in the world collect and find a vogue. First, then, the confessed members of the sect were arrested; next, on their disclosures, vast numbers were convicted, not so much on the count of arson as for hatred of the human race. And derision accompanied their end: they were covered with wild beasts' skins and torn to death by dogs; or they were fastened on crosses, and, when daylight failed were burned to serve as lamps by night....Hence, in spite of a guilt which had earned the most exemplary punishment, there arose a sentiment of pity, due to the impression that they were being sacrificed not for the welfare of the state but to the ferocity of a single man.[8]

It appears that Nero chose Christians because they were already despised. Blame could be diverted to them because they were mistrusted by much of the populace. Moreover, the types of executions that Tacitus describes for Christians (being killed by dogs, crucified, or burned to death) were those reserved for the lower-classes of society. As Clifton Black notes, "Roman law forbade such means of executions for citizens of the state."[9] It is no wonder that the author of 1 Peter refers to Christians as "aliens and exiles" (2:11) and acknowledges that they will be maligned as evildoers (2:12). He exhorts them, saying, "In this you rejoice, even if now for a little while you have

had to suffer various trials, so that the genuineness of your faith—
being more precious than gold that, though perishable, is tested by
fire—may be found to result in praise and glory and honor when Jesus
Christ is revealed" (1:6-7).

In fact, Mark's Gospel may address the very Christians who were
threatened by Nero's persecution. Many writers have understood
Mark's Gospel to have a Roman origin,[10] and this is certainly the
tradition expressed in patristic references to Mark's provenance.[11] In
modern scholarship, Roman provenance was more prominently represented prior to the publication of Willi Marxsen's *Der Evangelist Marcus*
in 1956.[12] Since Marxsen's book, a Roman location for the writing
of Mark has largely (though not completely) fallen out of favor, and
a number of scholars have located Mark in Galilee or in the adjacent
Roman province of Syria, usually around the time of the destruction
of the temple in 70 C.E.[13] For example, Marcus argues that the conflict
to which Mark's Gospel gives expression is not between Christians and
Rome, but between Christians who lived in Gentile regions near Galilee and Jews involved in the revolt of 66–74 C.E.: "Mark may thus be
situated along a time line of developing opposition between Christian
communities and the Jewish world from which they sprang."[14] Theories abound with regard to the specific circumstances that account for
the language in Mark's Gospel that suggests persecution. As Robert
Guelich notes, determining the provenance with any certainty is very
difficult: "The evidence permits one to place the audience in various
time periods and locales."[15]

Yet, regardless of disagreements with regard to Mark's provenance and the specific circumstances in which it was written, there
is a widespread scholarly consensus that Mark's audience was under-
going some type of persecution.[16] More detailed discussions of the
possibility that Mark was written for a group of persecuted Christians
are available elsewhere, but it will be helpful at this point to recount
some of the more important passages that appear to confirm this position.[17] First of all, Mark 4:16-17, part of the explanation of the Parable of the Sower, relates that the seed that is sown on the rocky
ground (*petrōdēs*) represents people who hear the word and "immediately receive it with joy." These people, however, "have no root and
are short-lived, and when trouble or persecution comes on account

of the word, immediately they are scandalized [*skandalizontai*]" (my translation). The NRSV translates *skandalizō* as "fall away" and offers an alternate translation of "stumble" in a footnote. Such a translation, however, does not capture the social significance of this term, the sense of offense and scandal—and thus dishonor—that it connotes. As Morna Hooker points out, *to skandalon* "is used frequently in the New Testament, especially by Paul, of the offence of the Cross."[18] Mark's use of *skandalizō*, then, connotes not simply apostasy, but a sense of social scandal and dishonor that is caused by the persecution of followers of Jesus.

It is very likely that an ancient audience would hear the resonance between the word *petrōdēs* (4:5, 16), "rocky ground," and the name *Petros*. Peter's threefold denial of Jesus in 14:66-72 shows exactly the kind of pattern represented in the parable and its explanation: Peter shows great promise initially, only to wither away when being a follower of Jesus becomes too perilous. Yet Peter is no different than the other disciples: by the time Jesus stands before the council (14:53ff.), all of his followers have abandoned him. Apostasy seems to have been a significant problem in the early church, and it is very reasonable to see the pattern described in the parable and borne out in the actions of Peter and the other disciples as representative of temptations facing the Markan audience.[19]

Mark 10:30, with its strange reference to "fields with persecutions," is another key passage. In this pericope, Jesus refers to the hundredfold reward that those who have sacrificed for him are to receive in "this age": "houses and brothers, and sisters and mothers and children and fields with persecutions." The reference to persecutions simply does not fit the context of Jesus' saying, and both Matthew and Luke omit this reference (see Matt 19:29//Luke 18:29-30). It is reasonable to postulate that Mark's abrupt and seemingly misplaced reference to persecutions in this passage reflects the experience of the Christians for whom Mark was writing. In other words, because the reference to persecutions does not fit the narrative context, one might account for it by claiming that it fits the historical context that the narrative addresses.

Shortly thereafter, Mark alludes to the martyrdom of the sons of Zebedee (10:38-39), which closely follows the third of Jesus' three predictions of his own suffering and death (8:31; 9:31; 10:33-34). Each of these passages is part of a general emphasis on suffering that is represented more strongly after 8:31, as the Gospel moves toward the passion narrative. Joel Marcus holds that Jesus "is presented as a paradigm of the way in which his disciples, including the Markan audience, should endure suffering."[20] Although the sons of Zebedee do not seem to realize that to drink from the cup from which Jesus will drink and to be baptized with his baptism will lead them on the way of the cross, to those hearing this story the reference was likely very clear. In the Old Testament the image of the cup can be used to convey what will befall an individual for good or ill (see, for example, Pss 16:5; 23:5; 75:8; 116:13; Jer 25:15-29; 49:12) and Mark's Jesus uses this very image with reference to his own suffering (14:36; cf. John 18:11).[21] Likewise, the language of baptism is used in contemporary Greek to convey the idea of being overwhelmed or "flooded" with calamity (see also Luke 12:50).[22] It may be that the misunderstanding to which James and John give voice—that glory should be the result of following Jesus (10:37)—and Jesus' claim that James and John will share in his "cup" and "baptism" reflect the situation of the Markan audience. Those who follow Jesus must be prepared to endure the suffering that will accompany their doing so.

Chapter 13 offers perhaps the strongest internal textual evidence for persecution, especially in verses 1-13. In verse 9, Jesus references the disciples' being handed over to councils, beaten in synagogues, and being made to stand before governors and kings "because of me, as a witness to them." Mark 13:10 speaks of the necessity of proclaiming the good news to all the nations, and then with verse 11 Mark turns again to warnings about particular trials: the disciples are not to worry about what to say when they are brought to trial and handed over. The Holy Spirit will give them the appropriate words at that time. In verse 12, Jesus speaks of divisions that will occur among family members, and in verse 13 he states that they "will be hated by all because of my name; but the one who endures to the end will be saved." Referring to Mark 13, Marcus states that "it seems likely that the prophecies of false messiahs, war, persecution, and betrayal in vv. 6-13 (cf. vv. 21-22) are part of the present experience of Mark's community."[23] Such circumstances may also account for the reference to "suffering" (*thlipsis*) in 13:19 and 24.

THE FICTIVE FAMILY

First-century Christians constituted a small minority group that faced a deep and serious social dislocation from the non-Christian culture. The ancient Mediterranean context was one in which those outside of one's group were distrusted, considered rivals, and even scorned. In times of persecution, the social dislocation experienced by Christians would become even more immediate and acute. To be dragged into court, publicly beaten, betrayed by one's own family members, and "hated by all" (all described in Mark 13:9-13) would be shaming in the extreme, as would being publicly executed by such means as Tacitus describes. The hardships and social disdain that early Christians had to endure frequently resulted in the rupturing of kinship bonds (cf. Mark 3:31-35) and a disconnection from commonly held social values. Ascribed honor (obtained through one's family) and the possibility of acquiring honor as social eminence were thus no longer live options. These early Christians had broken with traditional symbols of authority and respect, and they would not have received acceptance within their former social groups, including that most basic of social groups, the family.

The third chapter of Mark's Gospel may provide a window into the kinds of conflicts that followers of Jesus experienced with their own family members.[24] Mark 3:21 and 3:31-35 form a frame around an episode in which Jesus enters into debate with the scribes. This framing material offers a reinterpretation of the family. In 3:21, Jesus' family comes out to restrain him because, as the NRSV puts it, "people were saying 'He has gone out of his mind.'"[25] It appears that Jesus' family saw him as bringing dishonor on the family and intended to stop him from doing further harm.[26] Jesus, however, is undaunted by the fact that the members of his family—on whom he should himself depend for honor—do not approve of his conduct. In 3:32-35, when the members of the crowd around Jesus tell him that his mother and brothers and sisters are outside asking for him, Jesus replies, "'Who are my mother and my brothers?' And looking around at those sitting around him in a circle, he said, 'Look! [These are] my mother and my brothers. For whoever does the will of God, this one is my brother and sister and mother.'" The main criterion for kinship with Jesus is no longer a blood relationship, but doing the will of God. In other words, in Mark's story fictive kinship based on doing God's will supplants natural kinship. Mark 10:29-30 (and possibly 1:20) indicates that leaving one's natural family was a common part of following Jesus.[27] Halvor Moxnes argues that, while "[c]onflicts with [the] family were common among the first followers of Jesus, . . . the Christian communities became 'surrogate families' or 'fictive kinship' [groups] (Mark 3:31-35)."[28] Mark 3:21 and 3:31-35, then, may address a very acute need among the members of Mark's audience. The family was the most basic unit in the honor-and-shame culture of the ancient Mediterranean basin. Without a family, one lacked those closest associates through whom honor was assigned. Christians, however, were often cut off from their natural family members, and so they formed a new family, a family based on doing the will of God. Such a fictive family would serve as a new court of public opinion, displacing the natural family in importance. This new court of public opinion would function as the primary context in which Christians secured honor.

The new Christian family was not, for the most part, made up of the rich and powerful individuals who could claim high honor ratings according to conventional standards. Rather, the Christian family was made up largely of lower-strata individuals who worshiped a crucified criminal and regarded him a savior, rejected the gods of the pantheon, and would not pay divine honors to the emperor. They drew the suspicion of their non-Christian neighbors, and at times were publicly humiliated through torture and execution. Being a Christian was not the way to a high-honor rating within the wider culture. David deSilva holds that, because Christians proclaimed a message that contradicted some of the core values within the contexts in which they lived, they were often subject to censure. Non-Christians

> subjected the early Christians to censure and other shaming techniques, designed to bring these deviant people back in line with the values and behaviors held dear by the surrounding culture (whether Jewish or Greco-Roman). The authors of the New Testament devote much of their attention, therefore, to insulating their congregations from the effects of these shaming techniques, calling the hearers to pursue lasting honor before that court of God whose verdict is eternal.[29]

The social significance of the Markan concealment passages, then, may have emerged from the social dislocation that Christians felt. The Christians of Mark's audience were cut off from honor in the wider culture, but Mark's Jesus demonstrates that such honor is insignificant. Jesus is depicted repetitively as attempting to avoid the honor that he is due, and then he offers new criteria for honorable behavior within his in-group: doing the will of God, becoming a servant, becoming "last," becoming like a child, taking up the cross—in other words, acting in ways entirely opposed to the reckoning of honor in the wider culture. The kinds of actions and attitudes that most people perceive to be honorable are in fact not so; God's own Son has shown this. What matters is honor within the new family, *honor among other Christians*, who have the proper criteria for the kinds of actions and attitudes of which God approves. Because God's understanding of honorable actions and attitudes differs significantly from those in the wider culture, the rejection of the non-Christian world becomes a mark of honor among Christians.[30] Within this group, the crucifixion of Jesus is no longer a symbol of shame, but of honor, since God has given the crucifixion new honor value and vindicated Jesus by raising him from the dead.[31]

LATER CHRISTIAN REJECTION OF COMMON UNDERSTANDINGS OF HONOR

J. E. Lendon notes that, along with the unconventional understandings of honor in the Greek philosophical literature, there was a similar reinterpretation of honor among the Christian fathers. On the one hand, there was honor that was conferred by God, and which would be enjoyed in heaven after death. He holds that "Christian views of honour offered the starkest possible challenge to aristocratic pagan attitudes. Activities prompted by the lust for honour in this life were ruled out; ideally the whole proud, competitive, jostling ethos of the ancient city was abandoned."[32] On the other hand, however, "Christian glory could also be enjoyed before death in the community of believers."[33]

The Christian martyrs were widely venerated among Christians (for example, Stephen, Ignatius, Polycarp, Perpetua). In the description of Polycarp's execution, we read that "he put his hands behind him and was bound, as a noble ram out of a great flock, for an oblation, a whole burnt offering made ready and acceptable to God."[34] His non-Christian executioners, however, do not see Polycarp in this light, and they go about their tasks with great zeal. Similarly, a Christian who was condemned to die, and who was later released (though not because of apostasy) and temporarily denied the glory and praise of God could in the meantime enjoy the praise of other Christians.[35] No doubt, most people from the pagan world would not consider the person who was condemned as a Christian to be honorable, but as we have seen, even rejection by the wider culture could itself be considered honorable. According to the *Epistle to Diognetus*, Christians "are dishonoured, and are glorified in their dishonour, they are spoken evil of and are justified."[36] Two centuries later, John Chrysostom wrote, "To us gentleness, scorn for wealth, scorn for reputation, mockery of honour from the many... this is respectability, this reputation, this honour."[37]

Christianity, then, continued as a countercultural force for some time, perhaps until the empire became thoroughly Christianized through the gradual process that began politically with the Edict of Milan in 313. After all, the attempt to eradicate Christianity from the empire under Diocletian and Galerius (303), perhaps the bloodiest of all of the persecutions, took place within a decade of the beginning of Constantine's reign (312). Yet the Christian counterculture—which judged honor and shame in ways that were markedly different from those employed in the wider culture—was already in place among the audience of our earliest extant Gospel.

CONCLUDING REMARKS

For over a century, scholars have puzzled over the group of passages to which William Wrede called attention, and yet no scholarly consensus has emerged regarding the significance or function of the passages with which his work dealt. Why, then, should anyone take seriously yet another account of these passages? Although social-scientific study of the New Testament has been around for some time, serious scholarly engagement with the cultural values of honor and shame is relatively new in the field of biblical studies. Consider, for example, that the first edition of Bruce Malina's *New Testament World*, one of the earliest works in this area, was published in 1981. *The Social World of Luke-Acts*, a programmatic work edited by Jerome Neyrey, was published in 1991. Other major works dealing with the honor-and-shame culture of the ancient Mediterranean basin were published even more recently. Yet the vast majority of work on the messianic secret was published prior to 1990. Vital data for understanding the concealing behavior of Mark's Jesus was simply not available to the scholarly community when most of the work on the messianic secret was being written.

"Perhaps secrecy is nothing more than our own bewilderment projected into the text," writes Frank Kermode.[38] I think there is some validity to this speculative comment. If the arguments that I have advanced in this book are valid on the whole, Mark's audience would not have heard most of the concealment passages as having to do primarily with secrecy, but with honor and shame. They are not, moreover, a theme unto themselves, but components of a larger theme in which Jesus reshapes common standards for deciding who is honorable and who is shameful. The notion of a "messianic secret" is a product of modern scholarly reflection, one that has become a part of the fabric of critical scholarship on Mark's Gospel. I fully expect that we will continue to use the language of the "messianic secret." Yet perhaps a contribution of this book may be a heightened awareness that the "messianic secret" is a technical term and scholarly construct. It is a placeholder that we use to create space for a puzzling set of passages. And puzzling they are; for like Wrede, who wrote about this Gospel centuries after it was first composed, Mark leaves us with more questions than answers.

APPENDIX

Some Structural Features of Mark's First Ten Chapters

As an oral-derived text, Mark often exhibits concentric and repetitive structures. Elements in one episode sometimes echo those in a previous one. Parallel episodes often form "frames" around other material, sometimes in the form of a chiasm. Further, concentric structures sometimes overlap one another. This analysis of Mark's structure is not intended to be exhaustive, but to point out some structural features of the narrative that are relevant to the arguments of this book. For a fuller account of the structure of Mark, see "Appendix A: Rhetorical Structure of Mark," in Mary Ann Tolbert, *Sowing the Gospel: Mark's World in Literary-Historical Perspective* (Minneapolis: Fortress Press, 1989).

1:1-15—Prologue

1:16—2:14

A. Call story demonstrating Jesus' authority (1:16-20)

- Jesus is beside the sea (1:16)
- "Follow me" (1:17)
- "Immediately they left their nets and followed him" (1:18)

B. Jesus casts out an unclean spirit (1:21-28)

- Performed before onlookers
- "He taught them as one having authority" (1:22; see also 27)
- "They were all amazed" (1:27)

C. Jesus heals Peter's mother-in-law, his fame spreads, and he silences demons (1:29-34)

- "[H]e would not permit the demons to speak, because they knew him" (1:34)

D. Jesus preaches throughout Galilee (1:35-39)

C'. Jesus heals a leper, commands silence, and his fame spreads (1:40-45)

- "See that you say nothing to anyone" (1:44)

B'. Jesus heals a paralytic (2:1-12)

- Performed before onlookers
- "So that you may know that the Son of Man has authority..." (2:10)
- "They were all amazed" (2:12)

A´. Call story demonstrating Jesus' authority (2:13-14)

- "Jesus went out again beside the sea" (2:13)
- "Follow me" (2:14)
- "And he got up and followed him" (2:14)

2:1—3:6[1]

A. Healing of the Paralytic (responsive *chreia* in the form of a miracle story) (2:1-12)

- "He said to the paralytic ..." (2:5, 10)
- Opponents' objection unspoken (2:6-7)
- Jesus' riposte: "the Son of Man has authority on earth to forgive sins"; he heals the paralytic
- Audience reaction: "they were all amazed and glorified God" (2:12)

B. Call of Levi and eating with sinners (responsive *chreia*, no miracle) (2:13-17)

- Call of Levi (2:13-14)
- Meal with tax collectors and sinners (2:15)
- Opponents' objection vocalized (2:16)
- Jesus' riposte: proverb and a saying of Jesus about himself (2:17)

C. Question about fasting (responsive *chreia*, no miracle) (2:18-22)
- Fasting question (2:18)

B´. Plucking grain on the Sabbath (responsive *chreia*, no miracle) (2:23-28)

- Plucking grain incident (2:23)
- Opponents' objection vocalized (2:24)
- Jesus' riposte: example of David eating, proverb, saying of Jesus about himself (2:25-28)

A'. Healing of the man with a withered hand (responsive *chreia* in the form of a miracle story) (3:1-6)

- "He said to the man . . ." (3:3)
- Opponents' objection unspoken (3:2, 4)
- Jesus' riposte: questions about the Sabbath; healing of the man (3:4-5)
- Audience reaction: Pharisees conspire with Herodians to destroy Jesus (3:6)

3:7-12—Jesus heals multitudes, but he will not allow the unclean spirits to speak because they know him

3:13—6:13

A. Jesus appoints the twelve (3:13-19a)

- The twelve are to be sent out to proclaim the message and to have authority to cast out demons (3:14-15)

B. Responsive *chreia* in which Jesus is challenged by his family (3:19b-35)

- Statement regarding kinship: "Whoever does the will of God is my brother and sister and mother" (3:35)

C. Teaching section (4:1-34)

D. Miracles section (4:35—5:43)

- Jesus stills a storm (4:35-41)
- Jesus exorcises the Gerasene demoniac and instructs the former demoniac to proclaim God's beneficence (5:1-20)
- Intercalated healing episodes, one with silence command, one without and in public (5:21-43)

B′. Responsive *chreia* in which Jesus is rejected by people in his hometown (6:1-6a)

- Statement regarding kinship: "Prophets are not without honor, except in their hometown, and among their own kin, and in their own house" (6:4)

A′. Jesus sends the twelve (6:6b-13)

- The twelve are given authority over unclean spirits; they exorcise and proclaim that all should repent (6:7, 13)

6:14—8:31

A. Speculation regarding Jesus' identity; John the Baptist killed shamefully (6:14-29)

- People say Jesus is John the Baptist, Elijah, or one of the prophets (6:14-16)
- John is killed in a shaming manner by the ruling authorities (6:27)

B. Jesus' brokerage followed by misunderstanding (6:30-52)

- Jesus feeds five thousand (6:30-42)
- Sea journey (6:45)
- Jesus' status revealed (6:48)
- The disciples lack comprehension, reference to bread; "their hearts were hardened" (6:52)

C. Jesus performs a mass healing (6:53-56)

- His fame has already spread: "People at once recognized him" (6:54)
- No silence command

D. Teaching about properly honoring God and parents; teaching about defilement (=dishonor) from within (7:1-23)

C´. Jesus casts out a demon from the Syrophoenician woman's daughter (7:24-30)

- His fame has already spread: "He could not escape notice" (7:24)
- No silence command

    E. Jesus cures a deaf man (7:31-37)

- Jesus takes the man aside (7:33)
- Use of saliva and touching in healing (7:33)
- Silence command (7:36)

B´. Jesus' brokerage followed by misunderstanding (8:1-21)

- Jesus feeds four thousand (8:1-10)
- Sea journey (8:10, 13)
- The disciples lack comprehension; reference to bread; "Are your hearts hardened?" (8:16-17)

    E´. Jesus cures a blind man (8:22-26)

- Jesus takes the man outside of the village (8:23)
- Use of saliva and touching in healing (8:23)
- Command not to go back into the village (8:26)

A´. Question regarding Jesus' identity. Jesus foretells his shameful death and vindication in the resurrection (8:27-31)

- People say Jesus is John the Baptist, Elijah, or one of the prophets (8:28)
- Identification of Jesus as the Messiah (8:29)
- Jesus will be shamed and killed by the religious authorities (8:31)

8:22—10:52

A. Healing of the blind man (8:22-26)

B. Jesus' status revealed (8:27-30)
- Peter identifies him as the Messiah, silence command (8:29-30)

C. Teaching section (8:31—9:1)
- First prediction of Jesus' shameful death and his vindication in the resurrection (8:31)
- Teaching about honor (8:34, 9:1)

B′. Jesus' status revealed (9:2-29)
- Transfiguration, silence command (9:2-13)
- Jesus casts a spirit out of a boy (9:14-29), no attempt at concealment, elicits a statement of trust from the father (9:24)

C′. Teaching section (9:30-37)
- Second prediction of Jesus' shameful death and his vindication in the resurrection (9:30-31)
- Teaching about honor (9:33-35)
- Jesus assigns honor to a child (9:36-37)

B″. Jesus' status revealed (9:38-41)
- An exorcist is casting out demons in his name; no attempt to stop this from occurring (9:38-41)

C″. Teaching section (9:42—10:45)
- Jesus assigns honor to a child (10:13-16)
- Third prediction of Jesus' shameful death and his vindication in the resurrection (10:32-34)
- Teaching about honor (10:35-45)

A′. Healing of blind Bartimaeus (10:46-52)
- Bartimaeus follows Jesus "on the way," illustrating the proper understanding of honor (10:52)

NOTES

Introduction

1. William Wrede, *Das Messiasgeheimnis in den Evangelien: zugleich ein Beitrag zum Verständnis des Markusevangeliums* (Göttingen: Vandenhoeck & Ruprecht, 1901); the English translation used in this book is *The Messianic Secret*, trans. J. C. G. Greig (Cambridge: James Clarke, 1971).

2. Cf. M. Eugene Boring, *Mark: A Commentary,* New Testament Library (Louisville: Westminster John Knox, 2006), 264–65.

3. Although he offers category headings somewhat different from those offered here, Wrede treats basically the same set of passages as those I have listed; see *Messianic Secret*, 24–66, 231–36.

4. Christopher Tuckett writes, "The earlier studies of Holtzmann and others had convinced the majority of scholars of the literary priority of Mark's Gospel. However, this was then often taken as an indication of Mark's historical reliability. In particular, discussion of the secrecy texts in Mark was assumed to concern only the historical question of why Jesus might have enjoined secrecy

on others. A number of 'lives of Jesus' were written, all based for their chro-
nology on the Marcan outline, and many of these centred on the idea of Jesus'
gradual revelation to others of his own basic conviction that he was the Messiah" ("Introduction: The Problem of the Messianic Secret," in *The Messianic
Secret*, ed. Christopher Tuckett [Philadelphia: Fortress Press, 1983], 1).

5. Wrede, *Messianic Secret*, 131.

6. Wrede dealt with the other canonical Gospels as well, though the bulk of
his work and of subsequent scholarship on the messianic secret related primarily
to Mark; for a discussion of the messianic secret in Matthew and Luke, see Neil
Elliott, "The Silence of the Messiah: The Function of 'Messianic Secret' Motifs
across the Synoptics," in *Society of Biblical Literature Seminar Papers, 1993*, ed.
Eugene H. Lovering Jr. (Atlanta: Society of Biblical Literature, 1993), 604–22.

7. Wrede holds that Jesus' wonder-working would disclose his messiahship,
and that the content of Jesus' teaching is that he is the Son of God; see *Messianic
Secret*, 80.

8. See ibid., 34–53; see also 80.

9. See ibid., 53–79.

10. See ibid., 231–36.

11. Ibid., 33; see also 50.

12. See ibid., 50–51.

13. Ibid., 17.

14. See ibid., 218.

15. William Sanday, *The Life of Christ in Recent Research* (New York: Oxford
University Press, 1907), 70.

16. For a fuller treatment up through the mid-1970s, see James L. Blevins,
The Messianic Secret in Markan Research, 1901–1976 (Washington, D.C.: University Press of America, 1981).

17. See, for example, Julius Schniewind, *Das Evangelium nach Markus* (Göttingen: Vandenhoeck & Ruprecht, 1933); idem, *Das Selbstzeugnis Jesu nach den
ersten drei Evangelien* (Berlin: A. Deichert, 1922); Erik Sjöberg, *Der verborgene
Menschensohn in den* Evangelien (Lund: C. W. K. Gleerup, 1955); Martin Hengel, *Studies in the Gospel of Mark* (Philadelphia: Fortress Press, 1985), 41–45.

18. See Oskar Holtzmann, *The Life of Jesus*, trans. J. T. Bealby and Maurice
A. Canney (London: Adam and Charles Black, 1904), 30, 32, 70–71.

19. Ibid., 70.

20. Ibid.

21. Albert Schweitzer, *The Quest of the Historical Jesus: A Critical Study of
Its Progress from Reimarus to Wrede*, trans. W. Montgomery (New York: Collier,
1969); James D. G. Dunn, "The Messianic Secret in Mark," in Tuckett, ed.,
Messianic Secret, 116–31.

22. Ulrich Luz, "The Secrecy Motif and the Marcan Christology," in
Tuckett, ed., *Messianic Secret*, 75–96; see also Francis J. Moloney, *The Gospel of
Mark: A Commentary* (Peabody, Mass.: Hendrickson, 2002), 58 n.55; 111; H.
N. Roskam, *The Purpose of the Gospel of Mark in Its Historical and Social Context*
(Leiden: Brill, 2004), 170–81.

23. Boring, *Mark*, 270–71.

24. See Martin Dibelius, *From Tradition to Gospel*, trans. Bertram Lee Woolf (New York: Charles Scribner's Sons, n.d.); Rudolf Bultmann, *The History of the Synoptic Tradition*, trans. John Marsh (New York: Harper & Row, 1963), especially 346–48.

25. Adela Yarbro Collins, *Mark: A Commentary*, Hermeneia (Minneapolis: Fortress Press, 2007), 172; see also ibid., "Messianic Secret and the Gospel of Mark: Secrecy in Jewish Apocalypticism, the Hellenistic Mystery Religions, and Magic," in *Rending the Veil: Concealment and Secrecy in the History of Religions*, ed. Elliot R. Wolfson (New York: Seven Bridges, 1999), 11–30.

26. See Joel Marcus, *Mark 1–8: A New Translation with Introduction and Commentary*, The Anchor Bible Commentary (New York: Doubleday, 2000), 525–27; see also Nils Alstrup Dahl, "The Purpose of Mark's Gospel," in Tuckett, ed., *Messianic Secret*, 30–31.

27. Marcus, *Mark 1–8*, 527.

28. For a redaction-critical reworking of Wrede's position, see Günther Bornkamm, *Jesus of Nazareth*, trans. Irene and Fraser McLuskey with James M. Robinson (New York: Harper & Row, 1960), especially 171–78; for a summary of Bornkamm's position, see Blevins, *Messianic Secret in Markan Research*, 172–74.

29. T. A. Burkill, "Mysterious Revelation," in Tuckett, ed., *Messianic Secret*, 44–48; see also Morna D. Hooker, *The Gospel according to Saint Mark*, Black's New Testament Commentaries (Peabody, Mass.: Hendrickson, 1991), 66–69.

30. Burkhill, "Mysterious," 44.

31. Ibid.

32. Joseph B. Tyson, "The Blindness of the Disciples in Mark," in Tuckett, ed., *Messianic Secret*, 35–43; see also Theodore J. Weeden, "The Heresy That Necessitated Mark's Gospel," in *The Interpretation of Mark*, ed. William Telford (Philadelphia: Fortress Press, 1985), 64–77; idem, *Mark: Traditions in Conflict* (Philadelphia: Fortress Press, 1971); Heikki Räisänen, "The 'Messianic Secret' in Mark's Gospel," in Tuckett, ed., *Messianic Secret*, 132–40.

33. See Heikki Räisänen, *The 'Messianic Secret' in Mark*, trans. Christopher Tuckett (Edinburgh: T. & T. Clark, 1990), 254; for an assessment of and dialogue with some of Räisänen's arguments, see Christopher Tuckett, "The Disciples and the Messianic Secret in Mark," in *Fair Play: Diversity and Conflicts in Early Christianity: Essays in Honor of Heikki Räisänen*, ed. Ismo Dunderberg, Christopher Tuckett, and Kari Syreeni (Leiden: Brill, 2002), 131–49.

34. See Blevins, *Messianic Secret in Markan Research*, 48–52.

35. Robert H. Stein, *Mark* (Grand Rapids: Baker Academic, 2008), 25–26; for an older representation of this position, see Johannes Weiss, *Das älteste Evangelium: Ein Beitrag zum Verständnis des Markus-Evangeliums und der ältesten evangelischen Überlieferung* (Göttingen: Vandenhoeck & Ruprect, 1903); idem, *Jesus von Nazareth, Mythus oder Geschichte? eine Auseinandersetzung mit Kalthoff, Drews, Jensen* (Tübingen: J. C. B. Mohr [Paul Siebeck], 1910); see also Blevins, *Messianic Secret in Markan Research*, 48–52.

36. Frank Kermode, *The Genesis of Secrecy: On the Interpretation of Narrative* (Cambridge: Harvard University Press, 1979).

37. Mary Ann Tolbert, *Sowing the Gospel: Mark's World in Literary-Historical Perspective* (Minneapolis: Fortress Press, 1989), 229, emphasis hers.

38. Dennis R. MacDonald, "Secrecy and Recognitions in the *Odyssey* and Mark: Where Wrede Went Wrong," in *Ancient Fiction and Early Christian Narrative*, ed. Ronald F. Hock, J. Bradley Chance, and Judith Perkins (Atlanta: Scholars, 1998), 153; see also idem, "Recognitions," chap. 6 in *The Homeric Epics and the Gospel of Mark* (New Haven: Yale University Press, 2000).

39. See Gerd Theissen, "Die pragmatische Bedeutung der Geheimnis-motive im Markusevangelium," in *Secrecy and Concealment: Studies in the History of Mediterranean and Near East Religions,* ed. Hans G. Kippenberg and Guy G. Stroumsa (Leiden: Brill, 1995), 225–45.

40. See Bruce J. Malina, *The New Testament World: Insights from Cultural Anthropology*, 3d ed. (Louisville: Westminster John Knox, 2001), 125; John J. Pilch, "Secrecy in the Gospel of Mark," *PACE* 21 (1992): 150–53; idem, "Lying and Deceit in the Letters to the Seven Churches," *BTB* 22 (1992): 126–35; idem, "Secrecy in the Mediterranean World: An Anthropological Perspective," *BTB* 24 (1994): 151–57.

41. See also Tolbert, *Sowing*, 229; David A. deSilva, *Honor, Patronage, Kinship & Purity: Unlocking New Testament Culture* (Downers Grove, Ill.: Intervarsity, 2000), 106–7.

42. Thomas Barfield, ed., *The Dictionary of Anthropology* (Malden, Mass.: Blackwell, 1997), s.v. "anthropology, cultural and social."

43. Ibid.

44. For additional NT scholarship that utilizes insights from cultural anthropology, see, e.g., Jerome H. Neyrey, ed., *The Social World of Luke-Acts: Models for Interpretation* (Peabody, Mass.: Hendrickson, 1991); idem, "Despising the Shame of the Cross: Honor and Shame in the Johannine Passion Narrative," *Semeia* 69 (1996): 113–37; idem, *Honor and Shame in the Gospel of Matthew* (Louisville: Westminster John Knox, 1998); idem, "Questions, Chreiai, and Challenges to Honor: The Interface of Rhetoric and Culture in Mark's Gospel," *CBQ* 60 (1998): 657–81; idem, "The Sociology of Secrecy and the Fourth Gospel," in *What Is John?* vol. 2, *Literary and Social Readings of the Fourth Gospel*, ed. Fernando Segovia (Atlanta: Scholars, 1998), 79–109; Anselm C. Hagedorn and Jerome H. Neyrey, "'It Was Out of Envy that They Handed Jesus Over' (Mark 15:10): The Anatomy of Envy and the Gospel of Mark," *JSNT* 96 (1998): 15–56; Richard L. Rohrbaugh, ed., *The Social Sciences and New Testament Interpretation* (Peabody, Mass.: Hendrickson, 1996); deSilva, *Honor, Patronage*; Louise J. Lawrence, *Reading With Anthropology: Exhibiting Aspects of New Testament Religion* (Waynesboro, Ga.: Paternoster, 2005); Louise J. Lawrence and Mario I. Aguilar, eds., *Anthropology & Biblical Studies: Avenues of Approach* (Leiden: Deo, 2004).

45. For a seminal essay in this area, see Julian Pitt-Rivers, "Honor and Social Status," in *Honour and Shame: The Values of Mediterranean Society*, ed. J. G. Peristiany (Chicago: University of Chicago Press, 1966), 21–77; see also David D. Gilmore, ed., *Honor and Shame and the Unity of the Mediterranean* (Washington, D.C.: American Anthropological Association, 1987). For reasons to presume certain constant cultural values across the centuries in the circum-Mediterranean area, see Bruce J. Malina and Jerome H. Neyrey, "First-Century Personality: Dyadic, Not Individual," in *The Social World*, ed. Jerome H. Neyrey, 67–96, especially 69–72.

46. Malina, *New Testament World*, 30.

47. See, e.g., Robert Fowler, *Let the Reader Understand: Reader-Response Criticism and the Gospel of Mark* (Harrisburg, Pa.: Trinity Press International, 1996); Richard Horsley, *Hearing the Whole Story: The Politics of Plot in Mark's Gospel* (Louisville: Westminster John Knox, 2001), especially chap. 1, "Taking the Gospel as a Whole"; Donald H. Juel, *The Gospel of Mark*, Interpreting Biblical Texts (Nashville: Abingdon, 1999); idem, *A Master of Surprise: Mark Interpreted* (Minneapolis: Fortress Press, 1994); Kermode, *Genesis*; Mitzi L. Minor, *The Power of Mark's Story* (St. Louis: Chalice, 2001); David Rhoads, Joanna Dewey, and Donald Michie, *Mark as Story*, 2d ed. (Minneapolis: Fortress Press, 1999); Vernon K. Robbins, *Jesus the Teacher: A Socio-Rhetorical Interpretation of Mark* (Minneapolis: Fortress Press, 1992); Stephen H. Smith, *A Lion with Wings: A Narrative-Critical Approach to Mark's Gospel* (Sheffield: Sheffield Academic, 1996); Tolbert, *Sowing*; Joel F. Williams, *Other Followers of Jesus: Minor Characters as Major Figures in Mark's Gospel* (Sheffield: JSOT, 1994); Jack Dean Kingsbury, *The Christology of Mark's Gospel* (Philadelphia: Fortress Press, 1983).

48. See, for example, Paul J. Achtemeier, "*Omne verbum sonat:* The New Testament and the Oral Environment of Late Western Antiquity," *JBL* 109, no. 3 (1990): 3–27; Joanna Dewey, "The Gospel of Mark as an Oral-Aural Event: Implications for Interpretation," in *The New Literary Criticism and The New Testament*, ed. Elizabeth Struthers Malbon and Edgar V. McKnight (Sheffield: Sheffield Academic, 1994), 145–63; idem, "Mark as Aural Narrative: Structures as Clues to Understanding," *STRev* 36 (1992): 45–56; idem, "Oral Methods of Structuring Narrative in Mark," *Interpretation* 43 (1989): 32–44; idem, "Orality and Textuality in Early Christian Literature," *Semeia* 65 (1994): 1–216; Harry Y. Gamble, *Books and Readers in the Early Church: A History of Early Christian Texts* (New Haven: Yale University Press, 1995); Horsley, *Hearing*, especially chap. 3, "Mark as Oral"; Werner H. Kelber, *The Oral and the Written Gospel: The Hermeneutics of Speaking and Writing in the Synoptic Tradition, Mark, Paul, and Q* (Bloomington: Indiana University Press, 1997); Walter J. Ong, *Orality and Literacy: The Technologizing of the Word* (London: Routledge, 1982); Carolyn Osiek, "The Oral World of Early Christianity in Rome," in *Judaism and Christianity in First Century Rome*, ed. Karl P. Donfried and Peter Richardson (Grand Rapids: Eerdmans, 1998), 151–72; Lucretia B. Yaghjian, "Ancient Reading," in Rohrbaugh, *Social Sciences*, 206–30.

Chapter 1: Secrecy

1. The term "intentional concealment" is taken from Sissela Bok, *Secrets: On the Ethics of Concealment and Revelation* (New York: Pantheon, 1982), 5.

2. Ibid., 6.

3. Guy G. Stroumsa, "From Esotericism to Mysticism in Early Christianity," in *Secrecy and Concealment: Studies in the History of Mediterranean and Near Eastern Religions*, ed. Hans G. Kippenberg and Guy G. Stroumsa (Leiden: Brill, 1995), 291.

4. See LSJ, 9th ed., s.v. *pareiserpō, parekdidōmi.*

5. "*Kruphios* and its cognate *kruptos*, however, were notions that played little role in Greek religion for which the typical term was *mystērion.*" Luther H. Martin, "Secrecy in Hellenistic Religious Communities," in Kippenberg and Stroumsa, eds., *Secrecy*, 108.

6. Philo, *Sacr.* 62.

7. *1 Clem.* 18:6 (LCL); a similar usage of *apokruptō* occurs in LXX 4 Kgds 4:27.

8. Josephus, *Vita* 388.

9. *Aristeas to Philocrates*, trans. Moses Hadas (New York: Ktav, 1973), 132; see also Josephus, *A.J.* 17.38; Josephus, *Vita* 83; Ign. *Eph.* 15; *1 Clem.* 21:3; 27:6.

10. See LSJ, 9th ed., s.v. *arrētos.*

11. Plutarch, *Is.Os.* 360.

12. Philostratus, *V.A.* 3.15 (LCL); see also Euripides, *Bacch.* 472

13. Josephus, *B.J.* 1.470 (LCL).

14. Ign. *Eph.* 19 (LCL).

15. *Diog.* 11.2 (LCL).

16. In some Christian Era texts (Symmachus, Theodotion, and Origen's fifth column in Psalms [Quinta]), we find this term used in Job, Proverbs, Isaiah, and Psalms.

17. There are still a number of other terms that express secrecy. For example, various forms of the following words also express secrecy: *adēlos, aphanizō, apothetos, endomuchi, kleptō, orgia, phōlētērion, hēsuchasteon*; see the LSJ (9th ed.) definition for each of these terms.

18. I include in this group forms of the words *kruptō, apokruptō, kruptos, kruphaios, kruphē, kruptē,* and *apokruphos.*

19. Georg Simmel, *The Sociology of Georg Simmel*, trans. and ed. Kurt H. Wolff (Glencoe, Ill.: Free, 1950), 345, italics his.

20. Juvenal, *Sat.* 9.102-23.

21. Seneca, *Ira* 1.1.5 (LCL).

22. See the discussion of Roman law and magic in Hans G. Kippenberg, "Magic in Roman Civil Discourse: Why Rituals Could Be Illegal," in *Envisioning Magic: A Princeton Seminar and Symposium*, ed. Peter Schäfer and Hans G. Kippenberg (Leiden: Brill, 1997), 137–63.

23. See Hans Dieter Betz, "Introduction to the Greek Magical Papyri," in *The Greek Magical Papyri in Translation*, ed. Hans Dieter Betz (Chicago: University of Chicago Press, 1986), xli.

24. On high and low contexts, see Edward T. Hall, *Beyond Culture* (Garden City, N.Y.: Anchor, 1976), 34–35, and chap. 7, "Contexts, High and Low"; cf. Bruce J. Malina, *The New Testament World: Insights from Cultural Anthropology*, 3d ed. (Louisville: Westminster John Knox, 2001), 91.

25. See Plutarch, *Inim. Util.* 87C-D.

26. Achilles Tatius, *Leucippe and Clitophon*, trans. Tim Whitmarsh (Oxford: Oxford University Press, 2002), 6.10.

27. See Martin, "Secrecy."

28. Martin states that it is a mistake to assume that "such a reality as 'religion' existed in antiquity as a discrete cultural or institutional reality that may be measured over against the non-religious" (ibid., 104); on the religious nature of these associations, see the *Oxford Classical Dictionary*, 3d ed., s.v. "clubs, Roman."

29. See Martin, "Secrecy," 105–6.

30. See the discussion in ibid., 106.

31. See ibid, 108; Simmel, *Sociology*, 330.

32. Martin, "Secrecy," 109.

33. Ibid., 110.

34. Simmel, *Sociology*, 352.

35. Ibid., 359.

36. See Matthias Klinghardt, "Prayer Formularies for Public Recitation. Their Use and Function in Ancient Religion," *Numen* 46 (1999): 41–42.

37. Philostratus, *V.A.* 1.11 (LCL).

38. *Gos. Thos.* 1; this translation is from *The Gospel of Thomas*, trans. Thomas O. Lambdin, in *The Nag Hammadi Library*, ed. James M. Robinson (San Francisco: HarperSanFrancisco, 1990).

39. Anselm C. Hagedorn and Jerome H. Neyrey, "'It Was Out of Envy That They Handed Jesus Over' (Mark 15:10): The Anatomy of Envy and the Gospel of Mark," *JSNT* 96 (1998): 21.

40. Ibid., 51.

41. Malina, *New Testament World*, 125; see also Hagedorn and Neyrey, "It Was Out of Envy," 53.

42. John J. Pilch, "Secrecy in the Gospel of Mark," *PACE* 21 (1992): 150–53; idem, "Lying and Deceit in the Letters to the Seven Churches," *BTB* 22 (1992): 126–35; idem, "Secrecy in the Mediterranean World: An Anthropological Perspective," *BTB* 24 (1994): 151–57; this is a similar concept to the "aggressive defensive" mentioned in Simmel, *Sociology*, 330.

43. For other functions of secrecy, see Jerome H. Neyrey, "The Sociology of Secrecy and the Fourth Gospel," in *What Is John?* vol. 2, *Literary and Social Readings of the Fourth Gospel*, ed. Fernando Segovia (Atlanta: Scholars, 1998), 79–109, especially 81–87.

44. See Pilch, "Secrecy in the Mediterranean World," 154, as well as "Secrecy in the Gospel of Mark."

45. Pilch, "Secrecy in the Mediterranean World," 157.

46. Pilch, "Secrecy in the Gospel of Mark," 152.

47. Jerome H. Neyrey and Richard L. Rohrbaugh, " 'He Must Increase and I Must Decrease,' (John 3:30): A Cultural and Social Interpretation," *CBQ* 63 (2001): 480, italics theirs.

48. See LSJ, 9th ed., s.v. *arrētos*.

49. Walter Burkert, *Ancient Mystery Cults* (Cambridge: Harvard University Press, 1987), 69.

50. See Michael A. Williams, "Secrecy, Revelation, and Late Antique Demiurgical Myths," in *Rending the Veil: Concealment and Secrecy in the History of Religions*, ed. Elliot R. Wolfson (New York: Seven Bridges, 1999), 44.

51. Josephus, *Ant.* 8.45-49.

52. Cf. Joel Marcus, *The Mystery of the Kingdom of God* (Atlanta: Scholars, 1986), 92; Robert H. Gundry, *Mark: A Commentary on His Apology for the Cross*, vol. 1 (Grand Rapids: Eerdmans, 1993), 196.

53. Joel Marcus, "Mark 4:10-12 and Marcan Epistemology," *JBL* 103, no. 4 (1984): 559.

Chapter 2: Jesus Resists Honor

1. Daniel G. Bates and Fred Plog, *Cultural Anthropology*, 3d ed. (New York: McGraw-Hill, 1990), 7.

2. *Epistle* 7, 7-8; all quotations of the Cynic epistles are from Abraham J. Malherbe, ed., *The Cynic Epistles: A Study Edition* (Missoula: Scholars, 1977).

3. Plutarch, *Alex.* 42.2 (LCL).

4. Plutarch, *An seni* 786 E; Xenophon, *Mem.* 2.1.31.

5. Bruce J. Malina and Jerome H. Neyrey, "The First-Century Personality: Dyadic, Not Individual," in *The Social World of Luke-Acts: Models for Interpretation*, ed. Jerome H. Neyrey (Peabody: Hendrickson, 1991), 41. Female shame refers to a woman's proper modesty, especially with regard to the sexual advances of men other than her husband. See ibid., 41–44; Carol Delaney, "Seeds of Honor, Fields of Shame," in *Honor and Shame and the Unity of the Mediterranean*, ed. David D. Gilmore (Washington, D.C.: American Anthropological Association, 1987); Diane Bergant, " 'My Beloved is Mine and I am His' (Song 2:16)," *Semeia* 68 (1994): 23–40.

6. See, for example, Bruce J. Malina, *The New Testament World: Insights from Cultural Anthropology*, 3d ed. (Louisville: Westminster John Knox, 2001), 32–33.

7. Josephus, *A.J.* 6.80-81. The translation "returned in glory to his own land" depends upon an alternate reading of the text, which substitutes *lamprōs* for *lampros* in the phrase *lamprōs eis tēn oikeian hupestrepsen.*

8. Josephus, *B.J.* 1.199 (LCL). For other associations in Josephus of honor and royalty, see ibid., 1.461; 2.208; *A.J.* 1.6.67; according to Philo, Moses ascribes to others the honor of priesthood as a reward for virtuous warfare (*Mos.* 2.32.172-173). For an example of honor coming from widespread knowledge of one's virtue, see Plutarch, *Num.* 6.

9. For a criticism of ascribed honor, see Juvenal, *Sat.* 8.

10. See, for example, Plutarch, *Alex.* 34.1-4; idem, *Caes.* 5.8-9.

11. A wealthy, high-ranking individual might have a great deal of ascribed honor, but in order to acquire more honor he or she would have to use his or her resources for the benefit of others.

12. See J. E. Lendon, *Empire of Honour: The Art of Government in the Roman World* (Oxford: Clarendon, 1997), 86.

13. See Aelius Aristides, *Heracles* 40.12.

14. Xenophon, *Mem.* 2.1.28 (LCL).

15. Frederick W. Danker, *Benefactor: Epigraphic Study of a Graeco-Roman and New Testament Semantic Field* (St. Louis: Clayton, 1982), 26.

16. Dio Chrysostom 66.2; cf. London, *Empire* 86.

17. Plutarch, *Cupid. divit.* 525 D (LCL).

18. Plutarch, *Caes.* 5.8-9 (LCL).

19. Diogenes Laertius 8.69-70 (LCL).

20. Danker, *Benefactor,* 27.

21. Suetonius, *Aug.* 59 (LCL).

22. John H. Elliott, "Patronage and Clientage," in *The Social Sciences and New Testament Interpretation,* ed. Richard Rohrbaugh (Peabody, Mass.: Hendrickson, 1996), 144.

23. See Halvor Moxnes, "Patron-Client Relations and the New Community in Luke-Acts," in Neyrey, *Social World,* 248; E. A. Judge, *The Social Pattern of the Christian Groups in the First Century: Some Prolegomena to the Study of New Testament Ideas of Social Obligation* (London: Tyndale, 1960), 31.

24. Seneca, *Ben.* 3.1.4.

25. Ibid., 2.17.7.

26. Ibid., 2.10.4.

27. Elliott, "Patronage and Clientage," 149.

28. See Danker, *Benefactor,* 26; Elliott, "Patronage and Clientage," 144–56.

29. Apuleius, *Metam.* 5.10 (LCL).

30. Ibid. 11.6 (LCL).

31. Ibid. 4.9 (LCL)

32. Juvenal, *Sat.* 5.9-11 (LCL).

33. Ibid. 5.125-27.

34. Ibid. 5.156-60.

35. Lucian, *Nigr.* 23 (LCL).

36. See Bruce J. Malina and Richard L. Rohrbaugh, *Social-Science Commentary on the Synoptic Gospels* (Minneapolis: Fortress Press, 1992), 151, 177. The phrase *kai gonupetōn* in 1:40 is missing from some important texts, including B, D, and G, but it does show up in ℵ, A, C, L, Δ, Θ, and a number of other

manuscripts. The addition of *kai gonupetōn*, whether by the evangelist or a later copyist, merely underscores the idea that the leper comes as a client to Jesus.

37. Ibid., 55, 246.

38. In this case, however, the leper's acknowledgment of Jesus' power could well amount to a positive challenge since it is unlikely that they are in private. Honor challenges are public events; on positive and negative challenges, see Jerome H. Neyrey, *Honor and Shame in the Gospel of Matthew* (Louisville: Westminster John Knox, 1998), 45.

39. Ibid., 135.

40. With regard to the textual variant in 1:41, the manuscript evidence weighs heavily in favor of *splanchnistheis* (found in), A, B, C, L, W, and numerous other manuscripts) rather than the variant reading, *orgistheis* (found in D and a few Old Latin manuscripts). For arguments in favor of *splanchnistheis*, see Bruce M. Metzger, *A Textual Commentary on the Greek New Testament*, 2d ed. (Stuttgart: United Bible Societies, 1994), 65; John R. Donahue, S.J., and Daniel J. Harrington, S.J., *The Gospel of Mark,* Sacra Pagina (Collegeville: Liturgical, 2002), 89. Robert Gundry does not argue definitively for one reading over another, but offers several rebuttals to arguments in favor of *orgistheis* (see *Mark: A Commentary on His Apology for the Cross* [Grand Rapids: Eerdmans, 1993], 102–3). For arguments in favor of *orgistheis*, see William L. Lane, *The Gospel according to Mark,* The New International Commentary on the New Testament (Grand Rapids: Eerdmans, 1974), 84; Morna D. Hooker, *The Gospel according to Saint Mark,* Black's New Testament Commentary (Peabody, Mass.: Hendrickson, 1991), 79; Joel Marcus, *Mark 1–8: A New Translation with Commentary,* The Anchor Bible Commentary (New York: Doubleday, 2000), 206; and D. E. Nineham, *Saint Mark* (Philadelphia: Westminster, 1963), 86. Ben Witherington also leans in this direction, although he leaves the matter undecided (see *The Gospel of Mark: A Socio-Rhetorical Commentary* [Grand Rapids: Eerdmans, 2001], 103).

41. Seneca, *Ben.* 2.11.2 (LCL).

42. Ibid., 2.24.4 (LCL).

43. Although the subject of the verb *ērxato* is ambiguous, the verb almost certainly refers to the leper, and not to Jesus. For a discussion of this issue, see Donahue and Harrington, *Gospel of Mark*, 90.

44. Tacitus, *Hist.* 4.81 (LCL). This example of Vespasian is unusual. Erkki Koskenniemi writes that from "ca. 300 BCE to ca. 150 CE, there has not been a single important Gentile miracle worker identified in the literature" ("Apollonius of Tyana: A Typical ΘΕΙΟΣ ΑΝΗΡ?" *JBL* 117, no. 3 [1998]: 462). Koskenniemi holds that miracles performed by rulers form a special class, but notes, "The miracles of rulers seem not to have been as common as has been presumed. I know only of the miracles of Pyrrhos (Plutarch, *Pyrrh.* 3.3-4) and Vespasian (Tacitus, *Hist.* 4.81; Dio Cassius 65.8; Suetonius, *Vesp.* 7.23)" (ibid., n. 34); for a similar assessment of ancient pagan exorcists, see Barry Blackburn, Theios Anēr *and the Markan Miracle Traditions: A Critique of the* Theios

Anēr *Concept as an Interpretive Background of the Miracle Traditions Used by Mark* (Tübingen: J. C. B. Mohr [Paul Siebeck], 1991), 185.

45. On the connection between beneficent works and honor, see Cicero, *Off.* 2.3.1–2.3.2.

46. Cf. Acts 28:8-10.

47. See Apuleius, *Metam.* 2.28.

48. Cf. Mary Ann Tolbert, *Sowing the Gospel: Mark's World in Literary-Historical Perspective* (Minneapolis: Fortress Press, 1989), 229.

49. On Jarius's petition as a client, see Douglas Geyer, *Fear, Anomaly, and Uncertainty in the Gospel of Mark* (Lanham, Md.: Scarecrow, 2002), 163.

50. See Neyrey, *Honor and Shame in the Gospel of Matthew*, 45.

51. Seneca, *Ben.* 2.24.4.

52. See Plutarch, *Vit. pud.* 528E, 529E, 532D.

53. See Josephus, *Ant.* 5.144; TDNT, s.v. *gelaō*.

54. Juvenal, *Sat.* 10.31 (LCL).

55. Achilles Tatius, *Leucippe and Clitophon*, trans. Tim Whitmarsh (Oxford: Oxford University Press, 2002*)*, 2.29.

56. Juvenal, *Sat.* 13.11-12.

57. Presumably, the mourners later learn that the girl is alive (and thus receive Jesus' riposte), but Mark does not narrate their doing so.

58. Malina and Rohrbaugh, *Social-Science Commentary*, 359; cf. Bruce J. Malina and Jerome H. Neyrey, *Portraits of Paul: An Archaeology of Ancient Personality* (Louisville: Westminster John Knox, 1996), 165–66. Josephus uses the term this way, for example, in *Vita* 34; 104; 240; 293; 346; cf Jerome H. Neyrey, "Josephus' *Vita* and the Encomium: A Native Model of Personality," *JSJ* 25 (1994): 194–96.

59. Geyer, *Fear*, 170.

60. Eurpides, *Alc.* 1155 (LCL).

61. See Tolbert, *Sowing*, 228; David A. deSilva, *Honor, Patronage, Kinship & Purity: Unlocking New Testament Culture* (Downers Grove, Ill.: Intervarsity, 2000), 106–7.

62. Plutarch, *De laude* 540C-D.

63. Lucian, *De mort. Peregr.* 1 (LCL); for other unfavorable assessments of those who grasp at honor, see Seneca, *Ep.* 94.64-66; Euripides, *Phoen.* 529-30; Diogenes Laertius 8.69-70.

64. Philostratus, *Vit. Apoll.* 8.15. This translation is from David R. Cartlidge and David L. Dungan, *Documents for the Study of the Gospels*, rev. ed. (Minneapolis: Fortress Press, 1994), 235. I have used it because it better captures the sense of the Greek than does the Loeb translation, which reads, "[T]he attitude of Hellas towards him came near to that of actual worship; the main reason why they thought him divine being this, that he never made the least parade about the matter"; for another passage that conveys the idea that Apollonius was honored though he did not seek honor, see 8.7.7.

65. Apuleius, *Metam.* 3.11 (LCL).

66. Philostratus admits that there was some disagreement regarding whether the girl had actually died or was merely unconscious and near the point of death.

67. See Philostratus, *Vit. Apoll.* 4.45. Philostratus's sources are debated, but it may be that his accounts of Apollonius's great deeds were influenced by traditions about Jesus. Indeed, it is reasonable to see in Philosratus's *Life of Apollonius* a certain amount of anti-Christian polemic; see Blackburn, *Theios Anēr*, 74–75; cf. Simon Swain, "Defending Hellenism: Philostratus, *In Honour of Apollonius*," in *Apologetics in the Roman Empire: Pagans, Jews, and Christians*, ed. Mark Edwards et al. (New York: Oxford University Press, 1999), especially 194.

68. See Malina, *New Testament World*, 37–38.

69. For an account of the parallel structure of these passages, see Marcus, *Mark 1–8*, 476.

70. Ibid., 480.

71. *Corpus Inscriptiones Graecae*, 4.1.121-22, quoted in Wendy Cotter, *Miracles in Greco-Roman Antiquity: A Sourcebook for the Study of New Testament Miracle Stories* (New York: Routledge, 1999), 18.

72. Gundry holds that "[g]oing home, not into the village, does not imply going home instead of telling the villagers that he can now see (cf. vv.ll). It implies going home instead of begging from the villagers" (*Mark*, 419). Given that Jesus has already taken the man away from the village, however (8:23), this second reference to the village seems to indicate that Jesus wishes to maintain the isolation of the blind man from the villagers, at least temporarily. Further, Mark gives no indication that this man ever begged in the village.

73. Jerome H. Neyrey distinguishes between the male public-political sphere, the "private" sphere of male interaction, and the private sphere of the household; see "'Teaching You in Public and from House to House' (Acts 20:20): Unpacking a Cultural Stereotype," *JSNT* 26 (2003): 69–102, especially 75–83; idem, "Jesus, Gender, and the Gospel of Matthew," in *New Testament Masculinities*, ed. Stephen D. Moore and Janet Capel Anderson (Atlanta: Society of Biblical Literature, 2003), 46–49.

74. For another example of honor ascribed by God, see Philo, *Mos.* 2.8.67.

75. Hooker, *Saint Mark*, 64; Marcus holds a similar position: "The demons recognize Jesus, because they, like him, are spiritual beings" (*Mark 1–8*, 188); see also Witherington, *Gospel of Mark*, 91; Lane, *Mark*, 73; Robert A. Guelich, *Mark 1—8:26*, Word Biblical Commentary (Nashville: Thomas Nelson, 1989), 149.

76. See Graham H. Twelftree, *Jesus the Exorcist: A Contribution to the Study of the Historical Jesus* (Tübingen: J.C.B. Mohr, 1993), 67. See also Gundry's detailed discussion of this term and review of the scholarly debate surrounding it (*Mark*, 82–84). For further discussion, see Donahue and Harrington, *Gospel of Mark*, 80; Marcus, *Mark 1–8*, 188; Hooker, *Saint Mark*, 64; Otto Procksch and Karl Georg Kuhn, "*hagios*," *TDNT* 1:88–110, especially 101–2.

77. Malina and Rohrbaugh, *Social-Science Commentary*, 150. It is not clear whether Mark means by this term "Holy One who comes from God," or "the

One to whom God has ascribed holiness," but in either case it reflects Jesus' high status and connection with the divine.

78. See Ulrich Luz, "The Secrecy Motif and the Marcan Christology," in *The Messianic Secret*, ed. Christopher Tuckett (Philadelphia: Fortress Press, 1983), 81.

79. Twelftree, *Jesus the Exorcist*, 69. He also points to its use in the magical papyri as a term that is used in incantations for such purposes as keeping others from speaking against oneself, or "binding" another person, often in relation to that person's speech (ibid., 70).

80. Gundry comments on this passage, writing that "we should not think that Mark makes Jesus try to keep his messiahship secret. Besides, Mark has not given his audience any reason to think that Jesus wants to dampen publicity for purposes of avoiding misunderstanding, criticism, attack, or anything else of that sort. Mark portrays him, rather, as stopping the apotropaic use of his name and titles" (*Mark*, 84). Lane holds that the unclean spirit's recognition of Jesus is a "defensive address," but that Jesus' "sovereign command" renders the spirit powerless (*Mark*, 74).

81. For an instance of *phimo* that does not involve the same honor-related connotations, see Mark 4:39.

82. Cf. Hooker, *Saint Mark*, 65.

83. Witherington, *Gospel of Mark*, 91.

84. In the NT, the word often translated as "confess" is *homologeō*. Although this word refers in Matt 14:7 and Acts 7:17 to the making of a promise, and in 1 John 1:9 to the confession of sins, the most common usage of *homologeō* and related words in the NT has to do with the public acknowledgment of one's Christian faith (e.g., Matt 10:32; John 9:22; Rom 10:9-10; 2 Cor 9:13; Heb 3:1, 4:14, 10:23; 1 John 4:2-3). The word group *homologeō* and its cognates is absent from Mark.

85. Cf. Howard Clark Kee, "The Terminology of Mark's Exorcism Stories," *NTS* 14 (1968): 243.

86. Cf. ibid., 242.

87. Another figure who speaks with authority is Apollonius, whose authority comes in large part from his relationship to Asclepius; see Philostratus, *V.A.* 1.17.

88. Josephus, *Ant.* 8.45-48 (LCL). Kee notes also that "rabbinic exorcism stories are told in order to exalt the wonder-worker" ("Terminology," 243).

89. "Jesus' ministry of teaching could also be considered a gift (and not something the crowds endured in order to receive gifts!), since good advice and guidance were valued and valuable commodities. Seneca (*Ben* 1.2.4), for example, includes 'advice' and 'sound precepts' amidst the various kinds of assistance a friend or patron would give" (deSilva, *Honor, Patronage*, 134).

90. On the honor that could attend one who was widely perceived to be a prophet (even if a false one), see Philo's description of Balaam in *Mos.* 1.48.264-265.

91. Marcus argues, "This injunction to silence is reminiscent of the one in 1:25, though the motivations are slightly different: in the pre-Markan tradition taken up in 1:25, Jesus prevents the demon from manipulating his name to launch a demonic counter-attack, whereas in 1:34 he suppresses disclosure of his identity, because the time is not yet right for it" (*Mark 1–8*, 201). Yet it is hard to imagine that the Markan audience would draw such a distinction, especially in light of what Marcus points out: that the injunction to silence in 1:34 is reminiscent of the one in 1:25. While the silence command in the first episode (1:25) may have been heard initially as an exorcistic formula, its significance changes in light of the explanation in 1:34, that Jesus silenced the demons "because they knew him."

92. The term *phaneros* (3:12) sometimes connotes fame and reputation, both of which are connected with honor. For example, see Mark's use of this term in connection with Jesus' "name" (itself an honor-laden term) in 6:14; see also Xenophon, *Cyr.* 7.5.58.

93. See Seneca, *Clem.* 1.14.2.

94. Thus Guelich comments on 1:34, "[T]his command to silence stands in tension with a context that assumes a broad public 'knowledge' of Jesus, at least as one who heals and exorcizes (1:32-33)" (*Mark 1–8:26*, 67).

95. Gundry, *Mark*, 88; see also Lane, *Mark*, 79.

96. Cf. Guelich, *Mark 1–8:26*, 148–49.

97. As we have seen, philosophers were sometimes called "benefactors of humanity" by virtue of "inward excellence and prudent counsel" (Danker, *Benefactor*, 27). Moxnes holds that, in Luke, Jesus "gives access to God through proclaiming the kingdom (4:16-19)," which equates to brokerage through teaching ("Patron-Client Relations," 258).

Chapter 3: A New Vision of Honor

1. J. E. Lendon, *Empire of Honour: The Art of Government in the Roman World* (Oxford: Clarendon, 1997), 91.

2. Ibid., 92; see Cicero, *Arch.* 26.

3. See Diogenes Laertius 6, 72; see also F. Gerald Downing, "Cynics and Christians," *NTS* 30, no. 4 (1984): 584–93.

4. *Epistle 34* 1.15-19; all quotations of the Cynic epistles are from Abraham J. Malherbe, ed., *The Cynic Epistles: A Study Edition* (Missoula: Scholars, 1977).

5. Ibid., 2.1-3.

6. *Epistle 37*, 4.11-15.

7. See, e.g., *Epistle 7*, 103.9; *Epistle 8; Epistle 9.*

8. *Epistle 16*, 12.

9. See F. Gerald Downing, *Christ and the Cynics: Jesus and Other Radical Preachers in First-Century Tradition* (Sheffield: Sheffield Academic, 1988), 588.

10. In Mark's story world, not everyone recognizes that Jesus is due such honor (see 3:22-31; 6:1-6), but Mark's audience would.

11. Cf. Morna D. Hooker, *The Gospel according to Saint Mark,* Black's New Testament Commentary (Peabody, Mass.: Hendrickson, 1991), 89.

12. For a discussion of the theme of vindication in relation to the phrase "Son of Man," see Jack Dean Kingsbury, *The Christology of Mark's Gospel* (Philadelphia: Fortress Press, 1983), 170ff. The *Similitudes of Enoch* offer somewhat of a parallel, bringing together the imagery of Daniel 7 with the Servant of Deutero-Isaiah. The dating of the *Similitudes* is controversial, however, and it cannot be definitively established that the *Similitudes,* or ideas that were later incorporated into the *Similitudes,* influenced Mark. It may be that early Christian ideas influenced the *Similitudes*; see Hooker, *Saint Mark,* 90; Joel Marcus, *Mark 1–8: A New Translation with Commentary* (New York: Doubleday, 2000), 530–32; George E. Nickelsburg, "Son of Man," in *Anchor Bible Dictionary,* ed. David Noel Freedman (New York: Doubleday, 1992), 6:139.

13. See Bruce J. Malina and Richard L. Rohrbaugh, *Social-Science Commentary on the Synoptic Gospels* (Minneapolis: Fortress Press, 1992), 181.

14. See Bruce J. Malina, " 'Let Him Deny Himself' (Mark 8:34 and Par): A Social Psychological Model of Self-Denial," *BTB* 24 (1994): 106–19; idem, "Understanding New Testament Persons," in *The Social Sciences and New Testament Interpretation,* ed. Richard Rohrbaugh (Peabody, Mass.: Hendrickson, 1996), 41–61.

15. See Joanna Dewey, " 'Let Them Renounce Themselves and Take Up Their Cross': A Feminist Reading of Mark 8:34 in Mark's Social and Narrative World," in *A Feminist Companion to Mark,* ed. Amy-Jill Levine, with Marianne Blickenstaff (Sheffield: Sheffield Academic, 2001), 33–34; see also Bruce J. Malina and Jerome H. Neyrey, *Portraits of Paul: An Archaeology of Ancient Personality* (Louisville: Westminster John Knox, 1996), 165.

16. See Heb 12:2; Cicero, *Rab. Perd.* 16; Cicero, *In Verr.* 2.5.165; Josephus, *J.W.* 7.203; Origen, *Cels.* 6.10; see also Martin Hengel, *Crucifixion* (Philadelphia: Fortress Press, 1977); John J. Pilch, "Death with Honor: The Mediterranean Style Death of Jesus in Mark," in *BTB* 25 (1995): 65–70; Jerome H. Neyrey, "Despising the Shame of the Cross: Honor and Shame in the Johannine Passion Narrative," *Semeia* 68 (1994): 113–37; for a public trial as a status degradation ritual, see Neyrey, "Despising Shame"; cf. Cicero, *Rab. Perd.* 9-17.

17. Seneca, *Ira* 1.6.4.

18. Hence Plutarch writes, "[P]eople are often ashamed to receive benefits, but are always delighted to confer them" (*Max. Princ.* 778D [LCL]); see also Xenophon, *Mem.* 2.1.28; Dio Chrysostom 66.2.

19. See Suetonius, *Gramm.* 3.

20. See idem, *Rhet.* 1

21. See idem, *On Poet. Ter.* 1, 2; see also Horace, *Odes* 4.3.

22. See Juvenal, *Sat.* 10; Josephus, *A.J.* 6.80-81.

23. See, e.g., the commonplace ideal regarding satisfaction that Seneca argues against in *Ira* 2.32.1-2.34.5.

24. Suetonius, *Poet. Verg.* 11 (LCL).

25. See Dominic Montserrat, "Experiencing the Male Body in Roman Egypt," in *When Men Were Men: Masculinity, Power, and Identity in Classical Antiquity*, ed. Lin Foxhall and John Salmon (New York: Routledge, 1998), 160.

26. *Alexander Romance* 2.18.

27. Cicero, *Rab. Perd.* 16 (LCL).

28. Joel Marcus, "Crucifixion as Parodic Exaltation," *JBL* 125, no. 1 (2006): 78.

29. Ibid.

30. Apuleius, *Metam.* 1.6, my italics.

31. Plutarch, *Amic. mult.* 96B.

32. Malina and Rohrbaugh, *Social-Science Commentary*, 232.

33. See David A. deSilva, *Honor, Patronage, Kinship, and Purity: Unlocking New Testament Culture* (Downers Grove, Ill.: Intervarsity, 2000), 41–42.

34. Seneca, *Ira* 1.16.2.

35. Mark 8:27—9:1 is commonly cited as a passage in which Jesus redefines messiahship, but Jesus' teaching in this passage is open to various interpretations, and, as I have stated, I do not believe that this is its main purpose. Other than this passage, it is difficult to locate instances in Mark's Gospel that might qualify as teachings that redefine messiahship.

36. See Wilhelm Michaelis, "*leukos,*" *TDNT* 4:241–50.

37. Jerome H. Neyrey, *Honor and Shame in the Gospel of Matthew* (Louisville: Westminster John Knox, 1998), 64; in this quotation, he is dealing with the Matthean parallel to this Markan passage.

38. Mary Ann Tolbert, *Sowing the Gospel: Mark's World in Literary-Historical Perspective* (Minneapolis: Fortress Press, 1989), 205. For a different perspective, see Hooker, *Saint Mark*, 217.

39. Philostratus, *V.A.* 3.10. On the desire for a male to be fear-inspiring while in his prime, see Aristotle, *Rhet.*, 1.5.11; cf. Josephus, *A.J.* 19.344. Neyrey states that fear is a natural reaction to a demonstration of prowess (*Honor and Shame in the Gospel of Matthew*, 41). On fear as shameful (in contrast to courage, which was virtuous), see ibid., 114–16; 148–51, 154.

40. Neyrey, *Honor and Shame in the Gospel of Matthew*, 38; cf. 1 Pet 1:17.

41. Here the disciples refer to a scribal teaching on Mal 4:5.

42. See Gundry's detailed discussion of these verses in *Mark: A Commentary on His Apology for the Cross* (Grand Rapids: Eerdmans, 1993), 463–66, 483–86.

43. It may also be a reference to Ps 88:39 LXX.

44. Matt 17:13 makes this point explicit; cf. Hooker, *Saint Mark*, 220; B. M. F. van Iersel, *Mark: A Reader-Response Commentary*, trans. W. H. Bisscheroux (Sheffield: Sheffield Academic, 1998), 300; James R. Edwards, *The Gospel according to Mark*, Pillar New Testament Commentary (Grand Rapids: Eerdmans, 2002), 274; William L. Lane, *The Gospel according to Mark*, The New International Commentary on the New Testament (Grand Rapids: Eerdmans, 1974), 326–27.

45. See Gundry, *Mark*, 465.

46. See Mark 12:4 and 15:19; Bruce J. Malina and Jerome H. Neyrey, "Honor and Shame in Luke–Acts: Pivotal Values of the Mediterranean World," in *The Social World of Luke-Acts: Models for Interpretation*, ed. Jerome H. Neyrey (Peabody, Mass.: Hendrickson, 1991), 35.

47. On the threefold pattern of (1) passion prediction by Jesus, (2) misunderstanding by the disciples, and (3) clarification by Jesus, see Norman Perrin, *The Resurrection according to Matthew, Mark, and Luke* (Philadelphia: Fortress Press, 1977), 20–21.

48. Lane, *Gospel of Mark*, 339.

49. Hooker, *Saint Mark*, 228.

50. See also 10:13-15.

51. Aristotle, *Rhet.* 1.11.16.

52. See the *Alexander Romance,* 1.36, 38, 39; likewise, Seneca (*Ben.* 1.19.3) belittles anger by referring to it as "womanish and childish." "The term 'child/children' could...be used as a serious insult (cf. Matt 11:16-17; Luke 7:32)" (Malina and Rohrbaugh, *Social-Science Commentary*, 336).

53. Montserrat, "Experiencing," 153; cf. LSJ, s.v. *sōma* (II) and *pais* (III).

54. For example, see van Iersel, *Mark: A Reader-Response Commentary*, 335; Edwards, *Gospel according to Mark*, 324; Francis J. Moloney, *The Gospel of Mark: A Commentary* (Peabody, Mass.: Hendrickson, 2002), 206; Hooker, *Saint Mark*, 247; Gundry, *Mark*, 579.

55. See Jerome H. Neyrey and Richard L. Rohrbaugh, "'He Must Increase and I Must Decrease' (John 3:30): A Cultural and Social Interpretation," *CBQ* 63 (2001), especially 475–76.

56. Seneca, *Ira* 1.18.2.

57. Ibid., 2.8.2-3.

58. Plutarch, *Lat. viv.* 1128B.

59. Plutarch, *An seni* 788E-F (LCL).

60. On this issue, see John Painter, *Mark's Gospel: Worlds in Conflict* (New York: Routledge, 1997), 147.

61. See W. Grundmann, "*megas,*" *TDNT* 4:529–41, especially 529–30.

62. Wilhelm Michaelis, "*prōtos,*" *TDNT* 6:865.

63. Ibid., 866.

64. See John N. Collins, "*Diakonia: Re-interpreting the Ancient Sources*" (New York: Oxford University Press, 1990), 77–95, 169–76.

65. Ibid., 248.

66. Gerhard Kittel, "*eschatos,*" *TDNT* 2:698. Obviously, there are other meanings to this word as well. For example, it can have the sense of something's being last temporally, a sense that has given rise to its use in the NT as referring to the last days (its "eschatological" usage).

67. See Plato, *Gorg.* 492b; Seneca, *Ira* 2.21.3. Hermann W. Beyer writes that, for the Greeks, "serving is not very dignified," and that the basic attitude of the Greeks is summed up in the sophist's formula, "How can a man be happy when he has to serve someone?" ("*diakoneō,*" *TDNT* 2:82).

68. This type of "shift in expectancy" was a common ancient Greek rhetorical feature; see E. A. Nida et al., *Style and Discourse, with Special Reference to the Text of the Greek New Testament* (Cape Town: Bible Society, 1983), 36–44.

69. Xenophon, *Cyr.* 8.1.39 (LCL).

70. See Painter, *Mark's Gospel*, 149; Hooker, *Saint Mark*, 247-48.

71. See also the use of *thelō* in the episode of 6:14-29.

72. Compare with 10:36: "*Ti thelete [me] poiēsō humin?*"

73. On this link between faith and sight in the Bartimaeus story, see Moloney, *Gospel of Mark*, 210.

74. Plutarch, *Lat. viv.* 1129B-C.

75. Tolbert, *Sowing*, 227.

76. See Joanna Dewey, "Mark as Interwoven Tapestry: Forecasts and Echoes for a Listening Audience," *CBQ* 53 (1991): 236; David Rhoads, Joanna Dewey, and Donald Michie, *Mark as Story*, 2d ed. (Minneapolis: Fortress Press, 1999), 102. Vernon Robbins demonstrates that the failure of the disciple to understand the teacher is a common Greco-Roman motif (Vernon K. Robbins, *Jesus the Teacher: A Socio-Rhetorical Interpretation of Mark* [Minneapolis: Fortress Press, 1992], 136–67).

77. Jouette M. Bassler, "The Parable of the Loaves," *JR* 62 no. 2 (1986): 167.

78. Ibid.

79. William Wrede, *The Messianic Secret*, trans. J. C. G. Greig (Cambridge: James Clarke, 1971), 131.

Chapter 4: Honor in the Public Eye

1. William Wrede, *The Messianic Secret*, trans. J. C. G. Greig (Cambridge: James Clarke, 1971); see also, for example, James D. G. Dunn, "The Messianic Secret in Mark," in *The Messianic Secret*, ed. Christopher Tuckett (Philadelphia: Fortress Press, 1983), 116–31; John J. Pilch, "Secrecy in the Gospel of Mark," *PACE* 21 (1992): 150–53; Joel Marcus, *Mark 1–8: A New Translation with Introduction and Commentary,* The Anchor Bible Commentary (New York: Doubleday, 2000), 525–27; Scott Gambrill Sinclair, "The Healing of Bartimaeus and the Gaps in Mark's Messianic Secret," *SLJT* 33, no. 4 (1990): 249–57; Morna D. Hooker, *The Gospel according to Saint Mark,* Black's New Testament Commentary (Peabody, Mass.: Hendrickson, 1991), 68; Frank Kermode, *The Genesis of Secrecy: On the Interpretation of Narrative* (Cambridge: Harvard University Press, 1979), 141; M. Eugene Boring, *Mark: A Commentary,* New Testament Library (Louisville: Westminster John Knox, 2006), 264–71; Adela Yarbro Collins, *Mark: A Commentary,* Hermeneia (Minneapolis: Fortress Press, 2007), 170–72. The publicity motif is an important part of the concept of Mark as a book of "secret epiphanies," as described in Martin Dibelius, *From Tradition to Gospel,* trans. Bertram Lee Woolf (New York: Charles Scribner's Sons, n.d.); see also

Rudolf Bultmann, *The History of the Synoptic Tradition*, trans. John Marsh (New York: Harper & Row, 1963), especially 346–48.

2. Wrede, *Messianic Secret*, 124.

3. Ibid., 126.

4. Ibid., 128.

5. Joseph H. Hellerman, "Challenging the Authority of Jesus: Mark 11:27-33 and Mediterranean Notions of Honor and Shame," *JETS* 43, no. 2 (2000): 220.

6. Ibid., 220–21.

7. Cf. ibid., 242.

8. Another figure who speaks with authority is Apollonius, whose authority comes in large part from his relationship to Asclepius; see Philostratus, *V.A.* 1.17.

9. Josephus, *Ant.* 8.45-48 (LCL). Howard Clark Kee notes also that "rabbinic exorcism stories are told in order to exalt the wonder-worker" (Kee, "The Terminology of Mark's Exorcism Stories," *NTS* 14 (1968): 243.

10. See David A. deSilva, *Honor, Patronage, Kinship, and Purity: Unlocking New Testament Culture* (Downers Grove, Ill.: Intervarsity, 2000), 134.

11. Empedocles is another example of a miracle-worker who received honor from widespread beneficence; see Diogenes Laertius 8.60.

12. Hooker, *Saint Mark*, 86; cf. Robert H. Gundry, *Mark: A Commentary on His Apology for the Cross* (Grand Rapids: Eerdmans, 1993), 112.

13. Marcus, *Mark 1–8*, 222–23.

14. See Bruce J. Malina and Richard L. Rohrbaugh, *Social-Science Commentary on the Synoptic Gospels* (Minneapolis: Fortress Press, 1992), 154. If this is the case, the statement, "your sins are forgiven," may be an example of the "divine passive," a way of avoiding the use of the divine name; see B. M. F. van Iersel, *Mark: A Reader-Response Commentary*, trans. W. H. Bisscheroux (Sheffield: Sheffield Academic, 1998), 147. There are also other brokers of God mentioned in the Bible, such as kings and priests; see Jerome H. Neyrey, *Render to God: New Testament Understandings of the Divine* (Minneapolis: Fortress Press, 2004), 13–15.

15. Peder Borgen, "God's Agent in the Fourth Gospel," in *Religions in Antiquity: Essays in Memory of Erwin Ramsdell Goodenough*, ed. Jacob Neusner (Leiden: Brill, 1968), 138; texts that he cites for this principle are *m. Mek.* 12:3, 6; *m. Ber.* 5:5; *b. B. Meṣi'a* 96a; *b. Hag.* 10b; *b. Qidd.* 42b, 43a; *b. Menah.* 93b; *b. Naz.* 12b.

16. Ben Witherington, *The Gospel of Mark: A Socio-Rhetorical Commentary* (Grand Rapids: Eerdmans, 2001), 116–17; see also G. H. Boobyer, "Mark II, 10a and the Interpretation of the Healing of the Paralytic," *HTR* 47 (1954): 115–20; Robert Fowler, *Let the Reader Understand: Reader-Response Criticism and the Gospel of Mark* (Harrisburg: Trinity Press International, 1996), 102–3; William L. Lane, *The Gospel according to Mark,* New International Commentary on the New Testament (Grand Rapids: Eerdmans, 1974), 97; C. E. B. Cranfield, *The Gospel according to Saint Mark* (Cambridge: Cambridge University Press, 1959), 100.

17. Cf. Mary Ann Tolbert, *Sowing the Gospel: Mark's World in Literary-Historical Perspective* (Minneapolis: Fortress Press, 1989), 136 n.18; Marcus, *Mark 1–8*, 218.

18. See Jack Dean Kingsbury, *The Christology of Mark's Gospel* (Philadelphia: Fortress Press, 1983), 159ff., especially 171.

19. On "Son of Man" as an expression of the patron-client relationship between Jesus and God, see Neyrey, *Render*, 27; see also his discussion of Plutarch's fourfold meaning of names in ibid., 3–4.

20. See Jerome Neyrey's discussion of *chreiai* and native informants about them in "Questions, *Chreiai*, and Challenges to Honor: The Interface of Rhetoric and Culture in Mark's Gospel," *CBQ* 60 (1998): 657–81, especially 664–65.

21. For a similar perspective, although one that involves a "secrecy" motif, see Heikki Räisänen, *The 'Messianic Secret' in Mark*, trans. Christopher Tuckett (Edinburgh: T. & T. Clark, 1990), 225.

22. Some would suggest that the passage should be read as the evangelist's commentary rather than as a statement of Mark's Jesus. For example, Lane interprets 2:28 in the same way that he interpreted 2:10a: as a statement of the evangelist, rather than a statement that Jesus speaks within the narrative (see *Gospel of Mark*, 220). Yet without assuming the presence of a "secrecy motif" that Jesus must uphold, there is no reason to understand 2:28 as the evangelist's commentary. Luke chose to place these words on the lips of Jesus (Luke 6:5), and it seems likely that Mark's audience would do the same.

23. See Malina and Rohrbaugh, *Social-Science Commentary*, 54.

24. On "Lord of the Sabbath" as indicating authority on a par with that of Yahweh, see R. T. France, *The Gospel of Mark*, New International Greek Testament Commentary (Grand Rapids: Eerdmans, 2002), 148; van Iersel, *Mark: A Reader-Response Commentary*, 159; Francis J. Moloney, *The Gospel of Mark: A Commentary* (Peabody, Mass.: Hendrickson, 2002), 68; James R. Edwards, *The Gospel according to Mark*, Pillar New Testament Commentary (Grand Rapids: Eerdmans, 2001), 97.

25. France, *Gospel of Mark*, 148. He also states that "the 'messianic secret' is strained to the limits" (ibid.).

26. On the silence of the onlookers, see van Iersel, *Mark: A Reader-Response Commentary*, 161.

27. Tolbert, *Sowing*, 229, italics hers.

28. Cf. Cranfield, *Saint Mark*, 119; Gundry, *Mark*, 150.

29. Kingsbury, *Christology*, 18–19.

30. Gundry, *Mark*, 263.

31. J. Duncan M. Derrett, "Contributions to the Study of the Gerasene Demoniac," *JSNT* 3 (1979): 6.

32. See Wrede, *Messianic Secret*, 140–41.

33. Gerd Theissen, *The Miracle Stories of the Early Christian Tradition*, trans. Francis McDonagh (Philadelphia: Fortress Press, 1983), 146–47; originally published as *Urchristliche Wundergeschichten: Ein Beitrag zur formgeschichtlichen*

Erforschung der synoptischen Evangelien (Gütersloh: Gütersloher Verlagshaus Gerd Mohn, 1974).

34. See Wrede, *Messianic Secret*, 141.

35. See Marcus, *Mark 1–8*, 346.

36. Cf. Robert A. Guelich, *Mark 1—8:26,* Word Biblical Commentary (Nashville: Thomas Nelson, 1989), 285–86.

37. John R. Donahue and Daniel J. Harrington, *The Gospel of Mark,* Sacra Pagina (Collegeville, Minn.: Liturgical, 2002), 168; cf. Guelich, *Mark 1—8:26,* 285.

38. See Malina and Rohrbaugh, *Social-Science Commentary,* 166. Other scholars who hold that *ho kurios* refers to God rather than Jesus include Guelich, *Mark 1—8:26,* 285; Moloney, *Gospel of Mark,* 105. Hooker holds that *ho kurios* may refer to Jesus, but probably refers to God, as in the LXX (*Saint Mark,* 145). Marcus argues that *ho kurios* refers to God, but that, in Mark, "where Jesus acts, there God is acting" (*Mark 1–8,* 354). However, Gundry holds that in this passage, "Jesus has acted as the Lord," and therefore *ho kurios* refers to Jesus (*Mark,* 254; see also 255). Similarly, Edwards holds that *ho kurios* refers to Jesus, and that it serves as an indicator of Jesus' "divine status" (*Gospel according to Mark,* 160).

39. For an example of Moses offering up honors to God as a divine benefactor and exhorting others to do so, see Philo, *Mos.* 46.256.

40. Against Derrett, according to whom "it cannot be argued that he disobeyed Jesus' intention" ("Gerasene Demoniac," 3).

41. Cf. Hooker, *Saint Mark,* 151.

42. An ancient audience might well have seen the disciples' question as a challenge to Jesus, to which the woman's coming forward would function as a riposte. If their question does represent an honor challenge, this would advance the theme of the disciples' blindness.

43. See A. T. Robertson, *A Grammar of the Greek New Testament in Light of Historical Research* (New York: Hodder & Stoughton, 1914), 838.

44. See, e.g., van Iersel, *Mark: A Reader-Response Commentary,* 206; Timothy J. Geddert, *Watchwords: Mark 13 in Markan Eschatology* (Sheffield: Sheffield Academic, 1989), 49–50.

45. On high and low contexts, see Edward T. Hall, *Beyond Culture* (Garden City, N.Y.: Anchor, 1976), 34–35, and chap. 7, "Contexts, High and Low"; cf. Bruce J. Malina, *The New Testament World: Insights from Cultural Anthropology,* 3d ed. (Louisville: Westminster John Knox, 2001), 91.

46. See Malina and Rohrbaugh, *Social-Science Commentary* (Minneapolis: Fortress Press, 1992), 366–68; on the negative functions of gossip, see James C. Scott, *Domination and the Arts of Resistance: Hidden Transcripts* (New Haven: Yale University Press, 1990), 142.

47. Persius, *Sat.* 1.28 (LCL).

48. See deSilva, *Honor, Patronage,* 41–42.

49. Seneca, *Ira* 1.16.2 (LCL).

50. On the significance of these themes in this passage, see Tolbert, *Sowing*, 168–69.

51. Douglas Geyer, "Occluded Benefaction and Perspicuous Anomaly in the Gospel of Mark," presented at the annual meeting of the Society of Biblical Literature, Denver, Nov. 19, 2001, 19–20; Geyer is using "benefactor" where I would use "broker."

52. "A king imagined as a shepherd was, at the time of the Gospel of Mark, a well-known political and literary convention" (Douglas Geyer, *Fear, Anomaly, and Uncertainty in the Gospel of Mark* [Lanham, Md.: Scarecrow, 2002], 226). Geyer offers a thorough discussion of the image of a king as a shepherd; see ibid., 226ff.; see also Joachim Jeremias, *"poimēn k.t.l.,"* *TDNT* 6:485–502, especially 486–87.

53. Geyer, "Occluded Benefaction," 20–21.

54. See Fergus Millar, *The Roman Empire and Its Neighbours*, 2d ed. (New York: Holmes & Meier, 1981), 17–18.

55. Ibid., 18.

56. See Philo, *Spec.* 3.169ff.

57. See Hooker, *Saint Mark*, 222–23; Witherington, *Gospel of Mark*, 266; Gundry, *Mark*, 487–88; John Painter, *Mark's Gospel: Worlds in Conflict* (New York: Routledge, 1997), 132.

58. Cf. Joel Marcus, *The Way of the Lord: Christological Exegesis of the Old Testament in the Gospel of Mark* (Edinburgh: T. & T. Clark, 1992), 82–83; see also Philo, *Mos.* 14.68. For a contrasting opinion, see Georg Bertram, *"thambos,"* *TDNT* 3:4–7, especially 6.

59. France, *Gospel of Mark*, 364; cf. Lane, *Gospel of Mark*, 330.

60. Eduard Schweizer, *The Good News according to Mark* (Atlanta: John Knox, 1970), 187.

61. Hooker, *Saint Mark*, 222.

62. Other uses of *ekthambeō* in Mark's Gospel (14:33; 16:5; 16:6) are not especially helpful with regard to this issue.

63. Against France, who argues, "Verse 8 suggests an immediate return to normality" (*Gospel of Mark*, 364).

64. Hooker, *Saint Mark*, 224; cf. Schweizer, *Good News*, 187; D. E. Nineham, *Saint Mark* (Philadelphia: Westminster, 1963), 243.

65. See van Iersel, *Mark: A Reader-Response Commentary*, 304; Hooker, *Saint Mark*, 224; Witherington, *Gospel of Mark*, 267.

66. Gundry, *Mark*, 488.

67. See also 8:34-38, 10:35-45; cf. Donahue and Harrington, *Gospel of Mark*, 290.

68. See Gundry, *Mark*, 519–23.

69. Jerome H. Neyrey, *Honor and Shame in the Gospel of Matthew* (Louisville: Westminster John Knox, 1998), 58.

70. On "Son of David" as a messianic title, see Hooker, *Saint Mark*, 252; Painter, *Mark's Gospel*, 151; Nineham, *Saint Mark*, 47; Räisänen, *Messianic Secret*, 230; Edwards, *Gospel according to Mark*, 330; Malina and Rohrbaugh,

Social-Science Commentary, 194; Eduard Lohse, *"huios Dauid" TDNT* 8:478–88, especially 484–85. Lane holds that "it is probable that Mark's readers understood the epithet in this messianic context (cf. Rom. 1:3)" (*Gospel of Mark*, 387). On "Son of David" as a title that called to mind the benefaction and healing of Solomon, see Dennis Duling, "Solomon, Exorcism, and the Son of David," *HTR* 68 (1975): 235–52; idem, "The Therapeutic Son of David," *NTS* 24 (1978): 392–410; idem, "Matthew's Plurisignificant 'Son of David' in Social-Science Perspective: Kinship, Kingship, Magic and Miracle," *BTB* 22 (1992): 99–116; cf. Neyrey, *Honor and Shame in the Gospel of Matthew*, 44.

71. Cf. Earl S. Johnson, "Mark 10:46-52: Blind Bartimaeus," *CBQ* 40 (1978): 191–204; Donahue and Harrington, *Gospel of Mark*, 318.

72. Cf. Paul J. Achtemeier, " 'And He Followed Him': Miracles and Discipleship in Mark 10:46-52," *Semeia* 11 (1978): 118; Wrede, *Messianic Secret*, 280; Räisänen, *Messianic Secret*, 230–31; T. A. Burkill, *Mysterious Revelation: An Examination of the Philosophy of St. Mark's Gospel* (Ithaca: Cornell University Press, 1963), 190–91.

73. J. H. Charlesworth, "The Son of David: Solomon and Jesus (Mark 10.47)," in *The New Testament and Hellenistic Judaism*, ed. Peder Borgen and Søren Giversen (Peabody, Mass.: Hendrickson, 1997), 85; cf. Cranfield, *Saint Mark*, 344–45; for an example of an attempt to salvage the "messianic secret" in this passage, see G. H. Boobyer, "The Secrecy Motif in Mark's Gospel," *NTS* 6, no. 3 (1960): 225–35.

74. Donahue and Harrington, *Gospel of Mark*, 319.

75. See Jerome H. Neyrey, " 'Teaching You in Public and from House to House' (Acts 20:20): Unpacking a Cultural Stereotype," *JSNT* 26 (2003): 76, 81, 83.

76. See ibid., 83–84.

77. For a discussion of Mark's distinction between exorcisms and miracles of healing, see Hooker, *Saint Mark*, 71; cf. Marcus, *Mark 1–8*, 199.

78. Although Lane does not speak of a "gossip network," he expresses basically the same sentiment; see *Gospel of Mark*, 260.

79. See Wrede, *Messianic Secret*, 38.

80. Marcus, *Mark 1–8*, 467.

81. David Rhoads, "Jesus and the Syrophoenician Woman in Mark: A Narrative-Critical Study," *JAAR* 62, no. 2 (1994): 354.

82. Ibid., 358 n.3.

83. Cf. Guelich, *Mark 1—8:26*, 384. In fact, Guelich understands the entire journey to Tyre as an attempt to escape from the crowds.

84. Cf. Lane, *Gospel of Mark*, 260. Lane also sees 6:53-56 as another example of an interrupted attempt at rest.

85. On structural parallels between these two stories (as well as John 6:16-21), see Marcus, *Mark 1–8*, 424-25.

86. Rudolf Bultmann, *The History of the Synoptic Tradition*, trans. John Marsh (New York: Harper & Row, 1963), 215ff. The stories from Mark that he included in this category are two feeding miracles (6:34-44 and 8:1-9),

Jesus' walking on water (6:45-52), and the story of Jesus' cursing of the fig tree (11:12-14, 20). I discuss the two feeding stories below. Yet Hooker notes, "The difference between these [nature miracles] and healing miracles is probably more obvious to us than to Mark, for whom they are all indications of the authority of Jesus" (Hooker, *Saint Mark*, 138); see also Malina and Rohrbaugh, *Social-Science Commentary*, 164, 173.

87. On the issue of authority in this passage, particularly with regard to the use of *epitimaō*, see Kee, "Terminology," 243–44.

88. See, for example, Kingsbury, *Christology*, 74, 81; for another example of a scholar's understanding this question as primarily about identity, see William F. McInerny, "An Unresolved Question in the Gospel Called Mark: 'Who is This Whom Even Wind and Sea Obey?' (4:41)," *PRS* 23, no. 3 (1996): 258–59.

89. Isodorus, *Hymn One, The Four Hymns of Isodorus* 1.39, 43, 49, 50. Quoted in Wendy Cotter, *Miracle Stories in Greco-Roman Antiquity: A Sourcebook for the Study of New Testament Miracle Stories* (New York: Routledge, 1999), 136; see also Apuleius, *Metam.* 11.5.

90. See T. Snoy, "Marc 6,48: ". . . et il voulait les dépasser," in *L'Evangile selon Marc: Tradition et redaction*, ed. M. Sabbe (Louvain: Leuven University Press, 1974), 346–63, especially 361–62.

91. See LXX Exod 34:5-6: "*parēlthen kurios pro prosōpou autou.*"

92. See John Paul Heil, *Jesus Walking on the Sea: Meaning and Gospel Functions of Matt 14:22-33, Mark 6:45-52 and John 6:15b-21* (Rome: Biblical Institute Press, 1981), 69–70; Heil does not deal with the social-scientific terminology of acknowledgment of honor status, but the use of these terms is helpful in bringing his insights to bear on the arguments in this chapter. For interpretations that concur with Heil's, see Marcus, *Mark 1–8*, 426; Guelich, *Mark 1—8:26*, 350; Donahue and Harrington, *Gospel of Mark*, 213. For a similar interpretation, see Edwards, *Gospel according to Mark*, 198.

93. Heil, *Jesus Walking*, 70.

94. Donald H. Juel, *A Master of Surprise: Mark Interpreted* (Minneapolis: Fortress Press, 1994), 70.

95. Sinclair, "Healing," 249–57, especially 249–51.

96. Hooker, *Saint Mark*, 68.

97. On the issue that the "messianic secret" is one motif among many, see Räisänen, *Messianic Secret*, 228; Kingsbury, *Christology*, 11.

Chapter 5: Making the Parts into a Whole

1. Rosalind Thomas, *Literacy and Orality in Ancient Greece* (Cambridge: Cambridge University Press, 1992), 103; see also John D. Harvey, "Orality and Its Implications for Biblical Studies: Recapturing an Ancient Paradigm," *JETS* 45, no. 1 (2002): 102–3; Christopher Bryan, *A Preface to Mark: Notes on*

the Gospel in Its Literary and Cultural Settings (New York: Oxford University Press, 1993), 68–71; Richard Horsley, *Hearing the Whole Story: The Politics of Plot in Mark's Gospel* (Louisville: Westminster John Knox, 2001), 61; Paul J. Achtemeier, "*Omne verbum sonat:* The New Testament and the Oral Environment of Late Western Antiquity," *JBL* 109, no. 3 (1990): 15. For a history of the development of scholarship on oral theory, see John D. Harvey, *Listening to the Text: Oral Patterning in Paul's Letters* (Grand Rapids: Baker, 1998), 1–16; Eric Havelock, "The Oral-Literate Equation: A Formula for the Modern Mind," in *Literacy and Orality*, ed. David R. Olson and Nancy Torrance (Cambridge: Cambridge University Press, 1991), 11–27.

2. See John Miles Foley, *Traditional Oral Epic: The* Odyssey, Beowulf, *and the Serbo-Croatian Return Song* (Berkeley: University of California Press, 1990); Horsley, *Hearing the Whole Story*, 61.

3. Achtemeier, "*Omne*," 16; see also Whitney Shiner, *Proclaiming the Gospel: First-Century Performance of Mark* (Harrisburg: Trinity Press International, 2003), 18; Joanna Dewey, "The Survival of Mark's Gospel: A Good Story?" *JBL* 123, no. 3 (2004): 497–98.

4. See Achtemeier, "*Omne*," 16.

5. Jesper Svenbro postulates that reading aloud is also a function of the ancient Greek practice of writing in *scriptio continua*; see *Phrasikleia: An Anthropology of Reading in Ancient Greece* (Ithaca: Cornell University Press, 1993), 45.

6. See Achtemeier, "*Omne*," 11–12. Werner Kelber offers brief but helpful comments on the preponderance of texts in the ancient Near East; see Werner H. Kelber, *The Oral and the Written Gospel: The Hermeneutics of Speaking and Writing in the Synoptic Tradition, Mark, Paul, and Q* (Bloomington: Indiana University Press, 1997), 15–16.

7. William V. Harris, *Ancient Literacy* (Cambridge: Harvard University Press, 1989), 22.

8. Harry Y. Gamble, *Books and Readers in the Early Church: A History of Early Christian Texts* (New Haven: Yale University Press, 1995), 10.

9. See Joanna Dewey, "The Gospel of Mark as an Oral-Aural Event: Implications for Interpretation," in *The New Literary Criticism and the New Testament*, ed. Elizabeth Struthers Malbon and Edgar V. McKnight (Sheffield: Sheffield Academic, 1994), 146.

10. Carolyn Osiek, "The Oral World of Early Christianity in Rome," in *Judaism and Christianity in First Century Rome*, ed. Karl P. Donfried and Peter Richardson (Grand Rapids: Eerdmans, 1998), 160; see also Lucretia B. Yaghjian, "Ancient Reading," in *The Social Sciences and New Testament Interpretation*, ed. Richard L. Rohrbaugh (Peabody, Mass.: Hendrickson, 1996), 208–9.

11. See Richard L. Rohrbaugh, "The Social Location of the Marcan Audience," *BTB* 23 (1993): 114–27.

12. Joanna Dewey, for example, goes so far as to state, "It is indisputable that Mark was heard by early Christians, not read by them. *All* literature in antiquity was composed for the ear, not the eye" (Mark as Aural Narrative:

Structures as Clues to Understanding," *STRev* 36 [1992]: 46); see also Robert Fowler, *Let the Reader Understand: Reader-Response Criticism and the Gospel of Mark* (Harrisburg: Trinity Press International, 1996), 84.

13. For a brief discussion of particular characteristics of oral/aural culture that Mark bears, see Kelber, "Mark's Oral Legacy," chap. 2 in *Oral and Written Gospel*, especially 64–80.

14. See especially Walter J. Ong, *Orality and Literacy: The Technologizing of the Word* (London: Routledge, 1982), 36.

15. Dewey, "Oral-Aural Event," 149. "Literature that was meant to be heard, like the Gospel of Mark, is typically episodic and makes connections not so much by linear progression as by various forms of repetition" (David Rhoads, Joanna Dewey, and Donald Michie, *Mark as Story: An Introduction to the Narrative of a Gospel*, 2d ed. [Minneapolis: Fortress Press, 1999], 47); see also Whitney Shiner, "Creating Plot in Episodic Narratives: *The Life of Aesop* and the Gospel of Mark, in *Ancient Fiction and Early Christian Narrative*, ed. Ronald F. Hock, J. Bradley Chance, and Judith Perkins (Atlanta: Scholars, 1998), 155–76.

16. Ong, *Orality and Literacy*, 38.

17. See Rudolf Bultmann, *The History of the Synoptic Tradition*, trans. John Marsh (New York: Harper & Row, 1963), 209ff.

18. In fact, one goal of the form critics was to recover the earliest, oral form of the traditions that were recorded in written form in the Gospels; see Klaus Berger, "Form Criticism: New Testament," *Dictionary of Biblical Interpretation* (Nashville: Abingdon, 1999), 413–17.

19. For helpful analyses of redundancy in the NT, see also Ronald D. Witherup, "Functional Redundancy in the Acts of the Apostles: A Case Study," *JSNT* 48 (1992): 67–86; idem, "Cornelius Over and Over Again: 'Functional Redundancy' in the Acts of the Apostles," *JSNT* 49 (1993): 45–66; Janice Capel Anderson, "Double and Triple Stories, the Implied Reader, and Redundancy in Matthew," *Semeia* 31(1985): 71–90; Robert C. Tannehill, "The Composition of Acts 3–5: Narrative Development and Echo Effect," in *Society of Biblical Literature 1984 Seminar Papers*, ed. Kent Harold Richards (Chico, Calif.: Scholars, 1984), 217–40.

20. Ong also notes that redundancy is necessary in oral cultures because, throughout most of human history, orators have spoken without amplification. Repetition is a means of making sure that one speaking before a large crowd is heard; see *Orality and Literacy*, 40.

21. Kelber, *Oral and Written Gospel*, 67.

22. Frank Kermode, *The Genesis of Secrecy: On the Interpretation of Narrative* (Cambridge: Harvard University Press, 1979), 69.

23. Dewey remarks that to those who are "accustomed to print narrative, the additive style appears to have no clear plot at all" ("Mark as Aural Narrative," 49); see also idem, "Mark as Interwoven Tapestry: Forecasts and Echoes for a Listening Audience," *CBQ* 53 (1991), esp. 224.

24. Dewey, "Mark as Aural Narrative," 49, italics hers; see also Dewey, "Oral-Aural Event," 149–50; Horsley, *Hearing the Whole Story*, 75.

25. Wolfgang Iser, "The Reading Process: A Phenomenological Approach," in *Reader-Response Criticism: From Formalism to Post-Structuralism*, ed. Jane P. Tompkins (Baltimore: Johns Hopkins University Press, 1980), 55.

26. See also Meir Sternberg, "Gaps, Ambiguity, and the Reading Process," chap. 6 in *The Poetics of Biblical Narrative: Ideological Literature and the Drama of Reading* (Bloomington: Indiana University Press, 1985).

27. Ong, *Orality and Literacy*, 42.

28. Compare Chris Shea's account of "missing" details in Xenophon's *Ephesiaca*: "[T]he narrator had no need to supply details which his audience could see in front of them" ("Setting the Stage for Romances: Xenophon of Ephesus and the Ecphrasis," in *Ancient Fiction and Early Christian Literature*, ed. Ronald F. Hock, J. Bradley Chance, and Judith Perkins [Atlanta: Scholars, 1998], 72).

29. *Rhet. Her.* 1.9.14 (LCL).

30. For an article that discusses progression and changes in expectations in relation to Mark's Gospel, see Robert C. Tannehill, "The Disciples in Mark: The Function of a Narrative Role," *JR* 57, no. 4 (1977): 386–405, especially 388–89.

31. Meir Sternberg notes that gaps can occur from a narrative event's running counter to established norms; see *Poetics*, 249.

32. Tannehill, "Disciples," 396; see also Fowler's discussion of "incongruity" in *Let the Reader Understand*, 164.

33. For example, see Tannehill, "Composition"; idem, "Disciples"; David Rhoads, "Jesus and the Syrophoenician Woman in Mark: A Narrative-Critical Study," *JAAR* 62, no. 2 (1994): 343–75; Janice Capel Anderson, "Double and Triple Stories, the Implied Reader, and Redundancy in Matthew," *Semeia* 31 (1985): 71–89; Kelber, *Oral and Written Gospel*, 46ff.; Bryan, *Preface to Mark*, 75ff.; Sternberg, "The Structure of Repetition: Strategies of Informational Redundancy," chap. 11 in *Poetics*; Witherup, "Redundancy," 70; Dewey, "Mark as Interwoven Tapestry," 225; Eric Havelock, *Preface to Plato* (Cambridge: Harvard University Press, 1982), 147ff.

34. Rhoads, "Syrophoenician," 351.

35. Kelber, *Oral and Written Gospel*, 49. He does not refer to these as "healing stories," but as "heroic stories."

36. Ibid., 54. He refers to exorcism stories as "polarization stories."

37. Tannehill, "Composition," 229.

38. Ibid., 238.

39. Ibid., 231.

40. See Ong, *Orality and Literacy*, 40.

41. For a similar assessment of the patterns of repetition in Luke-Acts, see Tannehill, "Composition," 240.

42. See Iser, *Act of Reading*, 182.

43. See William Wrede, *The Messianic Secret*, trans. J. C. G. Greig (Cambridge: James Clarke, 1971), 124ff.

44. See Jack Dean Kingsbury, *The Christology of Mark's Gospel* (Philadelphia: Fortress Press, 1983), 21–22.

45. Heikki Räisänen, *The 'Messianic Secret' in Mark*, trans. Christopher Tuckett (Edinburgh: T. & T. Clark, 1990), 232.

46. Ibid., 240–41.

47. Jack Goody, *The Domestication of the Savage Mind* (Cambridge: Cambridge University Press, 1977), 49–50.

48. See, e.g., Aristotle, *Poet.* 25; Margaret M. Mitchell, "A Variable and Many-sorted Man: John Chrysostom's Treatment of Pauline Inconsistency," *JECS* 6 (1988): 93–111.

49. See José María Candau Morón, "Plutarch's Lysander and Sulla: Integrated Characters in Roman Historical Perspective," *AJP* 121, no. 3 (2000): 453–78.

50. *Rhet. Her.* 1.8.13 (LCL).

51. Fowler, *Let the Reader*, 155. For further discussion of indirection in the biblical texts, see Meir Sternberg, "Double Cave, Double Talk: The Indirections of Biblical Dialogue," in *"Not in Heaven": Coherence and Complexity in Biblical Narrative*, ed. Jason P. Rosenblatt and Joseph C. Sitterson Jr. (Bloomington: Indiana University Press, 1991), 28–57.

52. Fowler, *Let the Reader*, 155.

53. Ibid., 155–56.

54. Sternberg, *Poetics*, 249.

55. See Richard I. Pervo, "A Nihilist Fabula: Introducing *The Life of Aesop*," in Hock et al., eds., *Ancient Fiction*, 82.

56. See Lawrence M. Wills, *The Quest of the Historical Gospel: Mark, John, and the Origins of the Gospel Genre* (London: Routledge, 1997), 10, 16.

57. For other thematic similarities, see Pervo, "Nihilist," 77.

58. On the arrangement of the episodes in the *Life of Aesop*, see ibid., 83ff.

59. I discuss more about the social location of Mark's audience in the conclusion of this book. On the social class of Aesop's audience, Keith Hopkins writes, "Its simple prose style and unaffected humour suggest that it had a broader appeal among social strata well below the literary and power élites" (Keith Hopkins, "Novel Evidence for Roman Slavery," in *Past & Present* 138 (1993): 12.

60. On the views of slavery expressed in the *Life of Aesop*, see ibid.

61. See Aristotle, *Phgn.* 2.806b.38–807a.3.

62. References to the English translation of this story are from *The Aesop Romance*, trans. Lloyd W. Daly, in *Anthology of Greek Popular Literature*, ed. William Hanson (Bloomington: Indiana University Press, 1998); the Greek text I have used is found in Ben Edwin Perry, *Aesopica*, vol. 1 (New York: Arno, 1980); on issues of content in different recensions of the narrative, see Antonio La Penna, "Il romazo di Esopo," *Athenaeum* 40 (1962): 264–314; on theories regarding its composition and sources, see Niklas Holzberg, "Fable Books in Prose," chap. 3 in *The Ancient Fable: An Introduction* (Bloomington: Indiana University Press, 2002).

63. Aristotle, *Phgn.* 3.808a.30–31 (LCL).

64. Ibid. 6.811b.3–4.

65. Ibid. 6.812a.12. The author maintains that "excessively fair are also cowardly," while the "complexion that tends to courage is in between these two" (6.812a.13-15).

66. Aristotle, *Phgn.* 6.814a.1 (LCL).

67. Dominic Montserrat, "Experiencing the Male Body in Roman Egypt," in *When Men Were Men: Masculinity, Power, and Identity in Classical Antiquity*, ed. Lin Foxhall and John Salmon (New York: Routledge, 1998), 153; cf. LSJ, s.v. *sōma* (II) and *pais* (III).

68. See Aristotle, *Pol.* 1.2.3-5.

69. Susan (Elli) Elliott, "Phrygia," in *Eerdmans Dictionary of the Bible*, ed. David Noel Freedman, Allen C. Myers, and Astrid B. Beck (Grand Rapids: Eerdmans, 2000).

70. See Catherine Atherton, "Children, Animals, Slaves, and Grammar," in *Pedagogy and Power: Rhetorics of Classical Learning*, ed. Yun Lee Too and Niall Livingstone (Cambridge: Cambridge University Press, 1998), 214.

71. See Bruce J. Malina and Jerome H. Neyrey, "Honor and Shame in Luke-Acts: Pivotal Values of the Mediterranean World," in *The Social World of Luke-Acts*, ed. Jerome H. Neyrey (Peabody, Mass.: Hendrickson, 1991), 32.

72. Pervo, "Nihilist," 101.

73. Cf. Shiner, "Creating Plot," 175.

74. Suetonius, *Poet. Verg.* 28-30 (LCL).

75. Lucian, *Demon.* 11.

76. Ibid., 63.

77. Particularly, it may represent the consequence of offending Apollo, since Aesop has offended Apollo earlier in the story (100) and his death occurs at the home of Apollo's oracle. Pervo argues that the *Life of Aesop* involves a protest against the values of beauty and order represented by Apollo; see "Nihilist," 107ff.

78. Ibid., 80.

Conclusion: *Why* This *Story, Told in* This *Way*

1. See the discussion of this issue in Dwight Peterson, *The Origins of Mark: The Markan Community in Current Debate* (Boston: Brill, 2000).

2. Werner H. Kelber, *The Oral and the Written Gospel: The Hermeneutics of Speaking and Writing in the Synoptic Tradition, Mark, Paul, and Q* (Bloomington: Indiana University Press, 1997), 24.

3. Kirk Dombrowski, *Against Culture: Development, Politics, and Religion in Indian Alaska* (Lincoln: University of Nebraska Press, 2001), 11–12.

4. Abraham J. Malherbe, " 'Not in a Corner': Early Christian Apologetic in Acts 26:26," *SecCent* 5, no. 4 (1985/1986): 196.

5. Ibid.

6. See Richard Rohrbaugh, "The Social Location of the Marcan Audience," *BTB* 23 (1993): 114–27.

7. See John R. Donahue, "Windows and Mirrors: The Setting of Mark's Gospel," *CBQ* 57 (1995): 22; Malherbe, "Not in a Corner," 198; Bruce J. Malina and Jerome H. Neyrey, "Honor and Shame in Luke-Acts: Pivotal Values

of the Mediterranean World," in *The Social World of Luke-Acts*, ed. Jerome H. Neyrey (Peabody, Mass.: Hendrickson, 1991), 27.

8. Tacitus, *Hist.*, 15.44 (LCL).

9. C. Clifton Black, "Was Mark a Roman Gospel?" *ExpTim* 105 (1993): 37.

10. Scholars who posit Roman provenance include William L. Lane, *The Gospel according to Mark,* New International Commentary on the New Testament (Grand Rapids: Eerdmans, 1974); Donahue, "Windows"; Martin Hengel, *Studies in the Gospel of Mark* (Philadelphia: Fortress Press, 1985); D. E. Nineham, *Saint Mark* (Philadelphia: Westminster, 1963); Ernest Best, *Mark: The Gospel as Story* (Edinburgh: T. & T. Clark, 1983); C. E. B. Cranfield, *The Gospel according to Saint Mark* (Cambridge: Cambridge University Press, 1959); Black ("Roman Gospel") leans in this direction; for a summary and critique of the major arguments for Roman provenance, see Joel Marcus, *Mark 1–8: A New Translation with Introduction and Commentary,* The Anchor Bible Commentary (New York: Doubleday, 2000); see also E. Earle Ellis, "The Date and Provenance of Mark's Gospel," in *The Four Gospels 1992: Festschrift Frans Neirynck*, vol. 2, ed. F. Van Segbroeck et al. (Leuven: University Press, 1992), 801–15; John R. Donahue, "The Quest for the Community of Mark's Gospel," in ibid., 817–38; for an account of Mark as addressing the Neronic persecution, see Lane, *Gospel of Mark*, 15; Donahue, "Windows."

11. See Black, "Roman Gospel," 36; Ellis, "Date and Provenance," 801–7.

12. See, Donahue, "Quest," 817; Willi Marxsen, *Der Evangelist Markus: Studien zur Redaktionsgeschichte des Evangeliums* (Göttingen: Vandenhoeck & Ruprecht, 1956).

13. See, for example, Ellis, "Date and Provenance," 811ff.; Willi Marxsen, *Mark the Evangelist: Studies on the Redaction History of the Gospel*, trans. James Boyce, Donald Juel, and William Poehlmann, with Roy A. Harrisville (Nashville: Abingdon, 1969), 54–116; T. J. Weeden, *Mark: Traditions in Conflict* (Philadelphia: Fortress Press, 1971); H. C. Kee, *Community of the New Age: Studies in Mark's Gospel* (Macon, Ga.: Mercer University Press, 1983); Richard Horsley, *Hearing the Whole Story: The Politics of Plot in Mark's Gospel* (Louisville: Westminster John Knox, 2001); Gerd Theissen, *The Gospels in Context: Social and Political History in the Synoptic Tradition*, trans. Linda M. Maloney (Minneapolis: Fortress Press, 1991); for a summary of arguments for Galilean provenance, see Ellis, "Date and Provenance," 810ff.; see also Donahue, "Quest," *passim.*

14. Joel Marcus, "The Jewish War and the *Sitz im Leben* of Mark," *JBL* 111, no. 3 (1992): 462.

15. Robert A. Guelich, *Mark 1—8:26,* Word Biblical Commentary (Nashville: Thomas Nelson, 1989), xliii; see also xxx; cf. B. M. F. van Iersel, "The Gospel according to St. Mark—Written for a Persecuted Community?" *NedTT* 34 (1980): 16; Morna D. Hooker, *The Gospel according to Saint Mark*, Black's New Testament Commentary (Peabody, Mass.: Hendrickson, 1991), 8.

16. It is possible that the evangelist envisions a potential persecution, rather than an actual one, but evidence for a definitive conclusion is lacking; see van Iersel, "Persecuted Community," 35.

17. For a brief summary of the major arguments for a persecuted Markan community, see Marcus, *Mark 1–8*, 28–29; for a more detailed analysis, see van Iersel, "Persecuted Community," 15–36.

18. Hooker, *Saint Mark*, 131.

19. Cf. Mary Ann Tolbert, "The Good Earth and the Rocky Ground," chap. 9 in *Sowing the Gospel: Mark's World in Literary-Historical Perspective* (Minneapolis: Fortress Press, 1989); Donahue, "Windows," especially 17–19, 24–25.

20. Marcus, *Mark 1–8*, 29.

21. See R. T. France, *Gospel of Mark: A Commentary on the Greek Text*, New International Greek Testament Commentary (Grand Rapids: Eerdmans, 2002), 416–17; Hooker, *Saint Mark*, 246–47.

22. See France, *Gospel of Mark*, 416–17; Hooker, *Saint Mark*, 247.

23. Marcus, "Jewish War," 447.

24. See David M. May, "Mark 3:20-35 from the Perspective of Honor/Shame," *BTB* 17 (1987): 83–87.

25. It seems clear that *hoi par autou* refers to Jesus' relatives; see the discussion of this issue in John Dominic Crossan, "Mark and the Relatives of Jesus," *NovT* 15 (1973): 84–85.

26. Cf. May, "Mark 3," 85; see Bruce J. Malina and Richard L. Rohrbaugh, *Social-Science Commentary on the Synoptic Gospels* (Minneapolis: Fortress Press, 1992), 158.

27. J. Lambrecht, "The Relatives of Jesus in Mark," *NovT* 16 (1974): 257; cf. Matt 10:37-39//Luke 14:26-27.

28. Halvor Moxnes, "Honor and Shame," *BTB* 23 (1993): 172; see also Jerome H. Neyrey, *Honor and Shame in the Gospel of Matthew* (Louisville: Westminster John Knox, 1998), 52–55; Lambrecht, "Relatives," 257–58; Ernest Best, "Mark III. 20. 21, 31-35," *NTS* 22 (1976): 317–18; Malina and Rohrbaugh, *Social-Science Commentary*, 159, 377.

29. DeSilva, *Honor, Patronage*, 43. He takes up this issue more extensively in *The Hope of Glory: Honor Discourse and New Testament Interpretation* (Collegeville, Minn.: Liturgical, 1999).

30. Cf. Jerome H. Neyrey, "Despising the Shame of the Cross: Honor and Shame in the Johannine Passion Narrative," *Semeia* 68 (1994): 115; Malina and Neyrey, "Honor and Shame," 27.

31. Cf. Neyrey, "Despising the Shame," 119.

32. Lendon, *Empire of Honour*, 92–93.

33. Ibid., 93.

34. *Mart. Pol.* 14.1 (LCL).

35. See Lendon, *Empire of Honour*, 93.

36. *Diog.* 5.14 (LCL).

37. John Chrysostom, *De Inan. Glor.* 15; citation from Lendon, *Empire of Honour*, 92.

38. Frank Kermode, *The Genesis of Secrecy: On the Interpretation of Narrative* (Cambridge: Harvard University Press, 1979), 143.

Appendix

1. This account of the structure of 2:1—3:6 draws on the concentric structure identified by Joanna Dewey in "Mark as Aural Narrative: Structures as Clues to Understanding," *STRev* 36 (1992): 51.

ABBREVIATIONS

Journals

AJP	*American Journal of Philology*
BTB	*Biblical Theology Bulletin*
CBQ	*Catholic Biblical Quarterly*
ExpTim	*Expository Times*
HTR	*Harvard Theological Review*
JAAR	*Journal of the American Academy of Religion*
JBL	*Journal of Biblical Literature*
JECS	*Journal of Early Christian Studies*
JETS	*Journal of the Evangelical Theological Society*
JR	*Journal of Religion*
JSJ	*Journal for the Study of Judaism*
JSNT	*Journal for the Study of the New Testament*
NedTT	*Nederlands theologisch Tijdschrift*

NovT	*Novum Testamentum*
NTS	*New Testament Studies*
PACE	*Professional Approaches for Christian Educators*
PRS	*Perspectives in Religious Studies*
SecCent	*The Second Century*
SLJT	*St. Luke's Journal of Theology*
STRev	*Sewanee Theological Review*

Classical and Early Christian Literature

1 Clem.	*1 Clement*
A.J.	Josephus, *Antiquitates judaicae*
Alc.	Euripides, *Alcestis*
Alex.	Plutarch, *Alexander*
Amic. mult.	Plutarch, *De amicorum multitudine*
An seni	Plutarch, *An seni respublica gerenda sit*
Ant.	Josephus, *Jewish Antiquities*
Arch.	Cicero, *Pro Archia*
Aug.	Suetonius, *Divus Augustus*
Bacch.	Euripides, *Bacchae*
Ben.	Seneca, *De beneficiis*
B.J.	Josephus, *Bellum judaicum*
Caes.	Plutarch, *Caesar*
Cels.	Origen, *Contra Celsum*
Clem.	Seneca, *De clementia*
Cupid. divit.	Plutarch, *De cupiditate divitiarum*
Cyr.	Xenophon, *Cyropaedia*
De Inan. Glor.	John Chrysostom, *De inani gloria*
Demon.	Lucian, *Demonax*
De mort. Peregr.	Lucian, *De morte Peregrini*
Diog.	*Epistle to Diognetus*
Ep.	Seneca, *Epistulae morales*
Gorg.	Plato, *Gorgias*
Gos. Thos.	*Gospel of Thomas*
Gramm.	Suetonius, *De grammaticis*
Hist.	Tacitus, *Historiae*
Ign. Eph.	Ignatius, *To the Ephesians*
Inim. Util.	Plutarch, *De capienda ex inimicis utilitate*
In Verr.	Cicero, *In Verrem*
Ira	Seneca, *De Ira*
Is.Os.	Plutarch, *De Iside et Osiride*

J.W.	Josephus, *Jewish War* (*Bellum Judaicum*)
Lat. viv.	Plutarch, *De latenter vivendo*
Mart. Pol.	*Martyrdom of Polycarp*
Max. Princ.	Plutarch, *Maxime cum principibus philosophiam esse disserendum*
Mem.	Xenophon, *Memorabilia*
Metam.	Apuleius, *Metamorphoses*
Mos.	Philo, *De vita Mosis*
Nigr.	Lucian, *Nigrinus*
Num.	Plutarch, *Numa*
Off.	Cicero, *De Officiis*
On Poet. Ter.	Suetonius
Phgn.	Aristotle, *Physiognomonica*
Phoen.	Euripides, *Phoenissae*
Poet.	Aristotle, *Poetica*
Poet. Verg.	Suetonius
Pol.	Aristotle, *Politica*
Pyrrh.	Plutarch, *Pyrrhus*
Rab. Perd.	Cicero, *Pro Rabirio Perduellionis Reo*
Rhet.	Aristotle, *Rhetorica*
Rhet.	Suetonius, *De rhetoribus*
Rhet. Her.	*Rhetorica ad Herennium*
Sacr.	Philo, *De sacrificiis Abelis et Caini*
Sat.	Juvenal, *Satirae*
Sat.	Persius, *Satirae*
Spec.	Philo, *De specialibus legibus*
V.A.	Philostratus, *Vita Apollonii* (LCL)
Vesp.	Suetonius, *Vespasianus*
Vit. Apoll.	Philostratus, *Vita Apollonii*
Vit. pud.	Plutarch, *De vitioso pudore*

Other

LCL	Loeb Classical Library
LSJ	Liddell, H. G., R. Scott, and H. S. Jones. *A Greek-English Lexicon*. 9th ed. with rev. supp.
TDNT	*Theological Dictionary of the New Testament*.

Bibliography

I. Texts, Translations, and Reference Works

Achilles Tatius. *Leucippe and Clitophon*. Trans. Tim Whitmarsh. New York: Oxford University Press, 2002.

Aelius Aristides. *The Complete Works*. Trans. Charles A. Behr. Leiden: Brill, 1981.

Apostolic Fathers. Trans. Kirsopp Lake. 2 vols. Loeb Classical Library. Cambridge: Harvard University Press, 1959.

Apuleius. *The Golden Ass*. Trans. W. Adlington; rev. S. Gaselee. Cambridge: Harvard University Press, 1971.

Aristeas to Philocrates. Trans. Moses Hadas. Jewish Apocryphal Literature. New York: Ktav, 1973.

Aristotle. Trans. H. P. Cooke, et al. 23 vols. Loeb Classical Library. Cambridge: Harvard University Press, 1926–1995.

Barfield, Thomas, ed. *The Dictionary of Anthropology*. Oxford: Blackwell, 1997.

Betz, Hans-Dieter, ed. *The Greek Magical Papyri in Translation, Including the Demotic Spells.* Chicago: University of Chicago Press, 1986.

Cartlidge, David R., and David L. Dungan. *Documents for the Study of the Gospels.* Rev. ed. Minneapolis: Fortress Press, 1994.

Cassius Dio. *Roman History.* Trans. Earnest Cary and Herbert B. Foster. 9 vols. Loeb Classical Library. Cambridge: Harvard University Press, 1954–1961.

Charlesworth, James H., ed. *Old Testament Pseudepigrapha.* 2 vols. New York: Doubleday, 1983.

Cicero. Trans. H. M. Hubbell et al. 29 vols. Loeb Classical Library. Cambridge: Harvard University Press, 1900–1972.

Dio Chrysostom. Trans. J. W. Cohoon and H. Lamar Crosby. Loeb Classical Library. Cambridge: Harvard University Press, 1949–1962.

Diogenes Laertius. *Lives of Eminent Philosophers.* Trans. R. D. Hicks. Loeb Classical Library. Cambridge: Harvard University Press, 1995.

Euripides. Trans. David Kovacs. Loeb Classical Library. Cambridge: Harvard University Press, 1994–2002.

Freedman, David Noel, Allen C. Myers, and Astrid B. Beck, eds. *Eerdmans Dictionary of the Bible.* Grand Rapids: Eerdmans, 2000.

Freedman, David Noel, et al., eds. *Anchor Bible Dictionary.* 6 vols. New York: Doubleday, 1992.

Hansen, William, ed. *Anthology of Greek Popular Literature.* Bloomington: Indiana University Press, 1998.

Hornblower, Simon, and Antony Spawforth. *The Oxford Classical Dictoinary.* 3d ed. Oxford: Oxford University Press, 1999.

Josephus. Trans. H. St. J. Thackeray et al. 10 vols. Loeb Classical Library. Cambridge: Harvard University Press, 1926–1965.

Juvenal and Persius. Trans. G. G. Ramsay. Loeb Classical Library. Cambridge: Harvard University Press, 1993.

Kittel, Gerhard, and Gerhard Friedrich, eds. *Theological Dictionary of the New Testament.* Trans. Geoffrey W. Bromiley. 10 vols. Grand Rapids: Eerdmans, 1964–1976.

Liddell, H. G., R. Scott, and H. S. Jones. *A Greek-English Lexicon.* 9th ed. with rev. supp. New York: Oxford University Press, 1996.

Lucian. Trans. A. M. Harmon. 8 vols. Loeb Classical Library. Cambridge: Harvard University Press, 1955.

Malherbe, Abraham, ed. *The Cynic Epistles: A Study Edition.* Society of Biblical Literature Sources for Biblical Study 12. Missoula: Scholars, 1977.

Metzger, Bruce M. *A Textual Commentary on the Greek New Testament.* 2d ed. Stuttgart: United Bible Societies, 1994.

Nida, E. A., et al. *Style and Discourse, with Special Reference to the Text of the Greek New Testament.* Cape Town: Bible Society, 1983.

Perry, Ben Edwin, ed. *Aesopica,* vol. 1. New York: Arno, 1980.

Philo. Trans. F. H. Colson, G. H. Whitaker, and Ralph Marcus. 10 vols. Loeb Classical Library. Cambridge: Harvard University Press, 1929–1956.

Philostratus. Trans. Christopher P. Jones et al. 4 vols. Loeb Classical Library. Cambridge: Harvard University Press, 1922–2005.

Plato. Trans. H. N. Fowler. 12 vols. Loeb Classical Library. Cambridge: Harvard University Press, 1917–1962.

Plutarch's Lives. Trans. Bernadotte Perrin. 11 vols. Loeb Classical Library. New York: Macmillan, 1926.

Polybius. *Histories.* Trans. W. R. Paton. 6 vols. Loeb Classical Library. Cambridge: Harvard University Press, 1960.

Rhetorica ad Herennium. Trans. Harry Caplan. Loeb Classical Library. Cambridge: Harvard University Press, 1954.

Robinson, James, ed. *The Nag Hammadi Library.* San Francisco: HarperSanFrancisco, 1990.

Robertson, A. T. *A Grammar of the Greek New Testament in Light of Historical Research.* New York: Hodder & Stoughton, 1914.

Seneca. Trans. John W. Basore et al. 10 vols. Loeb Classical Library. Cambridge: Harvard University Press, 1913–2004.

Suetonius. Trans. J. C. Rolfe. 2 vols. Loeb Classical Library. Cambridge: Harvard University Press, 1997–1998.

Tacitus: The Histories and Annals. Trans. C. H. Moore and J. Jackson. 4 vols. Loeb Classical Library. Cambridge: Harvard University Press, 1937.

Vermes, Geza. *The Dead Sea Scrolls in English.* 4th ed. London: Penguin, 1995.

Xenophon. Trans. Carleton L. Brownson et al. 7 vols. Loeb Classical Library. Cambridge: Harvard University Press, 1918–2001.

II. Commentaries and Studies

Achtemeier, Paul J. "And He Followed Him: Miracles and Discipleship in Mark 10:46-52." *Semeia* 11 (1978): 115–45.

———. "*Omne verbum sonat:* The New Testament and the Oral Environment of Late Western Antiquity." *Journal of Biblical Literature* 109, no. 3 (1990): 3–27.

Adkins, A. W. H. *Merit and Responsibility.* Oxford: Clarendon, 1960.

Anderson, Janice Capel. "Double and Triple Stories, the Implied Reader, and Redundancy in Matthew." *Semeia* 31 (1985): 71–90.

Atherton, Catherine. "Children, Animals, Slaves, and Grammar." In *Pedagogy and Power: Rhetorics of Classical Learning*, ed. Yun Lee Too and Niall Livingstone. Cambridge: Cambridge University Press, 1998.

Atkins, G. Douglas, and Laura Morrow, eds. *Contemporary Literary Theory.* Amherst: University of Massachusetts Press, 1989.

Baroja, J. C. "Honour and Shame: A Historical Account of Several Conflicts." In *Honour and Shame*, ed. J. G. Peristiany, 79–137. London: Weidenfeld and Nicholson, 1966.

Bassler, Jouette. "The Parable of the Loaves." *Journal of Religion* 66, no. 2 (1986): 157–72.

Bates, Daniel G., and Fred Plog. *Cultural Anthropology.* 3d ed. New York: McGraw-Hill, 1990.

Bauckham, Richard. *The Gospels for All Christians: Rethinking the Gospel Audiences.* Grand Rapids: Eerdmans, 1998.

Bergant, Diane. "'My Beloved is Mine and I am His' (Song 2:16)." *Semeia* 68 (1994): 23–40.

Best, Ernest. *Mark: The Gospel as Story.* Edinburgh: T. & T. Clark, 1983.

———."Mark III. 20, 21, 31-35." *New Testament Studies* 22 (1976): 309–19.

Black, C. Clifton. *The Disciples according to Mark: Markan Redaction in Current Debate.* JSNT Supplement Series 27. Sheffield: Sheffield Academic, 1989.

———. "Was Mark a Roman Gospel?" *Expository Times* 105 (1993): 36–40.

Blackburn, Barry. Theios Anēr *and the Markan Miracle Traditions: A Critique of the* Theios Anēr *Concept as an Interpretive Background of the Miracle Traditions Used by Mark.* Tübingen: J. C. B. Mohr (Paul Siebeck), 1991.

Blevins, James L. *The Messianic Secret in Markan Research, 1901–1976.* Washington, D.C.: University Press of America, 1981.

Bok, Sissela. *Secrets: On the Ethics of Concealment and Revelation.* New York: Pantheon, 1982.

Boobyer, G. H. "Mark II, 10a and the Interpretation of the Healing of the Paralytic." *Harvard Theological Review* 47 (1954): 115–20.

———. "The Secrecy Motif in Mark's Gospel." *New Testament Studies* 6, no. 3 (1960): 225–35.

Borgen, Peder. "God's Agent in the Fourth Gospel." In *Religions in Antiquity: Essays in Memory of Erwin Ramsdell Goodenough,*" ed. Jacob Neusner, 138–48. Studies in the History of Religions. Leiden: Brill, 1968.

Boring, M. Eugene. *Mark: A Commentary.* New Testament Library. Louisville: Westminster John Knox, 2006.

Bornkamm, Günther. *Jesus of Nazareth.* Trans. Irene and Fraser McLuskey, with James M. Robinson. New York: Harper & Row, 1960.

Bowersock, G. W. Review of *Ancient Literacy,* by William V. Harris. *New Republic* 202, no. 14 (1990): 37–40.

Brandes, Stanley. "Reflections on Honor and Shame in the Mediterranean." In *Honor and Shame and the Unity of the Mediterranean,* ed. David D. Gilmore, 121–34. Washington, D.C.: American Anthropological Association, 1987.

Bruell, Christopher. "Literacy and Social Class in Antiquity." Review of *Ancient Literacy,* by William V. Harris. *Review of Politics* 52, no. 3 (1990): 466–69.

Brunt, P. A. *Roman Imperial Themes.* Oxford: Clarendon, 1990.

Bryan, Christopher. *A Preface to Mark: Notes on the Gospel in Its Literary and Cultural Settings.* New York: Oxford University Press, 1993.

Bultmann, Rudolf. *The History of the Synoptic Tradition.* Trans. John Marsh. New York: Harper & Row, 1963.

Burkert, Walter. *Ancient Mystery Cults.* Cambridge: Harvard University Press, 1987.

Burkill, T. A. "Mysterious Revelation." In *The Messianic Secret*, ed. Christopher Tuckett, 44–48. Philadelphia: Fortress Press, 1983.

Charlesworth, James H. "From Messianology to Christology: Problems and Prospects." In *The Messiah: Developments in Earliest Judaism and Christianity*, ed. James H. Charlesworth, 3–35. Minneapolis: Fortress Press, 1992.

————. "The Son of David: Solomon and Jesus (Mark 10.47)." In *The New Testament and Hellenistic Judaism*, ed. Peder Borgen and Søren Giversen, 72–87. Peabody, Mass.: Hendrickson, 1997.

Chronis, Harry L. "To Reveal and to Conceal: A Literary-Critical Perspective on 'the Son of Man' in Mark." *New Testament Studies* 51 (2005): 459–81.

Collins, Adela Yarbro. "The Apocalyptic Rhetoric of Mark 13 in Historical Context." *Biblical Research* 41 (1996): 5–36.

————. *The Beginning of the Gospel: Probings of Mark in Context*. Minneapolis: Fortress Press, 1992.

————. "The Eschatological Discourse of Mark 13." In *The Four Gospels, 1992: Festschrift Frans Neirynck*, vol. 2, ed. F. Van Segbroeck et al., 1125–40. Bibliotheca Ephemeridum Theologicarum Lovaniensium. Leuven: University Press, 1992.

————. *Mark: A Commentary*. Hermeneia. Minneapolis: Fortress Press, 2007.

————. "Mark and His Readers: The Son of God among the Jews." *Harvard Theological Review* 92, no. 4 (1999): 393–408.

————. "Messianic Secret and the Gospel of Mark: Secrecy in Jewish Apocalypticism, the Hellenistic Mystery Religions, and Magic," in *Rending the Veil: Concealment and Secrecy in the History of Religions*, ed. Elliot R. Wolfson (New York: Seven Bridges, 1999), 11–30.

Collins, John N. "*Diakonia: Re-interpreting the Ancient Sources*." New York: Oxford University Press, 1990.

Cotter, Wendy. *Miracles in Greco-Roman Antiquity: A Sourcebook for the Study of the New Testament Miracle Stories*. New York: Routledge, 1999.

Coutts, John. "The Messianic Secret and the Enemies of Jesus." In *Studia Biblica 1978 [2] II*, ed. E. A. Livingstone, 37–46. Sheffield: JSOT, 1980.

Cranfield, C. E. B. *The Gospel According to Saint Mark*. Cambridge: Cambridge University Press, 1959.

Crossan, John Dominic. "Mark and the Relatives of Jesus." *Novum Testamentum* 15 (1973): 81–113.

Dahl, Nils Alstrup. "The Purpose of Mark's Gospel." In *The Messianic Secret*, ed. Christopher Tuckett, 29–34. Philadelphia: Fortress Press, 1983.

Danker, Frederick W. *Benefactor: Epigraphic Study of a Graeco-Roman and New Testament Semantic Field*. St. Louis, Mo.: Clayton Publishing House, 1982.

Delaney, Carol. "Seeds of Honor, Fields of Shame." In *Honor and Shame and the Unity of the Mediterranean*, ed. David D. Gilmore, 35–48. Washington, D.C.: American Anthropological Association, 1987.

Derrett, J. Duncan M. "Contributions to the Study of the Gerasene Demoniac." *Journal for the Study of the New Testament* 3 (1979): 2–17.

de Tillese, C. Minette. *Le secret messianique dans l'évangile de Marc.* Lectio Divina 47. Paris: Cerf, 1968.

deSilva, David A. "Despising Shame: A Cultural-Anthropological Investigation of the Epistle to the Hebrews." *Journal of Biblical Literature* 113, no. 3 (1994): 439–61.

————. *Honor, Patronage, Kinship & Purity: Unlocking New Testament Culture.* Downers Grove, Ill.: InterVarsity, 2000.

————. *The Hope of Glory: Honor Discourse and New Testament Interpretation.* Collegeville, Minn.: Liturgical, 1999.

Dewey, Joanna. "The Gospel of Mark as an Oral-Aural Event: Implications for Interpretation." In *The New Literary Criticism and the New Testament,* ed. Elizabeth Struthers Malbon and Edgar V. McKnight, 145–63. JSNT Supplement Series 109. Sheffield: Sheffield Academic, 1994.

————. "Jesus' Healings of Women: Conformity and Non-Conformity to Dominant Cultural Values as Clues for Historical Reconstruction." *Biblical Theology Bulletin* 24 (1994): 122–31.

————. "'Let Them Renounce Themselves and Take Up Their Cross': A Feminist Reading of Mark 8:34 in Mark's Social and Narrative World." In *A Feminist Companion to Mark,* ed. Amy-Jill Levine, with Marianne Blickenstaff, 23–36. Sheffield: Sheffield Academic, 2001.

————. "Mark as Aural Narrative: Structures as Clues to Understanding." *Sewanee Theological Review* 36 (1992): 45–56.

————. "Mark as Interwoven Tapestry: Forecasts and Echoes for a Listening Audience." *Catholic Biblical Quarterly* 53 (1991): 221–36.

————. "Oral Methods of Structuring Narrative in Mark." *Interpretation* 43 (1989): 32–44.

————. "Orality and Textuality in Early Christian Literature." *Semeia* 65 (1994): 1–216.

————. "The Survival of Mark's Gospel: A Good Story?" *Journal of Biblical Literature* 123, no. 3 (2004): 495–507.

Dibelius, Martin. *From Tradition to Gospel.* Trans. Bertram Lee Woolf. New York: Charles Scribner's Sons, n.d.

Dombrowski, Kirk. *Against Culture: Development, Politics, and Religion in Indian Alaska.* Lincoln: University of Nebraska Press, 2001.

Donahue, John R. "The Quest for the Community of Mark's Gospel." In *The Four Gospels 1992: Festschrift Frans Neirynck,* vol. 2, ed. F. Van Segbroeck et al., 817–38. Leuven: University Press, 1992.

————. "Windows and Mirrors: The Setting of Mark's Gospel." *The Catholic Biblical Quarterly* 57 (1995): 1–26.

————, and Daniel J. Harrington. *The Gospel of Mark.* Sacra Pagina 2. Collegeville: Liturgical, 2002.

Douglas, Mary. *Purity and Danger: An Analysis of the Concepts of Pollution and Taboo.* London: Ark Paperbacks, 1984.

Downing, F. Gerald. *Christ and the Cynics: Jesus and Other Radical Preachers in First-Century Tradition.* Sheffield: Sheffield Academic, 1988.

————. "Cynics and Christians." *New Testament Studies* 30 (1984): 584–93.

Duling, Dennis. "Matthew's Plurisignificant 'Son of David' in Social-Science Perspective: Kinship, Kingship, Magic and Miracle." *Biblical Theology Bulletin* 22 (1992): 99–116.

————. "Solomon, Exorcism, and the Son of David." *Harvard Theological Review* 68 (1975): 235–52.

————. "The Therapeutic Son of David." *New Testament Studies* 24 (1978): 392–410.

Dunderberg, Ismo, Christopher Tuckett, and Kari Syreeni, eds. *Fair Play: Diversity and Conflicts in Early Christianity: Essays in Honor of Heikki Räisänen.* Leiden: Brill, 2002.

Dunn, James D. G. "The Messianic Secret in Mark." In *The Messianic Secret*, ed. Christopher Tuckett, 116–31. Philadelphia: Fortress Press, 1983.

Edwards, James R. *The Gospel according to Mark.* Grand Rapids: Eerdmans, 2002.

Elliott, John H. "Patronage and Clientage." In *The Social Sciences and New Testament Interpretation*, ed. Richard Rohrbaugh, 144–56. Peabody, Mass.: Hendrickson, 1996.

Elliott, Neil. "The Silence of the Messiah: The Function of 'Messianic Secret' Motifs across the Synoptics." In *Society of Biblical Literature Seminar Papers, 1993*, ed. Eugene H. Lovering, Jr., 604–22. Atlanta: Society of Biblical Literature, 1993.

Ellis, E. Earle. "The Date and Provenance of Mark's Gospel." In *The Four Gospels 1992: Festschrift Frans Neirynck*, vol. 2, ed. F. Van Segbroeck et al., 801–15. Leuven: University Press, 1992.

Ernst, Josef. "Das sog. Messiasgeheimnis—kein „Hauptschlüssel" zum Markusevangelium." In *Theologie im Werden: Studien zu den theologischen Konzeptionen im Neuen Testament*, ed. Josef Hainz, 21–56. Paderborn: Ferdinand Schöningh, 1992.

Foley, John Miles. *Traditional Oral Epic: The* Odyssey, Beowulf, *and the Serbo-Croatian Return Song.* Berkeley: University of California Press, 1990.

Fowler, Robert. *Let the Reader Understand: Reader-Response Criticism and the Gospel of Mark.* Harrisburg: Trinity Press International, 1996.

————. *Loaves and Fishes: The Function of the Feeding Stories in the Gospel of Mark.* Chico, Calif.: Scholars, 1981.

France, R. T. *Gospel of Mark: A Commentary on the Greek Text.* New International Greek Testament Commentary. Grand Rapids: Eerdmans, 2002.

Gamble, Harry Y. *Books and Readers in the Early Church: A History of Early Christian Texts.* New Haven: Yale University Press, 1995.

Geddert, Timothy J. *Watchwords: Mark 13 in Markan Eschatology.* Sheffield: Sheffield Academic, 1989.

Geyer, Douglas. *Fear, Anomaly and Uncertainty in the Gospel of Mark.* ATLA Monograph Series. Lanham: Scarecrow, 2001.

————. "Occluded Benefaction and Perspicuous Anomaly in the Gospel of Mark." Paper presented at the annual meeting of the Society of Biblical Literature. Denver, Nov. 19, 2001.

Gibson, Jeffrey B. "The Scribal Charge of Demonic Collusion in Mk 3.22: Evidence for a Break in the 'Secret'?" Paper presented at the annual meeting of the Society of Biblical Literature. Denver, Nov. 19, 2001.

Gilmore, David D. "Anthropology of the Mediterranean Area." *Annual Review of Anthropology* 11 (1982): 175–205.

————. "Introduction: The Shame of Dishonor." In *Honor and Shame and the Unity of the Mediterranean*, ed. David D. Gilmore, 2–21. Washington, D.C.: American Anthropological Association, 1987.

————, ed. *Honor and Shame and the Unity of the Mediterranean*. Washington, D.C.: American Anthropological Association, 1987.

Gilsenan, Michael. "Lying, Honor, and Contradiction." In *Transaction and Meaning: Directions in the Anthropology of Exchange and Symbolic Behavior*, ed. Bruce Kapferer, 191-219. Philadelphia: Institute for the Study of Human Issues, 1976.

Giovannini, Maureen J. "Female Chastity Codes in the Circum-Mediterranean Area: Comparative Perspectives." In *Honor and Shame and the Unity of the Mediterranean*, ed. David D. Gilmore, 61–74. Washington, D.C.: American Anthropological Association, 1987.

Goody, Jack. *The Domestication of the Savage Mind* (Cambridge: Cambridge University Press, 1977.

————. *The Interface between the Written and the Oral*. Cambridge: Cambridge University Press, 1987.

Green, William Scott. "Introduction: Messiah in Judaism; Rethinking the Question." In *Judaisms and Their Messiahs at the Turn of the Christian Era*, ed. Jacob Neusner, 1–13. New York: Cambridge University Press, 1987.

Guelich, Robert A. *Mark 1—8:26*. Word Biblical Commentary 34A. Nashville: Thomas Nelson, 1989.

Gundry, Robert. *Mark: A Commentary on His Apology for the Cross*. Grand Rapids: Eerdmans, 1993.

Hagedorn, Anselm C., and Jerome Neyrey. "'It Was Out of Envy That They Handed Jesus Over' (Mark 15:10): The Anatomy of Envy in the Gospel of Mark." *Journal for the Study of the New Testament* 69 (1998): 15–56.

Hall, Edward T. *Beyond Culture*. Garden City, N.Y.: Anchor, 1976.

Hanson, Anne E. "Ancient Illiteracy." In *Literacy in the Roman World*, ed. J. H. Humphrey, 159–98. Journal of Roman Archaeology Supplement 3. Ann Arbor: Journal of Roman Archaeology, 1991.

Hanson, K. C. "How Honorable! How Shameful! A Cultural Analysis of Matthew's Makarisms and Reproaches." *Semeia* 68 (1994): 82–111.

————. "Kinship." In *The Social Sciences and New Testament Interpretation*, ed. Richard Rohrbaugh, 62–79. Peabody, Mass.: Hedrickson, 1996.

Harris, William V. *Ancient Literacy*. Cambridge: Harvard University Press, 1989.

Harvey, John D. *Listening to the Text: Oral Patterning in Paul's Letters*. Evangelical Theological Society Studies 1. Grand Rapids: Baker, 1998.

————. "Orality and Its Implications for Biblical Studies: Recapturing an Ancient Paradigm." *Journal of the Evangelical Theological Society* 45, no. 1 (2002): 99–109.

Havelock, Eric A. *The Literate Revolution in Greece and Its Cultural Consequences.* Princeton: Princeton University Press, 1982.

————. "The Oral-Literate Equation." In *Literacy and Orality,* ed. David R. Olson and Nancy Torrance, 11–27. Cambridge: Cambridge University Press, 1991.

————. *Preface to Plato.* Cambridge: Harvard University Press, 1982.

Heil, John Paul. *Jesus Walking on the Sea: Meaning and Gospel Functions of Matt 14:22-33, Mark 6:45-52 and John 6:15b-21.* Rome: Biblical Institute Press, 1981.

Hellerman, Joseph H. "Challenging the Authority of Jesus: Mark 11:27-33 and Mediterranean Notions of Honor and Shame." *Journal of the Evangelical Theological Society* 43, no. 2 (2000): 213–28.

Henderson, Suzanne Watts. "'Concerning the Loaves': Comprehending Incomprehension in Mark 6.45-52. *Journal for the Study of the New Testament* 83 (2001): 3–26.

Hendrickson, G. L. "Ancient Reading." *Classical Journal* 25 (1929): 182–96.

Hengel, Martin. *Studies in the Gospel of Mark.* Philadelphia: Fortress Press, 1985.

Herzfeld, Michael. "'As In Your Own House': Hospitality, Ethnography, and the Stereotype of Mediterranean Society." In *Honor and Shame and the Unity of the Mediterranean,* ed. David D. Gilmore, 75–89. Washington, D.C.: American Anthropological Association, 1987.

Hobbs, T. R. "Reflections on Honor, Shame, and Covenant Relations." *Journal of Biblical Literature* 116, no. 3 (1997): 501–3.

Hock, Ronald F., J. Bradley Chance, and Judith Perkins, eds. *Ancient Fiction and Early Christian Literature.* Society of Biblical Literature Symposium Series. Atlanta: Scholars, 1998.

Holtzmann, Heinrich Julius. *Die synoptischen Evangelien, ihr Ursprung und geschichtlicher Charakter.* Leipzig: W. Engelmann, 1863.

Holtzmann, Oskar. *The Life of Jesus.* Trans. J. T. Bealby and Maurice A. Canney. London: Adam and Charles Black, 1904.

Holzberg, Niklas. *The Ancient Fable: An Introduction.* Bloomington: Indiana University Press, 2002.

Hooker, Morna D. *The Gospel according to St. Mark.* Black's New Testament Commentaries. Peabody, Mass.: Hendrickson, 1991.

Hopkins, Keith. "Novel Evidence for Roman Slavery." *Past & Present* 138 (1993): 3–27.

Horsley, Richard. *Hearing the Whole Story: The Politics of Plot in Mark's Gospel.* Louisville: Westminster John Knox, 2001.

Humphrey, J. H., ed. *Literacy in the Roman World.* Journal of Roman Archaeology Supplement 3. Ann Arbor: Journal of Roman Archaeology, 1991.

Iser, Wolfgang. *The Act of Reading: A Theory of Aesthetic Response.* Baltimore: Johns Hopkins University Press, 1978.

————. *The Implied Reader: Patterns of Communication in Prose Fiction from Bunyan to Beckett.* Baltimore: Johns Hopkins University Press, 1974.

————. "The Reading Process: A Phenomenological Approach." In *Reader-Response Criticism: From Formalism to Post-Structuralism,* ed. Jane P. Tompkins, 50–69. Baltimore: Johns Hopkins University Press, 1980.

Jauss, Hans Robert. *Toward an Aesthetic of Reception.* Trans. Timothy Bahti. Vol. 2 of *Theory and History of Literature,* ed. Wald Godzich and Jochen Schulte-Sasse. Minneapolis: University of Minnesota Press, 1982.

Johnson, Earl S. "Mark 10:46-52: Blind Bartimaeus." *Catholic Biblical Quarterly* 40 (1978): 191–204.

Johnson, Luke T. "On Finding the Lukan Community: A Cautious Cautionary Essay." In *Society of Biblical Literature Seminar Papers 1979,* ed. Paul J. Achtemeier, vol. 1, 87–100. Missoula: Scholars, 1978.

Judge, E. A. *The Social Pattern of the Christian Groups in the First Century: Some Prolegomena to the Study of New Testament Ideas of Social Obligation.* London: Tyndale, 1960.

Juel, Donald II. *The Gospel of Mark.* Interpreting Biblical Texts. Nashville: Abingdon, 1999.

_____. *A Master of Surprise: Mark Interpreted.* Minneapolis: Fortress Press, 1994.

Kealy, Seán P. *Mark's Gospel: A History of Its Interpretation; From the Beginning until 1979.* New York: Paulist, 1982.

Kee, Howard Clark. *Community of the New Age: Studies in Mark's Gospel.* Macon, Ga.: Mercer University Press, 1983.

_____. "The Terminology of Mark's Exorcism Stories." *New Testament Studies* 14 (1968): 232–46.

Kelber, Werner H. "Modalities of Communication, Cognition, and Physiology of Perception: Orality, Rhetoric, Scribality." In *Orality and Textuality in Early Christian Literature,* ed. Joanna Dewey, 193–216. Atlanta: Scholars, 1995.

_____. "Narrative and Disclosure: Mechanisms of Concealing, Revealing, and Reviling." *Semeia* 43 (1988): 1–20.

_____. *The Oral and the Written Gospel: The Hermeneutics of Speaking and Writing in the Synoptic Tradition, Mark, Paul, and Q.* Foreword by Walter J. Ong. Bloomington: Indiana University Press, 1997.

Kermode, Frank. *The Genesis of Secrecy: On the Interpretation of Narrative.* Cambridge, Mass.: Harvard University Press, 1979.

Kilgallen, John J. "The Messianic Secret and Mark's Purpose." *Biblical Theology Bulletin* 7, no. 2 (1977): 60–65.

Kingsbury, Jack Dean. *The Christology of Mark's Gospel.* Philadelphia: Fortress Press, 1983.

Kippenberg, Hans G. "Magic in Roman Civil Discourse: Why Rituals Could Be Illegal." In *Envisioning Magic: A Princeton Seminar and Symposium,* ed. Peter Schäfer and Hans G. Kippenberg, 137–63. Leiden: Brill, 1997.

Kippenberg, Hans G., and Guy G. Stroumsa, eds. *Secrecy and Concealment: Studies in the History of Mediterranean and Near Eastern Religions.* Studies in the History of Religions 65. Leiden: Brill, 1995.

Klinghardt, Matthias. "Prayer Formularies for Public Recitation. Their Use and Function in Ancient Religion." *Numen* 46 (1999): 39–52.

Koskenniemi, Erkki. "Apollonius of Tyana: A Typical ΘΕΙΟΣ ΑΝΗΡ?" *Journal of Biblical Literature* 117, no. 3 (1998): 455–67.

Lambrecht, J. "The Relatives of Jesus in Mark." *Novum Testamentum* 16 (1974): 241–58.

Lane, William L. *The Gospel according to Mark*. New International Commentary on the New Testament. Grand Rapids: Eerdmans, 1974.

La Penna, Antonio. "Il romanzo di Esopo." *Athenaeum* 40 (1962): 264–314.

Lawrence, Louise J. *Reading with Anthropology: Exhibiting Aspects of New Testament Religion*. Waynesboro, Ga.: Paternoster, 2005.

————, and Mario I. Aguilar, eds. *Anthropology & Biblical Studies: Avenues of Approach*. Leiden: Deo, 2004.

Lendon, J. E. *Empire of Honour: The Art of Government in the Roman World*. Oxford: Clarendon, 1997.

Luz, Ulrich. "The Secrecy Motif and the Marcan Christology." In *The Messianic Secret*, ed. Christopher Tuckett, 75–96. Philadelphia: Fortress Press, 1983.

MacDonald, Dennis. *The Homeric Epics and the Gospel of Mark*. New Haven: Yale University Press, 2000.

————. "Secrecy and Recognitions in the *Odyssey* and Mark: Where Wrede Went Wrong." In *Ancient Fiction and Early Christian Narrative*, ed. Ronald F. Hock, J. Bradley Chance, and Judith Perkins, 139–53. Society of Biblical Literature Symposium Series. Atlanta: Scholars, 1998.

Malbon, Elizabeth Struthers. "Fallible Followers: Women and Men in the Gospel of Mark." *Semeia* 28 (1983): 29–48.

Malherbe, Abraham J. "'Not in a Corner': Early Christian Apologetic in Acts 26:26." *The Second Century* 5, no. 4 (1985/1986): 193–210.

Malina, Bruce J. "'Let Him Deny Himself' (Mark 8:34): A Social Psychological Model of Self-Denial." *Biblical Theology Bulletin* 24 (1994): 106–19.

————. *The New Testament World: Insights from Cultural Anthropology*. 3d ed. Louisville: Westminster John Knox, 2001.

————. "Power, Pain and Personhood: Asceticism in the Ancient Mediterranean World." In *Asceticism*, ed. Vincent Wimbush and Richard Valantasis, 162–77. New York: Oxford University Press, 1995.

————. "The Social World Implied in the Letters of the Christian Bishop-Martyr (Named Ignatius of Antioch)." In *Society of Biblical Literature Seminar Papers 1978*, ed. Paul J. Achtemeier, vol. 2, 71–119. Missoula: Scholars, 1978.

————. *The Social World of Jesus and the Gospels*. London: Routledge, 1996.

————. "Understanding New Testament Persons." In *The Social Sciences and New Testament Interpretation*, ed. Richard Rohrbaugh, 41–61. Peabody, Mass.: Hendrickson, 1996.

————. *Windows on the World of Jesus: Time Travel to Ancient Judea*. Louisville: Westminster John Knox, 1993.

Malina, Bruce J., and Jerome H. Neyrey. "The First-Century Personality: Dyadic, Not Individual." In *The Social World of Luke-Acts: Models for Interpretation*, ed. Jerome H. Neyrey, 67–96. Peabody, Mass.: Hendrickson, 1991.

————. "Honor and Shame in Luke-Acts: Pivotal Values of the Mediterranean World." In *The Social World of Luke-Acts: Models for Interpretation*, ed. Jerome H. Neyrey, 25–65. Peabody, Mass.: Hendrickson, 1991.

————. *Portraits of Paul: An Archaeology of Ancient Personality.* Louisville: Westminster John Knox, 1996.

Malina, Bruce J., and Richard L. Rohrbaugh. *Social-Science Commentary on the Synoptic Gospels.* Minneapolis: Fortress Press, 1992.

Marcus, Joel. "Crucifixion as Parodic Exaltation." *Journal of Biblical Literature* 125, no. 1 (2006): 73–87.

————. "The Jewish War and the *Sitz im Leben* of Mark." *Journal of Biblical Literature* 111, no. 3 (1992): 441–62.

————. *Mark 1–8: A New Translation with Introduction and Commentary.* Anchor Bible 27. New York: Doubleday, 2000.

————. "Mark 4:10-12 and Marcan Epistemology." *Journal of Biblical Literature* 103, no. 4 (1984): 557–74.

————. *The Mystery of the Kingdom of God.* Society of Biblical Literature Dissertation Series 90. Atlanta: Scholars, 1986.

————. *The Way of the Lord: Christological Exegesis of the Old Testament in the Gospel of Mark.* Edinburgh: T. & T. Clark, 1992.

Martin, Luther H. "Secrecy in Hellenistic Religious Communities." In *Secrecy and Concealment: Studies in the History of Mediterranean and Near Eastern Religions,* ed. Hans G. Kippenberg and Guy G. Stroumsa, 101–21. Leiden: Brill, 1995.

Marxsen, Willi. *Der Evangelist Markus: Studien zur Redaktionsgeschichte des Evangeliums.* Göttingen: Vandenhoeck & Ruprecht, 1956.

————. *Mark the Evangelist: Studies on the Redaction History of the Gospel.* Trans. James Boyce, Donald Juel, and William Poehlmann, with Roy A. Harrisville. Nashville: Abingdon, 1969.

May, David M. "Mark 3:20-35 from the Perspective of Shame/Honor." *Biblical Theology Bulletin* 17 (1987): 83–87.

McInerny, William F. "An Unresolved Question in the Gospel Called Mark: 'Who Is This Whom Even Wind and Sea Obey?' (4:41)." *Perspectives in Religious Studies* 23, no. 3 (1996): 255–68.

McVann, Mark. "Reading Mark Ritually: Honor-Shame and the Ritual of Baptism." *Semeia* 67 (1994): 179–98.

Mearns, C. L. "Parables, Secrecy and Eschatology in Mark's Gospel." *Scottish Journal of Theology* 44 (1991): 423–42.

Meeks, Wayne A. *The Moral World of the First Christians.* Library of Early Christianity. Philadelphia: Westminster, 1986.

Millar, Fergus. *The Roman Empire and Its Neighbours.* 2d ed. New York: Holmes & Meier, 1981.

Mitchell, Margaret M. "A Variable and Many-sorted Man: John Chrysostom's Treatment of Pauline Inconsistency." *Journal of Early Christian Studies* 6 (1988): 93–111.

Moloney, Francis J. *The Gospel of Mark: A Commentary.* Peabody, Mass.: Hendrickson, 2002.

Montserrat, Dominic. "Experiencing the Male Body in Roman Egypt." In *When Men Were Men: Masculinity, Power, and Identity in Classical Antiquity,* ed. Lin Foxhall and John Salmon. New York: Routledge, 1998.

Moore, Stephen D. *Literary Criticism and the Gospels: The Theoretical Challenge.* New Haven: Yale University Press, 1989.

Morón, José María Candau. "Plutarch's Lysander and Sulla: Integrated Characters in Roman Historical Perspective." *American Journal of Philology* 121, no. 3 (2000): 453–78.

Moxnes, Halvor. "Honor and Shame." *Biblical Theology Bulletin* 23 (1993): 167–76.

―――――. "Honor and Shame." In *The Social Sciences and New Testament Interpretation*, ed. Richard L. Rohrbaugh, 19–40. Peabody, Mass.: Hendrickson, 1996.

―――――. "Honor, Shame, and the Outside World in Paul's Letter to the Romans." In *The Social World of Formative Christianity and Judaism: Essays in Tribute to Howard Clark Kee*, ed. Jacob Neusner, 207–18. Philadelphia: Fortress Press, 1988.

―――――. "New Testament Ethics—Universal or Particular? Reflections on the Use of Social Anthropology in New Testament Studies." *Studia Theologica* 47, no. 2 (1993): 153–68.

―――――. "Patron-Client Relations and the New Community in Luke-Acts." In *The Social World of Luke-Acts: Models for Interpretation*, ed. Jerome H. Neyrey, 241–68. Peabody, Mass.: Hendrickson, 1991.

―――――, ed. *Constructing Early Christian Families: Family as Social Reality and Metaphor.* London: Routledge, 1997.

Neyrey, Jerome H. "Despising the Shame of the Cross: Honor and Shame in the Johannine Passion Narrative." *Semeia* 68 (1994): 113–37.

―――――. *Honor and Shame in the Gospel of Matthew.* Louisville: Westminster John Knox, 1998.

―――――. "The Idea of Purity in Mark's Gospel." *Semeia* 35 (1986): 91–128.

―――――. "Jesus, Gender, and the Gospel of Matthew." In *New Testament Masculinities*, ed. Stephen D. Moore and Janet Capel Anderson, 43–66. Semeia Studies 45. Atlanta: Society of Biblical Literature, 2003.

―――――. "Josephus' *Vita* and the Encomium: A Native Model of Personality." *Journal for the Study of Judaism* 25 (1994): 194–96.

―――――. "The 'Noble Shepherd' in John 10: Cultural and Rhetorical Background." *Journal of Biblical Literature* 120, no. 2 (2001): 267–91.

―――――. "Questions, Chreiai, and Challenges to Honor: The Interface of Rhetoric and Culture in Mark's Gospel." *Catholic Biblical Quarterly* 60 (1998): 657–81.

―――――. *Render to God: New Testament Understandings of the Divine.* Minneapolis: Fortress Press, 2004.

―――――. "The Sociology of Secrecy and the Fourth Gospel." In *What is John?* Vol. 2, *Literary and Social Readings of the Fourth Gospel*, ed. Fernando Segovia, 79–109. Atlanta: Scholars, 1998.

―――――. " 'Teaching You in Public and from House to House' (Acts 20:20): Unpacking a Cultural Stereotype." *Journal for the Study of the New Testament* 26 (2003): 69–102.

―――――. "Unclean, Common, Polluted, and Taboo: A Short Reading Guide." *Forum* 4 (1988): 72–82.

————, ed. *The Social World of Luke-Acts: Models for Interpretation*. Peabody, Mass.: Hendrickson, 1991.

————, and Richard L. Rohrbaugh. "'He Must Increase and I Must Decrease' (John 3:30): A Cultural and Social Interpretation." *Catholic Biblical Quarterly* 63 (2001): 464–83.

Nineham, D. E. *Saint Mark*. Westminster Pelican Commentaries. Philadelphia: Westminster, 1963.

Ong, Walter J. *Orality and Literacy: The Technologizing of the Word*. London: Routledge, 1982.

Osiek, Carolyn. "The Oral World of Early Christianity in Rome." In *Judaism and Christianity in First-Century Rome*, ed. Karl P. Donfried and Peter Richardson, 151 72. Grand Rapids: Eerdmans, 1998.

Painter, John. *Mark's Gospel: Worlds in Conflict*. New York: Routledge, 1997.

Peristiany, J. G., ed. *Honour and Shame*. London: Weidenfeld and Nicholson, 1966.

Peristiany, J. G., and Julian Pitt-Rivers, eds. *Honour and Grace in Anthropology*. Cambridge: Cambridge University Press, 1992.

Perrin, Norman. *The Resurrection according to Matthew, Mark, and Luke*. Philadelphia: Fortress Press, 1977.

Pervo, Richard I. "A Nihilist Fabula: Introducing *The Life of Aesop*." In *Ancient Fiction and Early Christian Literature*, ed. Ronald F. Hock, J. Bradley Chance, and Judith Perkins, 77–120. Society of Biblical Literature Symposium Series. Atlanta: Scholars, 1998.

Peterson, Dwight. *The Origins of Mark: The Markan Community in Current Debate*. Boston: Brill, 2000.

————. "What has Versailles to do with Mark? Or, Problems with Constructing Hermeneutically Significant Markan Communities." Paper presented at the annual meeting of the Society of Biblical Literature. Toronto, Nov. 25, 2002.

Phillips, Thomas E. "Reading Theory and Biblical Interpretation." *Wesleyan Theological Journal* 35, no. 2 (2000): 32–48.

Pilch, John J. "Death with Honor: The Mediterranean Style Death of Jesus in Mark." *Biblical Theology Bulletin* 25 (1995): 65–70.

————. "Healing in Mark: A Social Science Analysis." *Biblical Theology Bulletin* 15 (1985): 142–50.

————. "Insights and Models from Medical Anthropology for Understanding the Healing Activity of the Historical Jesus." *Hervormde Teologiese Studies* 51, no. 2 (1995): 314–37.

————. *Introducing the Cultural Context of the Old Testament*. New York: Paulist, 1991.

————. "Lying and Deceit in the Letters of the Seven Churches: Perspectives from Cultural Anthropology." *Biblical Theology Bulletin* 22 (1992): 126–35.

————. "Secrecy in the Gospel of Mark." *PACE (Professional Approaches for Christian Educators)* 21 (1992): 150–53.

————. "Secrecy in the Mediterranean World: An Anthropological Perspective." *Biblical Theology Bulletin* 24 (1994): 151–57.

————. "Separating the Sheep from the Goats." *PACE (Professional Approaches for Christian Educators)* 21 (1992): 215–18.

————. "Understanding Biblical Healing: Selecting the Appropriate Model." *Biblical Theology Bulletin* 18 (1988): 60–66.

————. "Understanding Healing in the Social World of Early Christianity." *Biblical Theology Bulletin* 22 (1992): 26–33.

————, and Bruce J. Malina, eds. *Handbook of Biblical Social Values*. Peabody, Mass.: Hendrickson, 1998.

Pitt-Rivers, Julian. "Honor." In *International Encyclopedia of the Social Sciences*. 2d ed. Vol. 6, 503–11. New York: Macmillan, 1968.

————. "Honor and Social Status." In *Honour and Shame: The Values of Mediterranean Society*, ed. J. G. Peristiany, 21–77. Chicago: University of Chicago Press, 1966.

Powell, Mark Allan. *Jesus as a Figure in History: How Modern Historians View the Man from Galilee*. Louisville: Westminster John Knox, 1998.

Rabinowitz, Peter J. "Truth in Fiction: A Reexamination of Audiences." *Critical Inquiry* 4 (1977): 121–41.

Räisänen, Heikki. *The 'Messianic Secret' in Mark*. Trans. Christopher Tuckett. Edinburgh: T. & T. Clark, 1990.

————. "The 'Messianic Secret' in Mark's Gospel." In *The Messianic Secret*, ed. Christopher Tuckett, 132–40. Philadelphia: Fortress Press, 1983.

Rhoads, David. "Jesus and the Syrophoenician Woman in Mark: A Narrative-Critical Study." *Journal of the American Academy of Religion* 62, no. 2 (1994): 343–75.

————, Joanna Dewey, and Donald Michie. *Mark as Story*. 2d ed. Minneapolis: Fortress Press, 1999.

Robbins, Vernon K. *Jesus the Teacher: A Socio-Rhetorical Interpretation of Mark*. Minneapolis: Fortress Press, 1992.

————. "Writing as a Rhetorical Act in Plutarch and the Gospels." In *Persuasive Artistry: Studies in New Testament Rhetoric in Honor of George A. Kennedy*, ed. Duane F. Watson. Sheffield: Sheffield Academic, 1991.

Robinson, William C., Jr. "The Quest for Wrede's Secret Messiah." In *The Messianic Secret*, ed. Christopher Tuckett, 97–115. Philadelphia: Fortress Press, 1983.

Rohrbaugh, Richard, "The Social Location of the Marcan Audience." *Biblical Theology Bulletin* 23 (1993): 114–27.

————, ed. *The Social Sciences and New Testament Interpretation*. Peabody, Mass.: Hendrickson, 1996.

Roskam, H. N. *The Purpose of the Gospel of Mark in Its Historical and Social Context*. Supplements to Novum Testamentum. Leiden: Brill, 2004.

Sanday, William. "The Injunctions of Silence in the Gospels." *Journal of Theological Studies* 5 (1904): 321–29.

————. *The Life of Christ in Recent Research*. New York: Oxford University Press, 1907.

Schäfer, Peter, and Hans G. Kippenberg, eds. *Envisioning Magic: A Princeton Seminar and Symposium*. Studies in the History of Religions 75. Leiden: Brill, 1997.

Schniewind, Julius. *Das Evangelium nach Markus*. Göttingen: Vandenhoeck & Ruprecht, 1933.

————. *Das Selbstzeugnis Jesu nach den ersten drei Evangelien*. Berlin: A. Deichert, 1922.

Schweitzer, Albert. *The Quest of the Historical Jesus: From Reimarus to Wrede*. Trans. W. Montgomery. New York: Collier, 1969.

Shea, Chris. "Setting the Stage for Romances: Xenophon of Ephesus and the Ecphrasis." In *Ancient Fiction and Early Christian Literature*, ed. Ronald F. Hock, J. Bradley Chance, and Judith Perkins, 61–76. Society of Biblical Literature Symposium Series. Atlanta: Scholars, 1998.

Shiner, Whitney. "Creating Plot in Episodic Narratives: *The Life of Aesop* and the Gospel of Mark." In *Ancient Fiction and Early Christian Literature*, ed. Ronald F. Hock, J. Bradley Chance, and Judith Perkins, 155–76. Society of Biblical Literature Symposium Series. Atlanta: Scholars, 1998.

————. "The Gospel of Mark as Revelatory Event." Paper presented at the annual meeting of the Society of Biblical Literature. Denver, Nov. 19, 2001.

————. *Proclaiming the Gospel: First-Century Performance of Mark*. Harrisburg: Trinity Press International, 2003.

Simmel, Georg. *The Sociology of Georg Simmel*. Trans. and ed. Kurt H. Wolff. Glencoe, Ill.: Free, 1950.

Sinclair, Scott Gambrill. "The Healing of Bartimaeus and the Gaps in Mark's Messianic Secret." *Saint Luke's Journal of Theology* 33 (1990): 249–57.

Sjöberg, Erik. *Der verborgene Menschensohn in den Evangelien*. Lund: C. W. K. Gleerup, 1955.

Smith, Stephen H. *A Lion with Wings: A Narrative-Critical Approach to Mark's Gospel*. Sheffield: Sheffield Academic, 1996.

Snoy, T. "Marc 6,48: ". . . et il voulait les dépasser." In *L'Evangile selon Marc: Tradition et redaction*, ed. M. Sabbe, 346–63. Louvain: Leuven University Press, 1974.

Stein, Robert H. *Mark*. Baker Exegetical Commentary on the New Testament. Grand Rapids: Baker Academic, 2008.

Sternberg, Meir. "Double Cave, Double Talk: The Indirections of Biblical Dialogue." In *"Not in Heaven": Coherence and Complexity in Biblical Narrative*, ed. Jason P. Rosenblatt and Joseph C. Sitterson, Jr., 28–57. Bloomington: Indiana University Press, 1991.

————. *The Poetics of Biblical Narrative: Ideological Literature and the Drama of Reading*. Bloomington: Indiana University Press, 1985.

Stroumsa, Guy G. "From Esotericism to Mysticism in Early Christianity." In *Secrecy and Concealment: Studies in the History of Mediterranean and Near*

Eastern Religions, ed. Hans G. Kippenberg and Guy G. Stroumsa, 289–309. Leiden: Brill, 1995.

Suleiman, Susan R., and Inge Crosman. *The Reader in the Text: Essays on Audience and Interpretation*. Princeton: Princeton University Press, 1980.

Svenbro, Jesper. *Phrasikleia: An Anthropology of Reading in Ancient Greece*. Trans. Janet Lloyd. Ithaca: Cornell University Press, 1993.

Swain, Simon. "Defending Hellenism: Philostratus, *In Honour of Apollonius*." In *Apologetics in the Roman Empire: Pagans, Jews, and Christians*, ed. Mark Edwards et al., 157–96. Oxford: Oxford University Press, 1999.

Tannehill, Robert C. "The Composition of Acts 3-5: Narrative Development and Echo Effect." *Society of Biblical Literature 1984 Seminar Papers*, ed. Kent Harold Richards, 217–40. Chico, Calif.: Scholars, 1984.

————. "The Disciples in Mark: The Function of a Narrative Role." *Journal of Religion* 57, no. 4 (1977): 386–405.

Telford, W. R. *The Theology of the Gospel of Mark*. New Testament Theology. Cambridge: Cambridge University Press, 1999.

Theissen, Gerd. *The Gospels in Context: Social and Political History in the Synoptic Tradition*. Trans. Linda M. Maloney. Minneapolis: Fortress Press, 1991.

————. *The Miracle Stories of the Early Christian Tradition*. Trans. Francis McDonagh. Philadelphia: Fortress Press, 1983.

————. "Die pragmatische Bedeutung der Geheimnismotive im Markusevangelium." In *Secrecy and Concealment: Studies in the History of Mediterranean and Near East Religions*, ed. Hans G. Kippenberg and Guy G. Stroumsa, 225–45. Leiden: Brill, 1995.

————. *Social Reality and the Early Christians: Theology, Ethics, and the World of the New Testament*. Trans. Margaret Kohl. Minneapolis: Fortress Press, 1992.

Thomas, J. David. Review of *Ancient Literacy*, by William V. Harris. *English Historical Review* 108, no. 427 (1993): 429–30.

Thomas, Rosalind. *Literacy and Orality in Ancient Greece*. Key Themes in Ancient History. Cambridge: Cambridge University Press, 1992.

Tolbert, Mary Ann. *Sowing the Gospel: Mark's World in Literary-Historical Perspective*. Minneapolis: Fortress Press, 1989.

Tompkins, Jane P., ed. *Reader-Response Criticism: From Formalism to Post-Structuralism*. Baltimore: Johns Hopkins University Press, 1980.

Tuckett, Christopher. "The Disciples and the Messianic Secret in Mark." In *Fair Play: Diversity and Conflicts in Early Christianity; Essays in Honor of Heikki Räisänen*, ed. Ismo Dunderberg, Christopher Tuckett, and Kari Syreeni, 131–49. Leiden: Brill, 2002.

————. "Introduction: The Problem of the Messianic Secret." In *The Messianic Secret*, ed. Christopher Tuckett, 1–28. Philadelphia: Fortress Press, 1983.

————, ed. *The Messianic Secret*. Philadelphia: Fortress Press, 1983.

Twelftree, Graham H. *Jesus the Exorcist: A Contribution to the Study of the Historical Jesus*. Tübingen: J. C. B. Mohr, 1993.

Tyson, Joseph B. "The Blindness of the Disciples in Mark." In *The Messianic Secret*, ed. Christopher Tuckett, 35–43. Philadelphia: Fortress Press, 1983.

van Iersel, B. M. F. "The Gospel according to St. Mark—Written for a Persecuted Community?" *Nederlands theologisch Tijdschrift* 34 (1980): 15–36.

————. *Mark: A Reader-Response Commentary*. Trans. W. H. Bisscheroux. JSNT Supplement Series 164. Sheffield: Sheffield Academic, 1998.

Via, Dan O. "Irony as Hope in Mark's Gospel: A Reply to Werner Kelber." *Semeia* 43 (1988): 21–27.

Watson, Francis. "The Social Function of Mark's Secrecy Theme." *Journal for the Study of the New Testament* 24 (1985): 49–69.

Weeden, Theodore. "The Heresy That Necessitated Mark's Gospel." In *The Interpretation of Mark*, ed. William Telford, 145–58. Philadelphia. Fortress Press, 1985.

————. *Mark: Traditions in Conflict*. Philadelphia: Fortress Press, 1971.

Weiss, Johannes. *Das älteste Evangelium: Ein Beitrag zum Verständnis des Markus-Evangeliums und der ältesten evangelischen Überlieferung*. Göttingen: Vandenhoeck & Ruprect, 1903.

————. *Jesus von Nazareth, Mythus oder Geschichte? Eine Auseinandersetzung mit Kalthoff, Drews, Jensen*. Tübingen: J. C. B. Mohr (Paul Siebeck), 1910.

Williams, Joel F. *Other Followers of Jesus: Minor Characters as Major Figures in Mark's Gospel*. Sheffield: JSOT, 1994.

Williams, Michael A. "Secrecy, Revelation, and Late Antique Demiurgical Myths." In *Rending the Veil: Concealment and Secrecy in the History of Religions*, ed. Elliot R. Wolfson, 31–58. New York: Seven Bridges, 1999.

Wills, Lawrence M. *The Quest of the Historical Gospel: Mark, John, and the Origins of the Gospel Genre*. London: Routledge, 1997.

Witherington, Ben. *The Gospel of Mark: A Socio-Rhetorical Commentary*. Grand Rapids: Eerdmans, 2001.

Witherup, Ronald D. "Cornelius Over and Over Again: 'Functional Redundancy' in the Acts of the Apostles." *Journal for the Study of the New Testament* 49 (1993): 45–66.

————. "Functional Redundancy in the Acts of the Apostles: A Case Study." *Journal for the Study of the New Testament* 48 (1992): 67–86.

Wrede, William. *The Messianic Secret*. Trans. J. C. G. Greig. Cambridge: James Clarke, 1971.

Yaghjian, Lucretia B. "Ancient Reading." In *The Social Sciences and New Testament Interpretation*, ed. Richard Rohrbaugh, 206–30. Peabody, Mass.: Hendrickson, 1996.

INDEXES

Scripture / Ancient Source Index

Old Testament

215

New Testament

Apocrypha

Rabbinic Literature

Other Ancient Sources

Author Index

Subject Index